THE AMERICAN WEST AND THE WORLD

The American West and the World provides a synthetic introduction to the transnational history of the American West. Drawing from the insights of recent scholarship, Janne Lahti recenters the history of the U.S. West in the global contexts of empires and settler colonialism, discussing exploration, expansion, migration, violence, intimacies, and ideas. Lahti examines established subfields of Western scholarship, such as borderlands studies and transnational histories of empire, as well as relatively unexplored connections between the West and geographically nonadjacent spaces. Lucid and incisive, *The American West and the World* firmly situates the historical West in its proper global context.

Janne Lahti is Adjunct Professor of History at the University of Helsinki and the editor of *American Studies in Scandinavia*.

THE AMERICAN WEST AND THE WORLD

Transnational and Comparative Perspectives

Janne Lahti

Routledge
Taylor & Francis Group

NEW YORK AND LONDON

First published 2019
by Routledge
711 Third Avenue, New York, NY 10017

and by Routledge
2 Park Square, Milton Park, Abingdon, Oxon, OX14 4RN

Routledge is an imprint of the Taylor & Francis Group, an informa business

Library of Congress Cataloging-in-Publication Data
A catalog record for this title has been requested

ISBN: 978-1-138-18733-7 (hbk)
ISBN: 978-1-138-18734-4 (pbk)
ISBN: 978-1-315-64321-2 (ebk)

Typeset in Bembo
by codeMantra

CONTENTS

ACKNOWLEDGMENTS

When looking back and reflecting on how this book came to be, I want to start by showing my appreciation to my parents, Jouko and Marjatta Lahti. It was they, after all, who introduced me to great Western movies such as *Rio Bravo*, *The Man Who Shot Liberty Valance*, and *The Good, the Bad, and the Ugly* when I was growing up in 1980s Finland. And it was they who put up with my often noisy and frequently disruptive plays of "cowboys and Indians." And it was they as well who, back then, financed my seemingly endless appetite for Western comics and films. I am sure they had little idea of what it would all lead up to. Neither did I. As I went to college, got my PhD, and made myself a professional historian specializing in the American West, they have been per- haps a bit surprised and oftentimes somewhat puzzled by what exactly I do. But they have also shown true support and avid interest in my career choices, which I sincerely appreciate.

Academically, this book was generously supported by the Finnish Cultural Foundation. Its three-year postdoc fellowship provided much-valued time for research and writing at the University of Helsinki. There were several people who read parts of the manuscript or helped me in some other way as this book was in the works. I want to express my gratitude to Lance Blyth, Sebastian Conrad, Margaret Jacobs, James Leiker, Benjamin Madley, Sheila McManus, Roger Nichols, Markku Peltonen, Cynthia Culver Prescott, Robert Wooster, and David Wrobel. At Routledge, this project actually started as a proposal to put together a reader of relevant scholarly articles and then developed into what it is now, a monograph. Kimberly Guinta was instrumental in getting this project off the ground. She put a lot of faith in me and in this book, for which I am very grateful. In fact, it was her patience and guidance that got me to write this. I also want to thank Jack Censer for his beneficial feedback early on, as well as Margo Irvin. At present, Eve Mayer and Ted Meyer have proven friendly and supportive to work with. They have exhibited the fullest confidence in this book, which is something this author needs and values. Finally, it is time to remember what I, after all, need to be most thankful of. My wife Sanna is a true gem, and I should probably let her know that more frequently. Our two teenaged children Sofia and Juho have had to deal with my Western enthusiasm for a number of years now. They have listened aptly to my frequent ramblings about this or that historical subject. They have also proven amicable travel companions during the long car rides and endless walks throughout the West and its wonderful towns, nature, and historic sites. I hope all this has provided them some perspective on life and on the value and importance of history in our interconnected, globalizing world.

INTRODUCTION

The American West as Global History

I first visited the trans-Mississippi American West as a 23-year-old college student and have subsequently spent extended time (over three years in all) there as a student and as a scholar. Yet in many ways the West has been part of my life much longer. As a young boy growing up in a small, predominantly working-class, town in southern Finland in the 1980s, I consumed piles of Western comics, pulp novels, and movies (on VHS, of course). What's more I spent countless hours outdoors playing "cowboys and Indians," using my toy Colts, Winchesters, and bow and arrows. When the weather turned sour, as it so often does where I grew up, I staged Western holdups, shootouts, and Indian fights in the comfort of my room. I remember owning little replica stagecoaches, railroad cars and tracks, and quite a few dwellings – a saloon, an army fort, a sheriff's office, and a mercantile store, all made of wood, not plastic, spring to mind. I also had dozens of figurine cowboys, soldiers, and Indians to play with. In hindsight, the variety of Western-themed toys and apparel available in Finland in the 1980s seems striking as one is less and less likely to stumble on any in today's department stores and toy shops.

To a kid like me, the contemporary world looked pretty uninspiring and very serious. The Cold War was an all-too-real danger, and it was intensively present in the everyday lives of everyday people as Finland teetered between the communist East and the capitalist West. In contrast, the American West signaled colorful adventure with its Indians, buffalos, cowboys, and gunslingers. John Wayne, Randolph Scott, and Clint Eastwood made a lasting – and, in retrospect, quite possibly harmful – impression on a youngster trying to understand the world and figure out what it meant to become a man. So did the massively popular (in Europe, that is) Western comics *Lucky Luke* and *Tex Willer*. I only realized much later that *Lucky Luke* was actually a French-Belgian product and that *Tex Willer* came from Italy, and that neither had made much of a splash in the actual West. It also hit me afterward that the early Westerns of Clint Eastwood were similarly "made in Europe."

In school, I frequently stumbled on the West. I learned that thousands of Finns and millions of other Europeans had moved there. Many of those who became settlers in the West not only took the land and built their families, communities, and legacies there but also kept in touch and visited the "old country." More often than one would think, they also returned for good. This was the option my paternal great-grandfather took (luckily for me, as otherwise my grandmother would not have been born). Some of my other relatives stayed and became Americans. It is this history of (relatively) voluntary settler migration that most families in Finland share with much of Europe, sections of Asia, and areas in Latin America. Pursuing my master's and, later, doctorate in Finland, I had the opportunity to live in the West as a visiting student, first in Berkeley, California, and then in Lincoln, Nebraska. Next I returned to the West as a visiting scholar, this time to Tucson, Arizona, and, most recently, to San Marino, California. These visits and my other travels as a tourist in the West have taken me to numerous national parks, reservations, battlefields, and other historical sites across the Plains, the Rocky Mountains, the desert Southwest, and the Pacific Northwest. They have made me respect the vast landscapes and diverse peoples in the process. These personal experiences have also nurtured less pleasant realizations that the conquest of other peoples' lands, subjugation and marginalization of indigenous peoples, the building of multicultural (yet racially hierarchical) settler societies, and the extraction of natural resources in order to fuel the industrial revolution and mass consumption have been essential ingredients in Western history. I have also realized that these things come with lasting legacies as well as intricate transnational connections.

For the purposes of this book, the European fascination with the West, the transnational mobility of people, and the multidirectional processes and legacies of empires and conquest – of trading, settling, and invading – demonstrate in their varied ways how the American West is not just a distant land out there, but part of our collective, global, history. Historian Patricia Limerick's definition of the West as a "place undergoing conquest and never escaping its consequences" and as "one of the great meeting zones of the planet"[1] not only hits the mark but is what I take as my point of departure in this book that aims to provide a short introduction to Western history as global history.

A significant domain of convergence and conquest, the West has been a crossroads of the Atlantic and the Pacific worlds shaped by globe-spanning

---

1 Limerick, *The Legacy of Conquest*, 26–27; Limerick, *Something in the Soil*, 19. In this book, "American West," "West," or "Western" is capitalized and used in reference to the area between the Pacific Ocean and the Mississippi River that presently belongs to the United States.

structured transformations and multidirectional entanglements; first as a shared world with an international cast and then as a settler colonial project with a globally interwoven history. The early West attracted Spanish, French, British, Russian, and U.S. empires, not to mention several groups of indigenous expansionists, who together formed highly competitive joint spaces of Native grounds and middle grounds. By the Mexican–American War and the American Civil War, however, the West turned into and has remained a prime example of the global phenomenon of settler colonialism. Settler colonialism is usually associated with conquest, long-range migration, permanent settlement, substitution of Native peoples, market revolution, nationalization of space, extension of state power, and the reproduction of one's own society on what used to be other people's lands. According to anthropologist Patrick Wolfe, settler colonialism differs from other forms of colonialism – including exploitation colonies like the Dutch East Indies or the British Raj – as it is not primarily an effort to build a master–servant relationship interested in exploitation of Native labor in the extraction of natural resources but instead is more concerned about replacement and access to territory, the land itself. Settler colonialism, Wolfe continues, "destroys to replace." It introduces "a zero-sum contest over land" and is characterized by "logic of elimination." Moreover, as "settlers come to stay: invasion is a structure not an event" or a series of isolated events.[2] To discuss the West as a settler colonial project is to link it to shared stories of transnational settler colonialism taking place within the British Wests (primarily Australia, New Zealand, Canada, and South Africa), French Algeria, the Russian Caucasus and Siberia, and German Southwest Africa, among other places.

Over the years, several scholarly works have examined particular aspects of Western history in a comparative and/or transnational framework. Historians representing different specialties, applying multiple theories and research concepts, and coming from various backgrounds – a long list of authors that includes, but is not limited to, Margaret Jacobs, Glenda Riley, David Wrobel, Gregory Smithers, Roger Nichols, Benjamin Madley, Erika Lee, Kornel Chang, Ann McGrath, Katherine Ellinghaus, James Gump, James Belich, Robert Rydell, and David Weber – have opened productive terrain with more expansive analytical possibilities that reach beyond national boundaries and toward more open-ended horizons and global contexts. They have discussed cross-border assertions of indigenous power, border control, global color lines, and migration. Others have probed the multilayered histories of exploration and travel writings, and still others the comparative aspects of violence, wars, armies, and genocide. Some scholars have in turn looked at the various facets of intimate colonialism: the civilizing mission and the global portability of white middle-class cultures,

---

2 Wolfe, "Land, Labor, and Difference," 868; Wolfe, "Settler Colonialism and the Elimination of the Native," 388.

domesticity, and respectability. Scholars have also debated the worldwide ideological ramifications of the American West, its influence on settler regimes and imperial dreams elsewhere, as well as its role in shaping the imagination of masses and forms of popular culture.

Until now, there exists no synthesis that would introduce or pull together the main lines of these investigations in a concise manner. This study strives for inclusivity by discussing borderlands histories crossing national borders (mainly taking the present borders as reference) as well as scholarship linking the American West with geographically nonadjacent spaces. While it stresses newer studies published since the emergence of "New Western History" in the late 1980s, it will also touch on older works on comparative frontiers and hemispheric influences. Furthermore, set on charting what has already been achieved, this book also comes with a second aim: to inspire new research by exposing themes and networks not yet fully explored that carry further global possibilities. In all, this short book strives to demonstrate that the West matters in the histories of the modern world. More specifically, it holds that the West proves quintessential in the investigations of empires, colonialism, and settler colonialism: in the momentous and highly uneven transnational movements, flows, and networks of peoples, ideas, practices, goods, and pathogens that shaped not just the West but also the world during the last centuries. Indeed, the West and the world seem pretty much inseparable.

Frontiers and Borderlands

It is quite common among academic historians to acknowledge that a tendency toward exceptionalism has traditionally shaped much of American historical thinking. For Western history, this line of thought has been traced to Frederick Jackson Turner's 1893 frontier thesis. Turner's view of Western history centered on a westbound process where the existence of free land, its continuous recession, and the advancing Anglo settlement explained a profoundly national development. In short, the frontier was uniquely American, and it made America unique. At the heart of it all stood a vibrant democracy made distinct by individuality, pragmatism, and egalitarianism. As a historical explanation of national experience, identity, and disposition, the frontier process initially had little room for racial diversity, cultural cross-fertilization, or critical analysis of violence and exploitation. Neither did it leave much space for the agency of women or nonwhite peoples. Importantly, Turner's thesis seemed to insulate American development by proclaiming a fundamental difference, a dichotomy, against Europe and its modes of empire and colonialism.

While Turner's doctrine of frontier exceptionalism has lost much of its currency among academic historians today, it needs to be said that it never prevented a tradition of comparative investigations. One of those who wanted to link the West to the world was Herbert Eugene Bolton. While in hindsight he perhaps leaned too much toward the romantic and the uncritical in his analysis of exploration and the Spanish mission and the presidio, Bolton nevertheless viewed national history as a thread in a much larger strand and emphasized North America as a meeting point of Spanish and English civilizations. Other historians too have examined what the American West had in common with other parts of the world, while not necessarily making a substantial break with Turner or escaping the contours of national history. Earl Pomeroy, Jerome Steffen, Walter Nugent, Richard Slatta, and others have taken Turner's frontier on a world tour, discussing, for instance, differences in national development, the characteristics of cowboy cultures, or the tragedies and triumphs of indigenous resistance and Anglo expansion. Walter L. Williams in turn showed how U.S. policies in the West established precedents for American imperial policies overseas. These authors approached the frontier as the shifting outer limit of white expansion with which to compare other non-American frontiers. They also developed typologies of farming and extractive frontiers, or, like Howard Lamar and Leonard Thompson, reinterpreted the frontier as a meeting point between peoples of different polities and cultures. Furthermore, sensing the largely untapped scholarly potential that existed in linking the West and the world, scholars such as W. Turrentine Jackson in the 1970s and Michael P. Malone in the 1990s urged their colleagues to pursue comparative investigations with increased vigor.

If studies on comparative frontiers proposed to look at the American West in a bigger picture, what New Western historians brought to the table was interpretive realignments, shifts in perspectives, and alterations in emphasis. Patricia Limerick, Richard White, William Cronon, Donald Worster, and others generally sought to break from the Turnerian notions of frontier process, which had made 1890 the terminus of Western history. New Western historians wanted to tell more complex and grimmer stories and went on exploring themes such as dependency, exploitation, and violence. They underlined conquest and convergence and directed attention to the interplays of race, class, and gender – habitually viewed as social constructions and as contested sites of power – and to environmental history and to the lives of ordinary peoples. While they spent much time and energy debating the regional identity of the West in the national context, the subject matters and emphasis in their works also indicated that the American West was seldom isolated from the transnational, globetrotting epics of the modern era: empires and colonialism. Limerick's more current call for "going global" and Stephen Aron's appeal of "returning the West to the world" offer recent indicators of the budding desire of historians to move the field toward world-embracing narratives of parallels, networks, and circulations.

In many ways it has been borderlands historians who have expanded the field of vision in Western history. In the 1970s and 1980s, borderlands scholars – inspired by Chicano/a studies – looked at cross-cultural relations, social and economic struggle, and racism in the national period. They habitually applied comparative outlooks while zooming in on places close to the U.S.–Mexican border. David Weber expanded the field temporally, knitting together Bolton's Spanish borderlands and the national period in an endeavor to produce culturally subtle relational histories. Scholars such as James Brooks and Ramón Gutiérrez wove ethnohistory and gender and cultural studies into increasingly multivocal portraits of the borderlands. Seeking an overarching, national history-focused, framework for borderlands histories, Jeremy Adelman and Stephen Aron suggested that as empires turned into nations, borderlands also became bordered lands.

Today, borderlands scholarship has gone continental, hemispheric, and global. It is no longer confined to the U.S.–Mexican border, but spans different time periods and various spaces of plural sovereignty – the edges of nations and empires – around the world: from the Great Lakes to the German–Polish or Habsburg–Russian borderlands, from the Caucasus to the Pyrenees, and elsewhere. Importantly, it expands our grasp of global history through analysis of many transnational local histories. It strives to reveal hitherto veiled stories by pushing previously neglected subjects to the center of discussion. It often reads as a history of entanglements and convergences, of shifting transnational adaptations and nuanced dialogues involving spatial mobility, cultural mixing, situational identities, and political contestation. Borderlands history, as historians Pekka Hämäläinen and Samuel Truett remark, was previously "the marker of a particular place" but has today "become a way of seeing the world."[3]

Transnational Turn and Global Empires

Much of the current impetus for researching the American West in transnational and global settings can be traced to larger developments in the writing of academic history. Ongoing for nearly three decades now, the transnational turn in the humanities exemplifies our developing concern and desire to grapple with the global present and the processes of modern globalization. Coined to capture the present age of transformation, the term "globalization," according to historians Gary Magee and Andrew Thompson, is best understood as a set of processes that compress time and space and accelerate the interdependence of peoples, societies, and states. In some ways transnational history stands as the newest manifestation of an approach that has successively been branded as international, world, or, simply, comparative history. What all these conceptualizations share are attempts of interpretative and methodological realignments contradicting insular narratives. Comparative history is typically understood to point to broader patterns and to eschew parochialism as it maps the differences

---

3 Hämäläinen and Truett, "On Borderlands," 341.

and similarities of divergent yet interrelated realities functioning in an inter-linked world. Where transnational history differs from comparative history is in its emphasis on flows, networks, and circulations that span across national boundaries without ignoring their existence.

Transnational historians (such as Ian Tyrrell, David Thelen, Thomas Bender, and many others who fit the bill) have exhibited an attempt to break out of the nation-state paradigm. Part of this effort is undoubtedly fueled by a mounting criticism of the "developed" word and the growth of global inequalities, to-gether with the increased self-criticism inside academia. Transnational history has come to indicate a fresh attitude, a new start, and a wide field of endeavor where the central concern is with movements and circulation, a position of historical examination that opens up more spacious and inclusive analytical opportunities for grasping multifaceted networks. It enables a perspective, his-torian Sebastian Conrad writes, that avoids a tunnel vision and allows us to overcome the sharp division between the internal and the external. The em-phasis on the transnational permits us to recognize and draw links between dif-ferent scales of historical analysis from the local to the global. At best it offers a multiscopic approach where seemingly disparate local arenas are in fact shaped by similar global processes and movements.

When one looks at the outpouring of works from scholars such as Conrad, Jürgen Osterhammel, C. A. Baily, Frederick Cooper, Paul Kramer, Jane Burbank, Emily Rosenberg, Ann Laura Stoler, and John Darwin, among others, it is easy to draw the conclusion that, in present undertakings to pen transnational histories of the world, the history of empires and colonialism con-stitutes perhaps the most exciting ingredient and is commensurate with much of global history in the modern era. Empires were everywhere, and almost all societies in the world were in some form impacted by their ambitions and designs. There existed a global scramble for prestige, status, resources, markets, settler space, influence, and control as Britain, France, Germany, Russia, Japan, the United States, and others stretched their realms and coveted for power through colonial expansion.

Whether perceived as precursors to present globalization, or its early man-ifestations, empires hold the key to understanding globalization's historical roots. Empires and colonies, historians Tony Ballantyne and Antoinette Burton write, "were never fully self-contained or hermetically sealed systems."[4] Instead, different empires and their agents – administrators, scientists, entrepre-neurs, workers, soldiers, and settlers – produced forms of interconnectedness, intense competition, and imperial comparisons that operated on a variety of scales within and between empires as well as inside and beyond the boundaries of formal territorial rule. Also, while empires ruled much of world's surface

---

4 Ballantyne and Burton, *Empires and the Reach of the Global*, 12.

by 1914, their rule was seldom omnipotent or cohesive. Rather, their impact was uneven, penetrating and impacting different societies differently. They were diffused, contested, and fragile constructs and projects with, as Frederick Cooper and Jane Burbank note, varying repertoires of control and differentiated forms of rule, systems of power whose lines were seldom clear-cut.

Organization

Each chapter in this book builds a distinctive pathway toward understanding the varied strands in the shared histories of the West and the world. And while they are intended to be read in sequence – that is, as a book – the chapters are also meant to be quite free standing. As this is a short book meant to serve as an introduction, those readers who yearn for deeper discussion and more specific histories can find them in the bibliographies of key readings that follow each chapter. These bibliographies are by no means comprehensive, but hopefully whet the readers' appetite to learn more as well as enable them to pursue their interests further. In conjunction, and to save space, I have resisted my natural temptation as a historian to insert a long list of notes (basically only direct quotes are cited). Furthermore, when a historian pursues a broad topic in a concise space, like I do here, it is healthy to recognize that full coverage is unattainable, that there is always some line of investigation or some groups of scholars you do not do full justice to. I confess that I have concentrated on pre-World War II times and perhaps focused on certain topics at the expense of others. The choices I have made are certainly selective and they undoubtedly reflect my own limitations and preferences. I accept this. Hopefully the readers can live with them as well.

I hope that this small book will for its part encourage historians and students to think big, to explore in a transnational and global vein, and to avoid isolationist perspectives, insular paradigms, and unnecessary divisions. There are many historians already at work with transnational and comparative topics, and their lead can help us steer toward broader horizons and wider understandings. We historians of the American West still have plenty of room to improve, many lively scholarly horizons to explore, and fresh connections and parallels to unravel while extending the realms of our perspectives and thinking.

Bibliography

Frontiers

Billington, Ray Allen, ed. *The Frontier Thesis: Valid Interpretation of American History?* New York: Krieger, 1966.

———. *America's Frontier Heritage*. Albuquerque: University of New Mexico Press, 1975.

Cronon, William. "Revisiting the Vanishing Frontier: The Legacy of Frederick Jackson Turner." *Western Historical Quarterly* 18 (April 1987): 157–176.

Guy, Donna J., and Thomas E. Sheridan, eds. *Contested Ground: Comparative Frontiers on the Northern and Southern Edges of the Spanish Empire.* Tucson: University of Arizona Press, 1998.

Jackson, W. Turrentine. "A Brief Message for the Young and/or Ambitious: Comparative Frontiers as a Field for Investigation." *Western Historical Quarterly* 9 (January 1978): 5–18.

Klein, Kerwin Lee. *Frontiers of Historical Imagination: Narrating the European Conquest of Native America, 1890–1990.* Berkeley: University of California Press, 1997.

Lamar, Howard R., and Leonard Thompson, eds. *The Frontier in History: North America and Southern Africa Compared.* New Haven: Yale University Press, 1981.

Malone, Michel P. "Beyond the Last Frontier: Toward a New Approach to Western American History." In Patricia Nelson Limerick, Clyde A. Milner II, and Charles Rankin, eds. *Trails: Toward a New Western History.* Lawrence: University Press of Kansas, 1991: 139–160.

Mikesell, Marvin W. "Comparative Studies in Frontier History." *Annals of the Association of American Geographers* 50 (March 1960): 62–74.

Miller, David Harry, and Jerome O. Steffen, eds. *The Frontier: Comparative Studies.* Norman: University of Oklahoma Press, 1977.

Nugent, Walter. "Frontiers and Empires in the Late Nineteenth Century." In Patricia Nelson Limerick, Clyde A. Milner II, and Charles Rankin, eds. *Trails: Toward a New Western History.* Lawrence: University Press of Kansas, 1991: 161–181.

Pomeroy, Earl. "The West and New Nations in Other Continents." In John Alexander Carroll, ed. *Reflections of Western Historians.* Tucson: University of Arizona Press, 1969: 237–261.

Price, A. Grenfell. *White Settlers and Native Peoples: An Historical Study of Racial Contacts between English-Speaking Whites and Aboriginal Peoples in the United States, Canada, Australia and New Zealand.* Cambridge: Cambridge University Press, 1950.

Turner, Frederick Jackson. "The Significance of the Frontier in American History." In Frederick Jackson Turner, ed. *The Frontier in American History.* 1920; reprint, New York: Dover Publications, 1996: 1–38.

Sharp, Paul F. "Three Frontiers: Some Comparative Studies of Canadian, American, and Australian Settlement." *Pacific Historical Review* 24 (November 1955): 369–377.

Slatta, Richard W. *Cowboys of the Americas.* New Haven: Yale University Press, 1994.

Smith, Henry Nash. *Virgin Land: The American West as Symbol and Myth.* Cambridge, MA: Harvard University Press, 1950.

Steffen, Jerome O. *Comparative Frontiers: A Proposal for Studying the American West.* Norman: University of Oklahoma Press, 1980.

Webb, Walter Prescott. *The Great Frontier.* Boston: Houghton Mifflin, 1952.

Williams, Walter L. "United States Indian Policy and the Debate over Philippine Annexation: Implications for the Origins of American Imperialism." *Journal of American History* 66 (March 1980): 810–831.

New Western History

Aron, Stephen. "Returning the West to the World." *OAH Magazine of History* 20.2 (March 2006): 53–60.

Cronon, William. *Nature's Metropolis: Chicago and the Great West.* New York: W. W. Norton and Co., 1991.

Cronon, William, George Miles, and Jay Gitlin, eds. *Under an Open Sky: Rethinking America's Western Past.* New York: W.W. Norton & Co., 1992.

Limerick, Patricia Nelson. *The Legacy of Conquest: The Unbroken Past of the American West.* New York: W.W. Norton & Co., 1987.

———. *Something in the Soil: Legacies and Reckonings in the New West.* New York: W.W. Norton & Co., 2000.

———. "Going West and Ending up Global." *Western Historical Quarterly* 32 (Spring 2001): 4–23.

Limerick, Patricia Nelson, Clyde A. Milner II, and Charles Rankin, eds. *Trails: Toward a New Western History.* Lawrence: University Press of Kansas, 1991.

West, Elliott. *The Contested Plains: Indians, Goldseekers, and the Rush to Colorado.* Lawrence: University Press of Kansas, 1998.

White, Richard. *'It's Your Misfortune and None of My Own': A New History of the American West.* Norman: University of Oklahoma Press, 1991.

———. *The Middle Ground: Indians, Empires, and Republics in the Great Lakes Region, 1650–1815.* Cambridge: Cambridge University Press, 1991.

Worster, Donald. *Rivers of Empire: Water, Aridity, and the Growth of the American West.* New York: Pantheon, 1985.

———. "New West, True West: Interpreting the Region's History." *Western Historical Quarterly* 18 (April 1987): 141–156.

Modern Overviews of Western History (In a Predominately National Context)

Butler, Anne, and Michael J. Lansing. *The American West: A Concise History.* Oxford: Blackwell, 2008.

Deverell, William, ed. *A Companion to the American West.* Oxford: Blackwell, 2004.

Etulain, Richard W. *Beyond the Missouri: The Story of the American West.* Albuquerque: University of New Mexico Press, 2006.

Higham, Carol L., and William H. Katerberg. *Conquests & Consequences: The American West from Frontier to Region.* New York: Wiley-Blackwell, 2009.

Hine, Robert V., and John Mack Faragher. *The American West: A New Interpretive History.* New Haven: Yale University Press, 2000.

Borderlands

Adelman, Jeremy, and Stephen Aron. "From Borderlands to Borders: Empires, Nation-States, and the Peoples in between in North American History." *American Historical Review* 104 (June 1999): 814–841.

Baud, Michiel, and Willem Van Schendel. "Toward a Comparative History of Borderlands." *Journal of World History* 8 (Fall 1997): 211–242.

Bolton, Herbert E. *The Spanish Borderlands: A Chronicle of Old Florida and the Southwest.* New Haven: Yale University Press, 1921.

———. "The Epic of Greater America." *American Historical Review* 38 (April 1933): 448–474.

Brooks, James F. *Captives & Cousins: Slavery, Kinship, and Community in the Southwest Borderlands.* Chapel Hill: University of North Carolina Press, 2002.

DeLay, Brian, ed. *North American Borderlands.* New York: Routledge, 2013.

Evans, Sterling, ed. *The Borderlands of the American and Canadian Wests: Essays on Regional History of the Forty-ninth Parallel.* Lincoln: University of Nebraska Press, 2006.

Hämäläinen, Pekka, and Samuel Truett. "On Borderlands." *Journal of American History* 98 (September 2011): 338–361.

Johnson, Benjamin, and Andrew R. Graybill, eds. *Bridging National Borders in North America: Transnational and Comparative Histories.* Durham: Duke University Press, 2010.

Gutiérrez, Ramón A. *When Jesus Came the Corn Mothers Went Away: Marriage, Sexuality, and Power in New Mexico, 1500–1846.* Stanford: Stanford University Press, 1991.

Gutiérrez, Ramón A., and Elliott Young. "Transnationalizing Borderlands History." *Western Historical Quarterly* 41 (Spring 2010): 26–53.

Lee, John W.I., and Michael North. *Globalizing Borderlands Studies in Europe and North America.* Lincoln: University of Nebraska Press, 2016.

Readman, Paul, Cynthia Radding, and Chad Bryant, eds. *Borderlands in World History, 1700–1914.* New York: Palgrave Macmillan, 2014.

Weber, David J. *The Mexican Frontier, 1821–1846: The American Southwest under Mexico.* Albuquerque: University of New Mexico Press, 1982.

———. *The Spanish Frontier in North America.* New Haven: Yale University Press, 1992.

———. *Barbaros: Spaniards and their Savages in the Age of Enlightenment.* New Haven: Yale University Press, 2006.

Transnational/Global Histories

Baily, Christopher Alan. *The Birth of the Modern World, 1780–1914.* New York: Wiley-Blackwell, 2003.

Ballantyne, Tony, and Antoinette Burton. *Empires and the Reach of the Global, 1870–1945.* Cambridge, MA: The Belknap Press of Harvard University Press, 2012.

Beckert, Sven, and Dominic Sachsenmaier, eds. *Global History, Globally: Research and Practice around the World.* New York: Bloomsbury, 2018.

Bender, Thomas, ed. *Rethinking American History in a Global Age.* Berkeley: University of California Press, 2002.

———. *A Nation among Nations: America's Place in World History.* New York: Hill and Wang, 2006.

Burbank, Jane, and Frederick Cooper. *Empires in World History: Power and the Politics of Difference.* Princeton: Princeton University Press, 2011.

Coates, Ken S. *A Global History of Indigenous Peoples: Struggle and Survival.* Houndmills: Palgrave Macmillan, 2004.

Conrad, Sebastian. *Globalisation and the Nation in Imperial Germany.* Cambridge: Cambridge University Press, 2010.

———. *What Is Global History?* Princeton: Princeton University Press, 2016.

Darwin, John. *After Tamerlane: The Rise and Fall of Global Empires, 1400–2000.* New York: Bloomsbury Press, 2009.

Kramer, Paul A. "Power and Connections: Imperial Histories of the United States in the World." *American Historical Review* 116 (December 2011): 1348–1391.

Magee, Gary B., and Andrew S. Thompson. *Empire and Globalisation: Networks of People, Goods, and Capital in the British World, c. 1850–1914.* Cambridge: Cambridge University Press, 2010.

Osterhammel, Jürgen. *The Transformation of the World: A Global History of the Nineteenth Century.* Princeton: Princeton University Press, 2014.

Perry, Richard J. *From Time Immemorial: Indigenous Peoples and State Systems.* Austin: University of Texas Press, 1996.

Rosenberg, Emily S., ed. *A World Connecting, 1870–1945.* Cambridge, MA: Harvard University Press, 2012.

Stoler, Ann Laura. "Tense and Tender Ties: The Politics of Comparison in North American History and (Post) Colonial Studies." *Journal of American History* 88 (December 2001): 829–865.

Streets-Salter, Heather, and Trevor R. Getz. *Empires and Colonies in the Modern World: A Global Perspective.* Oxford: Oxford University Press, 2016.

Thelen, David. "The Nation and Beyond: Transnational Perspectives on United States History." *Journal of American History* 86 (December 1999): 965–975.

Tyrrell, Ian. "American Exceptionalism in an Age of International History." *American Historical Review* 96 (October 1991): 1031–1055.

——. *Transnational Nation: United States History in Global Perspective Since 1789.* New York: Palgrave Macmillan, 2007.

Wolfe, Patrick. "Land, Labor, and Difference: Elementary Structures of Race." *American Historical Review* 106 (June 2001): 866–905.

——. "Settler Colonialism and the Elimination of the Native." *Journal of Genocide Research* 8 (December 2006): 387–409.

PART I
Global Convergences

1

SHARED WORLDS

In 1833, a ship on a routine trip carrying rice and porcelain on the Japanese coast was dismasted and sent adrift on the Pacific Ocean by a powerful typhoon. In January 1834, that same vessel ran aground at Cape Flattery on the northernmost tip of the Olympic Peninsula, and the ship's three Japanese survivors found themselves enslaved by the indigenous Makahs. After being rescued some four months later by the Hudson's Bay Company (HBC) brigantine *Lama*, the Japanese sailors then adjusted to living at Fort Vancouver, the British company's factory on the Columbia River. This regional headquarters of a London-based trading consortium was international and multilingual; its diverse residents comprised Scots, English, Irish, French, Hawaiian, eastern Iroquois, northern Plains Cree, and local Chinook. But these Japanese men were not there to stay. In late 1834, the HBC dispatched them to London, and from there they continued to Macao, evidently with the intent of returning to Japan. However, the around-the-world trip was cut short as diplomatic tensions between Japan and Britain kept the sailors from their homes.

Located on the northeast corner of the contiguous United States in what today is Washington State, Cape Flattery offers breathtaking rock formations; a densely forested, steep-cliffed shoreline; an abundance of wildlife; and restless water where the Strait of Juan de Fuca joins the Pacific Ocean. It may easily be mistaken for a natural barrier, an end point insulating the American West from the world. But like the above description of the Japanese sailors attests, it has in fact functioned more as a dynamic gateway and a crossroads for peoples, goods, and ideas, with these circulations connecting the West with the Atlantic and Pacific worlds. Already in the late 1700s, the indigenous peoples of the cape, the Makahs, lived surprisingly international lives. Being highly skilled traders, fishermen, and whalers, they interacted regularly with other Natives of the coast to their north and south. They also saw the Russians coming from the direction of Alaska and encountered the Spanish regularly sailing their coastline. In 1790, Manuel Quimper even claimed Spanish possession of Cape Flattery and started the building of a fort on the coast. While this garrison lasted only for few months, more international visitors followed. James Cook, a flock of British traders and explorers following on his tail, and the Bostonians (New England traders) arrived with big ships laden with goods. To the south of the Makahs, on the Columbia River, the Americans Meriwether Lewis and William Clark reached the coast overland in 1805. The two famed explorers met Indians who already wore European clothes, cursed in English (and possibly in other European languages), and drove tough bargains. Six years later, the German emigrant John Jacob Astor set up an American trading operation, the Pacific Fur Company, near the mouth of the Columbia. He planned to collect furs inland from Indian hunters, ship the pelts to China, and monopolize the provisioning of the Russian settlements to the far north. By then, the Makahs, like the Chinook and other local Natives, engaged in high-volume trade in sea otter pelts and whale oil, as historian Joshua L. Reid notes. The HBC ships often purchased more than 100 gallons of whale oil at a time. Toward the mid-1800s, the Makahs sold some 30,000 gallons of whale oil a year. Furthermore, not only did the Makahs become players in far-reaching inland and maritime trade networks, but they also found work aboard non-Native ships that took them to Spanish California, Hawaii, and across the world, even as far as Africa.

One notable episode revealing the scope and intensity of the transnational entanglements in the Pacific Northwest happened in 1809. The Makahs held one Anna Petrovna, the wife of a Russian sea captain employed by the Russian–American Company. Anna and her husband had been on board the schooner *Sv. Nikolai* as it sailed from New Archangel (now Sitka), Russian Alaska and as it wrecked south of Cape Flattery. The survivors were soon attacked by Hoh Indians, after which some fled further inland. One of the men, Timofei Tarakanov, later wrote a popular account of his ordeal, which went through at least five different editions in Russia and gained international fame as it was translated to several other languages. In one section of his book, Tarakanov noted that when they met the Makahs, Anna refused to leave her captors and chose a Makah man referred to as Ulatilla (Yutramaki), much to the anger and horror of her Russian husband. Seeing their options were limited, Tarakanov and four other Russians also surrendered themselves to the Makahs. They became slaves, captives, or family members, depending on individual circumstances, notes historian David Igler. A year later, both Anna and her Russian husband had died, whereas Tarakanov and the others were sold to an American trading ship visiting from Boston. Thus what we have is one white European woman and several European men taken captive by Natives and rescued by Americans. But this was not the whole extent of the entanglement. Igler and historian Kenneth Owens posit that Tarakanov was actually a serf from Kursk and Anna Petrovna probably a mestizo with an Aleut or Kodiak mother.

They also ponder if Ulatilla's father might have been an Irish surgeon named John McKay who had been left behind by the British ship *Captain Cook* in 1786.

Whether the latter was the case or not, it seems clear that in the early 1800s, a full-blown transnational convergence of empires, peoples, and goods was taking place in the Pacific borderlands of the American West. Many similar transnational meetings were also happening in the inland West. In fact, in the 1700s and early 1800s, an international cast of explorers, traders, workers, captives, animals, microbes, and goods converged and circulated throughout the West, making it a meeting ground and a crossroads of the Atlantic and Pacific worlds. People crossed over to the West to expand their empires, to save souls, and to trade and profit in furs, hides, horses, captives, and a broad range of other items. They also arrived to locate a global shortcut from Europe to Asia (the Northwest Passage). What they found was a shared, yet highly competitive, world of indigenous power and plural sovereignty. This early West was an intermingled racial world where kin relations and alliances straddled ethnic and "national" lines. In these spaces, independent Indians controlled much of the land, and traders, trappers, and missionaries representing different empires, companies, and families operated in webs of multiethnic communities. This early West was a place where European empires negotiated in realities they could not control nor dictate, had they wanted to. It was a realm that Napoleon Bonaparte gave up voluntarily, preferring instead to build his empire in continental Europe. This West was international before it became national, and it became known and placed in a global context of empires, markets, epidemics, and knowledge before it was claimed by the United States and its brand of settler colonialism.

Contact Zones

Early Flows and Shortcuts

Native Americans were the West's first transnational expansionists, making their presence known, claiming territory, and crossing over in search of empowerment. Scholars point to a series of migrations some 10,000 and 20,000 years ago across the then solid land route in the Bering Strait. Making the move were peoples from northeastern Asia, possibly from the present borderlands of Russia, China, Mongolia, and Kazakhstan, who edged toward today's American West driven by hunger, curiosity, and violence. Others, possibly from Southeast Asia, also may have reached the Americas by sailing across the Pacific Ocean thousands of years ago. Native crossings attained diverse forms, took various routes, and happened at different times. Many followed a north–south trajectory, while others, like the migrations of the Cheyenne and the Sioux, took eastern detours before reaching the West later on. Take, for example, the Athapascans. Dropping southward from Artic Canada (where many Athapascans still reside) into the Southwest borderlands and southern Plains, the ancestors of today's Navajos and Apaches migrated piecemeal in small groups over extensive periods of time (between the 1200s and 1600s) and over various routes: through the Rocky Mountains, Great Plains, and Great Basin. Stopping and building communities that spanned from northern Mexico to Kansas in the 1600s, some Apaches were on the move again in the 1700s. This time they were pushed south by southwest from the Plains in a series of wars by the expansionist Comanches, who descended from the Rockies to the Plains. This ethnogenesis saw Apache groups vanish, integrate new members, or as individuals and families melt into different Apache, other indigenous, or Hispanic communities on both sides of today's U.S.–Mexico border. Numerous Apaches were also forced to live as captives within their rival indigenous groups and in Hispanic homes in New Mexico and Texas, households and plantations of French Louisiana, Spanish mines in Zacatecas, other locales in northern New Spain, Mexico City, and the sugar plantations in Cuba. In short, many Apaches lived intensely transnational lives in the early West.

From the opposite direction of the Apaches came the Spanish, spreading from Hispaniola to Puerto Rico and Jamaica in 1508 and to Cuba and Central America in 1511. In 1513, the Spanish landed in Florida. Thinking they were on the edge of Asia, entering the lands of Cathay (China), the Spanish took on the ostensibly powerful Aztec Empire in the 1520s. Coming out triumphant, the Iberians soon spread to all directions in the Americas, thirsting for riches, converts for the church, and power. The first Spanish reached the West in the late 1520s. They did not move into the region on purpose, as historian Andrés Reséndez demonstrates. It was the Andalusian explorer and minor noble Álvar Núñez Cabeza de Vaca, and his two Spanish compatriots and one black African slave, who entered the West after their excursion went astray on the Gulf Coast. These disoriented men represented what remained of the disastrous Narváez expedition, which had started with some 400 people to explore and colonize Florida. Delayed by a hurricane near Cuba, knocked off course by an error of navigation, and marred by a disastrous decision to separate the men – trekking overland – from their ships, the Narváez expedition turned desperate. Scrambling to get back to Mexico City, the survivors endured a horrific march through Florida, a harrowing raft passage along the Louisiana coast, and years of enslavement in the Southwest. They brought dysentery to the Indians, decimating half of the population at the Texas coastal villages of the Capoques and the Hans. They were also the first Europeans to see bison, immediately comparing them to the cows of Morocco and Spain.

After making it to Mexico City, the center of New Spain built by indigenous labor and imposed on the ruins of the Aztec capital Tenochtitlan, de Vaca and his compatriots shared tales of their trials and the Indians and animals they had met. They also fueled rumors of golden cities awaiting bold explorers in the continental interior. It was the fantastic dream of Cibola and the seven cities of gold that spurred ambitious Spanish explorers to various reaches of the Americas, from Rio del Plata and the Amazon to the early West. Obviously, the conquest of the gold-rich Aztecs and Incas only added stimulation to these dreams promulgated by the Spanish. So did the discovery of silver at Zacatecas in 1546. While de Vaca's adventures would continue in the Rio del Plata region, others headed north.

In the 1540s, Hernando de Alarcón ventured some 90 miles up the Colorado River. Moving overland toward the Upper Rio Grande Valley was another minor nobleman, this time from Castile and León: Francisco Vázquez de Coronado. He came accompanied by 300 Spanish, including mounted troops, as well as 800 Tlaxcalans recruited from central Mexico. The Tlaxcalans, once fierce enemies of the Aztecs, had become allies of the Spanish, participating as fighters and settlers in the conquest of the Chichimecas in northeastern Mexico and also in Guatemala. Now they witnessed Coronado bring Spanish might on the Pueblos. They partook in violence and in treks that spanned from the Grand Canyon deep to the Plains, experienced exhaustion and disappointment, and returned home disgusted and goldless. The disillusioned Coronado reverted to his comfortable "desk job" as an administrator in Nuevo Galicia and later in Mexico City.

The next wave of Spanish on the move were the missionaries who traveled from central Mexico to the Pueblos in the 1580s. While these Franciscans extended across much of Spanish America and worked up the Rio Grande, the globe-spanning networks of Jesuits spread not only to China, Japan, and India but also to Nueva Vizcaya and Sonora, including today's Arizona, until expelled from the Americas in 1767. The first European settlers reached the West in 1598. Actually, historian Marc Simmons records, many of those first potential settlers were Tlaxcalan warriors, servants, and their families. Led by the son of Spanish-Basque colonists and silver mine owners from Zacatecas, Don Juan de Oñate, a mixed bag of settlers, soldiers, and priests made their homes in the Upper Rio Grande Valley, establishing Santa Fe.

The Spanish arrival in the early West involved elaborate ritual laden with significant transnational meanings and ramifications. The Spanish customarily erected a cross and read aloud the *requerimiento*, a degree issued in 1513 by the Spanish monarchy. It was a customary Spanish practice that was performed all over the Americas when the Spanish made their rights of conquest known to the Native communities. It involved the absolute religious supremacy of the Christian faith and the political superiority of Spain, as based on the 1493 papal bull (Treaty of Tordesillas), which announced nothing less than the split of the western hemisphere between Portugal and Spain. In New Mexico, the Spanish told the Natives that they were there to stay and that the Pueblo Indians could fight or submit, or, to put it differently, choose between heaven, meaning conversion into Christianity, or hell, denoting the war and slavery that would result from resistance. While the *requerimiento* was normally read in Latin and with no interpreters present, it could also be delivered from shipboard to some empty shoreline the Spanish coveted. Thus, especially after the Spanish started sailing the coastal Pacific, many Native Americans (in theory, at least) became subjects of a European monarch and subject to a European religion without necessarily meeting any Europeans. Of course, even when hearing the *requerimiento* in person many Natives have failed to understand (or care about) these ceremonies and proclamations of "international law."

Not only expanding the realm of the crown and the church and setting up government and communities along the Rio Grande, but also hoping to find some golden cities, Onate's men went on to explore the Great Plains and the Colorado River. While mountains of gold continued to elude the Spanish in the West, their arrival connected numerous Native communities to all sorts of transnational circulations. Imported Euro-Asiatic diseases quickly decimated many Pueblo villages, while the Churra sheep from the Iberian Peninsula rapidly made it into the hands of independent Indians, especially the Navajos, who surrounded the Spanish settlements. Then there were the horses the Spanish had introduced to the Americas. Traded and raided, a large-scale horse diffusion followed, especially after the 1680 Pueblo revolt. Different indigenous communities, historian Pekka Hämäläinen comments, created different horse cultures. Horses reached the Shoshones by 1700 and facilitated the Comanche invasion from the Rocky Mountains to the plains grasslands from the 1710s onward. The animals also spread to the Blackfeet and Crows by 1740s, and to all reaches of the Northern Plains of today's Canada by the mid-1700s.

By the early 1700s, the transnational crossing of peoples, as well as of bacteria, animals, and material goods, was in full swing in the West. So were the transnational dreams of the Northwest Passage. There were many elusive destinations in modern world history – for instance, Terra Australis in the 1700s, or the source of the White Nile in the 1800s – that drew daredevils, romantics, and self-promoters from Europe. They became the stuff of feverish dreams among glory-hungry explorers, the sources of seemingly endless mystique among the broader public, as well as sites for intense competition between empires. While one such legend touching the West related to the cities of gold, another concerned the elusive Northwest Passage. Before the Norwegian Roald Amundsen first navigated the route in 1903–1906, the search for a shortcut between the Atlantic and the Pacific, from Europe to Asia, had been ongoing for centuries.

In 1524, the Italian explorer Giovanni de Verrazano thought he saw the Pacific Ocean when zooming across North Carolina's Outer Banks. In Mexico, Hernán Cortés – a globetrotting servant of the empire whose resume included being the conqueror of the Aztecs, the first governor of New Spain, the leader in Spanish expeditions against Honduras and Algiers, and the head of ocean voyages to first spot the tip of Baja California – felt positive that a waterway connected the Atlantic and the Pacific. He was not alone. While Columbus had thought he had arrived on the outskirts of Asia, others in his wake still believed that they were close to China. They supposed that America was slender, the Pacific narrow, and that both would be easy to cross. This notion proved extremely persistent. Exploring and setting up numerous Jesuit missions in Sonora in the 1680s and in Tumacácori and San Xavier del Bac (Tucson), Arizona, in the 1690s, Father Eusebio Kino was just one learned man among many who still dreamed of reaching China overland via California. He presumed that a slim strait, at worst, would have to be crossed to get there.

Elsewhere, the quest for a global shortcut had prompted the Frenchman Jacques Cartier up the St. Lawrence in the 1530s. Beginning in the 1570s, the English were also in the game, and in the 1610s, Englishman Henry Hudson went to look for a path and wintered in the bay that now bears his name. While no passage was found, the race to locate it only escalated, somehow surviving every disappointment and discarding all logical arguments made against it. For instance, the HBC men, after expanding inland from York Factory on Hudson's Bay and setting up factories on the Saskatchewan River in 1774 and Lake Athabasca in 1778, soon realized there was no waterway westward from the bay. The Scot Alexander MacKenzie attempted in 1789 to locate a watercourse to the Pacific on a river now named after him (which flows to the north). He then became the first European to cross the continent overland from east to west in 1793. Recommending that Britain plant settlements in the Pacific Northwest, he proclaimed that no water route existed through the continental interior. Still, the quest for the passage drew numerous parties in the 1800s, particularly in the Arctic waters. Some, like the expedition by the British John Franklin, perished in the world of ice and became legendary because of that.

MacKenzie was just one explorer among many to involve the interior West in this quest for a global shortcut. In 1681, the French nobleman from Rouen, René-Robert Cavelier, Sieur de La Salle, launched an expedition down the Mississippi River and the Gulf of Mexico from New France. A one-time Jesuit novice as a youth, and later, a fur trader and an agriculturalist near Montreal, La Salle dreamed, as historian Robert Weddle points out, of a great river system, which he thought would flow into the Pacific and provide passage to China. Thirsting to find the Northwest Passage, he also planned setting up French trading posts in the West for future settlements. What La Salle found was a route to the Atlantic. Although Hernando De Soto had explored and claimed this area for Spain some 140 years prior, La Salle now claimed the Mississippi River Valley for Louis XIV, naming the territory Louisiana. He also sailed defiantly in the Gulf of Mexico, which was considered by Spain to be theirs.

In 1684, La Salle continued the search. He sailed from Rochefort, France, to locate the mouth of the Mississippi River by sea. His agenda also included plans to establish a settlement and a post for striking against New Spain, afflicting Spanish shipping, and blocking potential English expansion, as well as providing a French port for the Mississippi Valley fur trade. While losing more than half of his 500 would-be settlers early on, he did not find the mouth of the

Mississippi. He did establish a colony, Fort St. Louis, on Garcitas Creek near the southern Texas coast in February 1685. By the end of summer, half of the residents had perished, possibly from poor rations and overwork. In 1686, La Salle himself moved west overland. Looking in vain for the Mississippi River and the great western waterways, he made it as far as the Pecos River or the Rio Grande. Lost, frustrated, and desperate, he next trekked east hoping that the Mississippi would turn out and his party could get back to the French settlements at the Great Lakes. Meanwhile, motivated by fears of French advancements, the Spanish in turn sought La Salle's French in Texas with five sea voyages and six land marches. Waiting for somebody to rescue them, the residents of Fort St. Louis instead faced a massacre at the hands of the Karankawa Indians. The settlement destroyed, La Salle's outfit in turn came apart. La Salle himself was assassinated by his own men somewhere near the Brazos River. The Northwest Passage had eluded him to the end.

While only five Frenchmen from La Salle's party eventually made it back to France, the few survivors played key roles in the exploration of the Southwest. Some joined Diego de Vargas in the Spanish reconquest of New Mexico in the 1690s, while others functioned as guides and interpreters for Louis Juchereau de St. Denis on an exploration across Texas to the Rio Grande in 1714. Crossing in the opposite direction, the Spanish missionaries who reached East Texas in 1690s were driven out by the Caddos. In 1716, a fresh crop of Spanish missionaries arrived, founding Nacogdoches close to the Red River. By 1722, the Spanish had a foothold of 12 missions and several presidios between San Antonio and East Texas.

The Great Pacific Rendezvous

Several historians (among them Warren Cook, James Gibson, Derek Pethick, and, more recently, David Igler) have shown how the Spanish, British, Russians, and Americans stepped up exploring the major oceans of the world during the late eighteenth century and how these empires met on the Pacific Coast of North America.

Starting in 1565 with the voyage of Andres de Urdaneta, the Spanish, with their large multiple-deck galleons that sailed between Mexico and the Philippines, had engaged in the trans-Pacific and global commodity exchanges. They traded silver mined in Mexico and in Potosi, Bolivia for Chinese goods like silk, spices, and porcelain. Initially, these galleons skirted the beaches of California. In the mid-1700s, Spain grew more and more wary that the "West" would be lost to competition. They worried over French extensions from Louisiana, British moves from Hudson's Bay, Russian advances from Alaska, and all of their activities in the Pacific. While making the folly of allying with France, Spain also seized the initiative while France and Britain clashed in the Seven Years' War. After France was defeated globally in Europe, India, and North America, Spain gained French Louisiana in 1763, while Britain took hold of New France. Six years later, the Spanish sent four expeditions made up of soldiers, settlers, and Franciscan priests to California (two by land and two by sea). They established the first missions in San Diego in 1769 and in Monterrey the next year. The space in between was gradually dotted with missions approximately a day's journey apart, while the northernmost Spanish bastion was Mission Dolores in the small village of Yerba Buena, better known, after 1847, as San Francisco.

Once it got going, Spain moved further north. In fact, already in 1539, Francisco de Ulloa had studied the California coast, proving it was not an island (although this popular belief persisted decades later). Three years later, Juan Rodriguez Cabrillo reconnoitered the coastline of today's California and Oregon. In 1602, Juan de Fuca, a Greek navigator in service of the Spanish, claimed he found the fabled Strait of Anián, a waterway believed to be the western entrance of the Northwest Passage. De Fuca also asserted that this watercourse started on the coast of modern-day Washington State. Hearing rumors of a Russian presence nearby, in 1774, Juan Perez sailed to establish a Spanish claim as far north as Vancouver Island. The next year, Bruno Heceta sailed to up to the 58th parallel, what is now Alaska, to claim it for Spain. Others would soon follow, and by 1790, the Spanish occupied Nootka Sound and set up what would be a short-lived settlement of Santa Cruz de Nuca on Vancouver Island.

On the move was also the British explorer James Cook. He was searching for the great southern continent, Terra Australis, and sailed the eastern coast of Australia, bumping into Hawaii. On his third trip, 1776–1779, he reached Oregon and advanced to the Bering Strait, trying, like so many of his contemporaries, to locate the western entry of the Northwest Passage. Since 1745, the British government had promised a £20,000 reward to the first captain who sailed through this mysterious watercourse. The money had no takers as the passage eluded the numerous British vessels hovering around Nootka Sound, Vancouver Island, Strait of Juan de Fuca, and Puget Sound. Several American (New England) trappers and mariners were also on the Pacific coast. In 1791, Boston sea captain Robert Gray took possession of the lower Columbia River on behalf of the United States.

The Russians were also coming. After moving east across Siberia to the Pacific, they went to the seas. Vitus Bering, a Dane in service of the Czar, reached the Aleutian Islands in 1741. The Russians soon had various companies engaged in sea otter trade, which made Alaska as attractive as sables made Siberia. Exhausting the Aleutian chain of furs, the Russians reached mainland North America in 1762. They continued the hunt, but they also established missions and some settlements on the coastline of Alaska. By 1788, the Spanish met Russians using Indian canoes on Prince William Sound and learned that some local Indians had visited St. Petersburg and were dressed in Russian clothing. By 1799, the Russian–American Company had gained a trading monopoly and sent ships south the coast all the way to California.

Already in 1790, an international conflict had nearly emerged in the Pacific Northwest as the Spanish seized British trading ships. This did nothing to diminish the buzzing activity, however. The busiest season so far, 1792 saw 21 vessels from five different countries trading on the Northwest coast. Rival claims and the continued threat of armed conflicts resulted in the Nootka Conventions. Diplomacy led to Spain abandoning its claims to exclusive sovereignty in the Pacific and opening the coast for European traders. The conventions also undermined the notion that an empire could claim exclusive sovereignty without establishing some kind of actual occupation or settlements. The seed for the settler colonial West had been planted.

In the 1810s, the international melee picked up speed. There were the Russians negotiating with John Jacob Astor's Pacific Fur Company, an American operation with its headquarters, Fort Astoria, on the Columbia River. There was David Thompson of the North West Company, who declared the portion of the Columbia River above its confluence with the Snake River for the British. Then the British ousted the Americans from the Columbia as a consequence of the War of 1812, and sorted their inner rivalries as the HBC merged with the North West Company. In the 1820s, the HBC's new regional factory, Fort Vancouver, was erected on the shores of the Columbia. Along with it, dozens of lesser HBC sites dotted the coastline to the north, making it look like the Pacific Northwest might become British. Or perhaps it would be Russian. In 1812, the Russians were busy establishing Rossiya, or Fort Ross, a trading post and potential seed of settlement some 50 miles north of the Spanish Yerba Buena. Russian California lasted until 1841. By then, Russian America had lost its main reason for existence due to the slaughtering of marine mammals for the market in such volume that there were too few left (Figure 1.1).

The great trans-Pacific hunt stretched from the New Zealand shoreline to North America, and it often came with devastating costs to the animal populations, among them sea otters, river otters, beavers, fur seals, and whales. By the 1830s, the trade also involved hides of California cattle. While the hunt grew to hundreds of thousands of skins per year, the commercial activity also quickly diversified to include provisions and various manufactured goods. Seamen restocked their ships with wood and water, exchanged manufactured goods for nutrition, as well as sought specific commodities such as whale oil. Able Native hunters exploited maritime and terrestrial resources from Alaska to Cape Flattery and California, and actually all the way to Chile, empowering themselves and filling the cargo holes of large non-Native trading ships. The Pacific Northwest maritime furs were sold mainly in China in exchange for tea, spices, silk, porcelain, and other Chinese goods. These were then sold to white consumers across Europe and North America (foremost in New England). The greatest fortunes from the sea otter trade tended to gravitate toward England

FIGURE 1.1 Fort Ross. Courtesy of Library of Congress Prints and Photographs Division (from Society of California Pioneers, before 1840, photographer unknown. HABS CAL,49-FORO,1—5).

and New England. While porcelain spread to well-to-do European homes like wildfire, in China, sea otter furs turned into a status symbol for the elite, including the royal household. Thousands of gallons of whale oil procured by Northwest-coast Natives also reached Europe, where, distilled into benzene, it lit the homes and businesses of cities such as London. Natives in turn received weapons, hardware, metal items (including knives, nails, and chisels), and blankets (they preferred British-made over New England-produced). As savvy consumers, Natives also wanted tea, rice, tobacco, sugar, and salt, as well as more luxurious items such as coral and Chinese-made sandalwood and camphor boxes.

Trade networks linked the early West with Russian Alaska, Spanish Peru and Chile, Hawaii, Polynesian ports, as well as with the burgeoning market center and open port of Canton (Guangzhou) in China. Facing stiff international competition in China from the 1780s onward, the British East India Company had established its factory in Canton in 1751, one of dozens of such factories linking the Atlantic Ocean to the Indian Ocean and to China. From Canton, trade linkages also spanned to ports in Fiji; the Gulf of Siam; Burma, Sumatra, and Java in the Dutch East Indies; the Netherlands; and, of course, to Calcutta, India, to London, and all the vast reaches of the British Empire.

Transnational commerce also brought new people to Pacific coast communities, and it moved local peoples from one place to the next across the vast oceans. While many Makahs found jobs on European ships sailing across the Pacific, numerous East Coast Indians did so as well. Some Native American seamen not only sailed across the Pacific but also stayed for good, making their homes and living in places such as Fiji and Hawaii. Hawaiian trappers in turn secured employment in the HBC inland posts. In 1787, Ka'iana, a high-ranking Hawaiian royal, and Comekala, a Mowachant Indian from Nootka Sound, spent over a year sailing the Pacific on a British ship *Felice Adventurer*. They visited both China and Hawaii. Also on board were Chinese carpenters, who built the first non-Native boat made in the Pacific Northwest in 1788. Besides these and other Chinese workers, at least 30 Japanese sailors reached the shores of North America or Mexico as a consequence of shipwrecks before the mid-1800s.

The number of vessels on the Pacific coast of North America increased each decade, so that hundreds of them had entered the coastal waters by the 1820s. David Igler writes that nearly half of these ships came from the United States, while Britain, Spain, Mexico, and Russia were pretty evenly matched (approximately 10% each). But there were trading vessels from 17 other polities, including France, Prussia, Hamburg, Canton, Sweden, Denmark, Sardinia, Bengal, and Mauritius. The list of most-visited ports was topped by Hawaii, where nearly half of the ships stopped. Hawaii quickly emerged as a central destination in these webs of trans-Pacific trade. It also became yet another fancy of imperial dreams. It drew British and French interest and an ill-fated attempt of colonization by the Russians long before it was annexed by the United States in the 1890s.

Terrestrial Circulations

Overland fur trading networks also placed the West firmly with global webs of production, exchange, and consumption. In the Rocky Mountains, scholars including Eric Dolin and David Wishart write, trading centered on beaver pelts. The felted fur provided soft yet resilient material that could be easily combed to make a variety of fashionable hat shapes; these included the familiar top hat, highly popular among many social classes in the eastern United States and especially in Europe. The northern Plains trade in turn revolved around buffalo hides, which were tanned into leather and then used as machine belts. Bison bones, fat – used for manufacturing tallow – and meat were also utilized internationally. Furs were low bulk and high value commodities that could bear transportation over long distances. Also, relatively little capital was needed, as overhead costs were low, especially if the Indians acted as primary producers.

Overland fur trade thought and functioned in global terms. Wishart explains that on the Plains, the annual cycle went something like this: winter hunts by mostly Native American hunters provided most bison robes, while supplies and trade goods originated in the factories of the eastern United States and Europe, and exchanges took place in trading posts dotting the Plains. Trade goods were often specially requested by Natives, their orders relayed by St. Louis via winter express and by steamboat in the summer. There were standardized products and standing orders. Here, again, most Natives – contrary to stereotypes – proved very picky and knowledgeable customers. They, for example, preferred Chinese vermillion over American and demanded woolen goods from England. Like the coastal Indians, they did not settle for blankets from Lowell, Massachusetts, but favored blankets and cloth provided by Leeds and Manchester textile companies. It was also the Loubat Company of Le Havre that made the kind of blue and scarlet blankets the Plains Indians wanted, while beads should come from Venice and guns from Britain, Belgium, and Germany.

There were three main routes to markets, and all led through New York. One was by steamboat to New Orleans and thence to New York, but on this route, heat and humidity could damage the furs. Other courses took to the Ohio River and either went on to Pittsburgh and the Pennsylvania Canal or to Buffalo and the Erie Canal. The final destination of the furs was decided each time after a thorough comparative market analysis. On the East Coast, furs were transported to markets in New York, Boston, and Montreal, and much was shipped to fur marts in London and Leipzig, Germany, from which the products were distributed all over Europe.

In the Rocky Mountains, it was the multinational and multiethnic mobile outfits of trappers who did much of the work, fall and spring being the main trapping seasons. They worked either as freelancers or on the payroll of companies, most notably William Ashley's Rocky Mountain Fur Company (until it was eliminated in the early 1830s by the American Fur Company). In the summer, they met for an annual rendezvous, with summer being the only season the supply wagon trains from St. Louis could move across the Plains. While the furs headed to the global markets from the rendezvous, company trappers also kept moving and divided into numerous parties delegated to various hunting grounds. Something of a "fur rush" was in full swing in the late 1820s, but the trade lacked stability: resource base was fragile and it renewed slowly. Competition also reduced prices and profits. The HBC was blamed as seeking to create a barren fur desert between the U.S and British operations. There was also a preference for short-term gain over long-term planning, and the markets habitually proved quite unstable. By the 1840s, the beaver population was depleted in the Rocky Mountains, but by then, trends were also changing in Europe, and silk hats were becoming the new fashion.

Like the Aleuts, Tlingits, Haidas, Nuu-chah-nulths, Makahs, Chinook, and other indigenous peoples of the Pacific Northwest, several Native American communities in the inland West encountered European crossings and became part of the global funneling of diseases, peoples, animals, and goods while staying at "home." Mandans were one of these sedentary, primarily horticultural, peoples whose lives these circulations revolutionized. Living in permanent villages on the eastern fringes of the Plains, close to the banks of the Missouri River in present-day North Dakota, their first face-to-face meetings with Europeans, historian Elisabeth Fenn shows, happened possibly in 1689. Then the French explorer and aristocrat Louis Armand de Lom d'Arce Lahontan made a foray from Michilimackinac, where Lake Huron and Lake Michigan meet, toward the Mississippi and Missouri Rivers. His account of the journey, published in 1703, proved wildly popular, seeing numerous reprints and translations. Apparently Thomas Jefferson, an avid expansionist, was among those who had a copy.

The first meeting could also have happened "abroad" in Saskatchewan between 1690 and 1692, when a group of Mandan or neighboring Hidatsa hunters met Henry Kelsey, an employee of the newly established HBC on an outing from York Factory. We do know that when searching for a great inland sea that would offer river links toward China, the Frenchman Pierre Gaultier de Varenne de La Vérendrye visited the Mandan villages in 1738. During the next decades, more and more traders started showing up. They were an international bunch, usually of French, English, and Scottish origin, many of them mestizos and quite a few aristocrats. Between 1787 and the coming of Lewis and Clark in 1804, at least 39 parties reached the Mandans from British Canada. Others made their appearance from St. Louis, seeking to secure the Mandans and their territories to the networks of the Spanish Empire.

By 1800, their communities awash with British goods, the Mandan villages and the York Factory functioned as principal permanent trade centers on the northern Plains. The Sioux, who soon eclipsed the Mandans, and the Comanches also commanded important trade centers on the opposite reaches of the Great Plains. The Cheyenne operated as middlemen. Working in small groups, they specialized in horses, manufactured weapons, and bison robes. Obviously, only the latter product originated from the Plains, with the others being transnational imports (although horse breeding was actively practiced by the Comanches). In the 1830s, some Cheyenne aligned with Bent's Fort, a new trading post on the Arkansas River. This fort was part of a trading nexus led by French, American, and mestizo men from St. Louis. These included William Bent, an American who married into the Cheyenne, becoming their ally and later their agent. Also involved was Ceran St. Vrain, a French businessmen and the son of French aristocrats who came to the United States when escaping the French Revolution.

Drawing an international crowd, the Plains trade centers were part of a wider web, some permanent, others annual meets, still others temporary gatherings, but all connecting dynamic regions and contributing to transnational webs and exchanges of manufactured goods, farm produce, livestock, germs, captives, and furs. Significant trade centers rising and falling in the West included the Dalles, on the Columbia River in today's Oregon; the Pueblos in New Mexico; and the Spanish Santa Fe. On the list were also the North West Company's and HBC's posts, which dotted southern Manitoba and the Minnesota-Ontario borderlands and advanced in the Pacific Northwest. Taken together, these networks spanned the Plains, the Southwest, the Great Basin, the Pacific Northwest, the Rocky Mountains, the eastern woodlands, the Mississippi, and the Great Lakes: the modern West and beyond. They also connected the Spanish, French, British, Russian, and U.S. realms in the Americas, in Europe, and elsewhere. They linked with New Orleans, St. Louis, Mexico City, Madrid, Montreal, New York, London, Canton, and beyond, and they tied to the Atlantic slave trade and thus with the Caribbean and Africa.

These circulations created and shaped communities in the early West that fused trapping, trading, and ethnic mixing. St. Louis was one such place, a fast-growing gateway town on the Mississippi River that sent traders and drew furs from the Rocky Mountains and the upper Missouri. Located amid powerful indigenous polities, foremost among them the Osages, St. Louis was a cosmopolitan community established by the French (1763), controlled by the Spanish (1770–1800), and then reclaimed by Napoleonic France (1800–1803) before it was purchased by the United States (1803). Although short on Iberian or other European settlers, the average Spanish settlement in New Mexico, Texas, and California was also populated by an international cast from at least three different continents. The community in these places usually comprised a mix of Europeans, Africans, and indigenous people from a variety of backgrounds in North and Latin America. The Tlaxcalans, for instance, remained fairly numerous and active settlers in various locales of New Spain. Their presence was most relevant on or just south of the Rio Grande. At El Paso, they were refugees from northern New Mexico after the Pueblo revolt of 1680, and they settled at San Juan Bautista near present Eagle Pass about 1700 to help instruct and control the Coahuiltecan Indians at nearby missions. In the 1750s, the Tlaxcalans were invited by José de Escandón to settle in his new colony of Nuevo Santander in the lower Rio Grande valley. Although there were plans to settle Tlaxcalans at several strategic places in Texas in the mid-1700s, relatively few actually made their homes there (few families arrived at San Saba Mission in 1757).

In California, Johann August (John) Sutter instituted yet another type of international community in the early West. Escaping debts in his native Switzerland in 1834, Sutter relocated to America, where he sought his luck as an entrepreneur in Kansas, Oregon, Hawaii, and Alaska before ending up in Mexican California in 1839. Inspired by what he saw at Fort Vancouver, Sutter wanted to build a Swiss colony, New Helvetia, on a Mexican land grant in the Sacramento Valley near the confluence of the American and Sacramento Rivers. What he actually ended up doing was combining a Hawaiian-style residential settlement with an international mix of hundreds of employees of

Hawaiian, Hispanic, European, and Native American descent, many of them working in conditions bordering on slavery. He had built an imposing adobe military fort and a trading post centering on maritime fur business. The settlement was defended by an army of some 200 local Miwok, Nisenan, and mission Indians and German-speaking white officers, dressed in Russian uniforms bought from Fort Ross. Sutter's downfall coincided with the Gold Rush, as his workers left to pan for gold and as miners and land speculators invaded his valley. Losing his fortune, Sutter settled in Pennsylvania with his Swiss family, which he had abandoned back in 1834 but brought to California in 1850.

St. Louis, the Spanish pueblos, Sutter's New Helvetia, and other communities were also sites through which notions of freedom and captivity were constantly negotiated as Europeans as well as indigenous peoples shared in the practice of captive-taking and slavery. Western captive networks embraced versions of a global phenomenon of slavery that saw the taking of individuals, enslavement of communities, breaking down of groups, and erasure of cultures across the Pacific, from Australia to Russian Alaska, the Caribbean, Africa, the Indian Ocean area, and elsewhere. The Spanish brought the first black African slaves to the West, and while numerous indigenous communities had engaged in some form of slavery before the coming of Europeans, human captives became one of the prime trade commodities through the West and its borderlands in the wake of Spanish arrival. Captives functioned as unpaid labor, as a way to gain access to other communities, and as a method for obtaining information on routes, peoples, and one's surroundings. While scores of people perished in captivity, others were integrated into their host communities. In the Spanish borderlands, former captives became a distinct social class known as *genizaros*.

Importantly for this book, networks of captive-taking and slavery made peoples in the West engage in involuntary crossings that connected the West with the British/American areas east of the Mississippi River, New Spain, and French Louisiana. Scores of indigenous peoples, including numerous Apaches and Pawnees, ended up as forced mining and plantation workers, house slaves, and as adopted community members from Louisiana to central Mexico and Cuba. In the shores and ports of the Pacific Northwest, ocean-going vessels carried enslaved Africans, stolen or purchased Native American women, other indigenous hostages, indentured servants, and a wide array of unfree people. From Alaska to Baja California and stretching from the Pacific Islands to New Zealand, a sexual marketplace developed where indigenous women, viewed as natural resources and cross-cultural assets, were bartered and prostituted. Thousands of white seafarers came for "native hospitality," for sexual companionship that overlapped with fur trade and captive-taking. Along with sexual commerce and hospitality, captivities became woven into the imaginative and spatial makeup of European empires in their Pacific voyages. James Cook, for instance, took as captives/hostages Tahitian and other Polynesian leaders, Tonga chiefs, Maori boys, and others, before being killed himself while trying to capture chief Kalani'opu'u at Kealakekua Bay, Hawaii. Cook was not alone: the British George Vancouver; Spanish Alejandro Malaspina; Russian Vasily Golovnin; French Jean-François de Galaup, comte de Lapérouse; and the American Charles Wilkes, all prominent explorers of the Pacific and its North American coastline in the late 1700s as well as men on the lookout for the Northwest Passage, each employed similar methods.

Long-distance exploration and transnational trade networks brought not only an international cast of people to the West but also an epidemiological chaos. Smallpox, dysentery, measles, typhus, and other deadly maladies traversed oceans and wreaked havoc among Native peoples, killing scores of adults, plummeting fertility levels, and increasing infant mortality rates. The impact was most extreme in places that had dense concentrations of people. Intended by the Spanish to become factories for agriculture and the conversion/civilizing of Natives, the Spanish missions in California and the average baptized Indians, or "neophytes," that lived there saw their mobility severely limited and their life fall under a stringent regime of labor and prayer. Friars enforced obedience through imposition of moral codes (although sexual abuse was also common), solitary confinement, and severe physical punishments that included the use of whippings, branding, and shackles. But it was the imported diseases that turned these sites of oppression into communities of death where the average resident could not expect to stay alive for more than a few years. A vicious cycle of apathy and death resulted as the Spanish amassed more and more Natives from the surrounding countryside to replace those who died in the missions.

Like the missions, many indigenous villages were ripe for turning into hotbeds of imported diseases that crossed borders with ease. In 1775, thousands of miles from the Mandans, smallpox was raging in Boston, while four years later it was destroying Mexico City. Traveling well, it covered much ground in Latin America. By December 1780, it had New Orleans, San Antonio, the Pueblos, and Santa Fe in its grip. In 1781, the pox struck the entire Great Plains. It also killed as much as one-third of the population of the Pacific Coast Tlingit, Haida, Chinook, and Nez Perce communities. Later this pandemic would make it all the way to Alaska. Lack of previous exposure, together with large and dense villages, made for vast suffering, confusion, and all-consuming grief and heartache among the Mandans. Of their thirteen clans, the Mandans were left with seven as the disease was through. Their neighboring Arikaras dropped from thirty-two towns to only two.

Transnational migrations of this type were far from over, however. Whooping cough and measles emerged in tandem in the winter of 1819. Norway rats, Elizabeth Fenn asserts, invaded the Mandans with force in 1825, coming on the keelboats of the U.S. Army. Originating nowhere near Norway, but possibly from the plains of central Asia, the rats were reported in Ireland in 1722, England in 1730, France in 1735, Germany in 1750, and Spain in

1800. The species went on to conquer nearly all continents, arriving in North America in the mid-1700s. Producing as many as 50 offspring per female per year, the rats stormed the Mandan grain storages with devastating effectiveness, displaying an insatiable appetite. The Mandans in turn went hungry. While the Indians tried to cope with the rats, so did the American Fur Company people at Fort Union, established in 1828 along the Missouri River some 120 miles north of the Mandans. From 1832, regular steamboat traffic linked Fort Union, the Mandans, and St. Louis. In 1833, cholera was on board. Arriving in Canada in 1832, it traveled west, reaching St. Louis by May 1833 and possibly the Mandans soon thereafter.

What is certain is that smallpox returned. HBC's brigantine *Lama* (the same vessel that redeemed the Japanese castaways from the Makahs) brought it to the Northwest Coast in 1836. Soon outbreaks of the disease hit everywhere in the Pacific, from Alaska to Chile and from California to Tahiti. The steamer *St. Peter's* dropped smallpox all along the upper Missouri. The epidemic exploded, killing some 10,000–15,000 Plains Indians. It wreaked havoc even among the more nomadic Lakota Sioux and Cheyenne. Unlike many other tribes in the area, the Mandans had been saved from the bouts of smallpox that had hit after 1781. Now, largely without immunity due to the long gap, smallpox killed as many as seven-eighths of the Mandans. Only some 300 survived.

In the bigger picture, the repeated strikes of "old world" pathogens led to a near total destruction among the Mandans. Many other indigenous villages also suffered irreplaceable loss. Among them were the Makahs, who lost three-quarters of their population to smallpox in 1853. Nomadic communities were also hit. These included the Blackfeet, a once powerful confederation of transborder peoples in Montana and Canada with strong ties to British traders. By the time the U.S. settler empire reached them, the Blackfeet were pale shadows of their former might.

Exploration and Expansion

Louisiana

Historians Robert Bush and Peter Kastor, among others, have claimed that as the new century dawned in 1800 it increasingly looked like the West had become a pawn on the chessboard of European politics. This notion applied equally to the Pacific Coast and to the massive landmass referred to as Louisiana. This Louisiana (unlike the present state) represented an area shaped like a triangle (the kind that stands on its head) spanning from the Rocky Mountains to the Mississippi River. The claim and the authority of Madrid, Paris, or (after 1804) Washington on this area certainly was contested by most of the area's indigenous peoples – including the Mandans, the Cheyenne, or the actively expanding Sioux. Many were probably not even aware of the international reshuffling of Louisiana, first in the mid-1700s and again in the early 1800s. Taken by Spain in 1763, the area returned to French hands in 1800 with the Third Treaty of San Ildefonso. This treaty represented one complex machination in a series of complex machinations by post-revolutionary and habitually chaotic France and its rising star Napoleon Bonaparte, who tried to reshuffle domestic and international politics to his liking. Kept secret until October 1802, the treaty involved French authority in Parma and Tuscany, put pressure on its ally Spain, and took measures against its enemy Britain. While the transfer of power in Louisiana to the French took place in November 1803, ten months earlier American negotiators had been sent to Paris to inquire if France would consider selling the area. A deal was struck in April and a formal cession to the United States made in New Orleans on December 20, 1803. Another ceremony was held in St. Louis on March 9–10, 1804. This event is remembered as Three Flags Day.

It is possible to argue that Napoleon's strong continental potential and visions in Europe led him to abandon any possible continental machinations in the West. During his rise to power, Napoleon had first entertained plans of French imperial expansion in Africa and the Middle East. He also had dreams of a French resurgence in the Americas. Louisiana would ideally form a strong French claim at the heart of the continent, checking U.S. expansion and providing food, fuel, and protection to the more profitable French sugar islands in the Caribbean. Political unrest inside France, the near-continuous fighting in continental Europe, the looming conflict with Britain, what had been a less-than-spectacular expedition into Ottoman Egypt, and campaigns of self-promotion to become the head of state in France made Napoleon rethink his priorities. Shaping his decisions was also the fate of the large expeditionary force he sent to regain control of the wealthy colony of Saint-Domingue (Haiti).

Influenced by the ideals of the French Revolution, in 1791 a slave insurrection had spread on Saint-Domingue, resulting in the abolition of slavery and the ousting of French rule. When it looked as if they would bring back slavery, the French and their efforts to retake the island became embroiled in a fresh round of rebellions. Soon French troops were frustrated and humiliated by the ravages of disease and fierce resistance. Deterred by these setbacks and worried about the resurgence of his potential enemies, a long list that included external threats from the British, Russian, Austrian, and Prussian rulers, Napoleon lost interest in North America. He sold Louisiana in April 1803 and withdrew the remaining French soldiers from Saint-Domingue in May. He was not weak, far from it. During this time, Napoleon also made himself the emperor of France and would soon crush coalition forces in Austerlitz and tighten his grip against Britain, and later, Russia. By 1807, he ruled a vast and still expanding continental empire in the heart of a continent. But that continent was Europe, not North America. For a while, it looked as if he would make Europe into a massive French settler empire, imposing, for example, the French language on his German subjects. If Napoleon had kept his sights on North America and the West instead of Europe, we might with good reason ask would this book be written in French?

Even after Napoleon had sold it, the boundaries of Louisiana proved vague. They rubbed against the Spanish claims in the south (Spain insisted that Texas was not part of the bargain) and with the British in the north, especially closer to the Rockies and to the burgeoning Metis communities around the Red River of the North. The Americans in turn tried to figure out the extent and nature of their purchase. At the advent of the Louisiana Purchase, President Thomas Jefferson had organized the Corps of Discovery, led by his private secretary Meriwether Lewis and the slaveholding planter and ex-soldier William Clark. Lewis and Clark were instructed by Jefferson to locate and map a practical route to the Pacific, ideally the fabled Northwest Passage that would open the equally fabled China trade to the United States. They should also establish relations between the United States and the independent Indians they met, and, as was the standard practice for explorers around the world, collect mountains of specimens of local flora and fauna.

As it turned out, the Rocky Mountains and the continental divide ensured that no rivers connected the Mississippi system with the Pacific. In order to reach the world's biggest ocean by crossing the West, one needed to take a very demanding overland trip across vast plains, arid basins, and mighty mountains. Obscuring this less than exciting and encouraging fact, Lewis and Clark nevertheless promoted the feasibility of the land passage they had carved to be the long-waited global shortcut. They conveyed that the (in reality, turbulent) Columbia River represented a potential avenue for funneling the furs from the Missouri River and the Rockies to awaiting ships on the Pacific coast and thence to the markets of China. They also predicted that this option would offer a faster route for inland furs to the global markets than the British system of shipping via Montreal to Europe.

Interior Thrusts

While Napoleon reshuffled the pack, and Lewis and Clark toured the West promoting U.S. rule, several indigenous peoples were also engaged in powerful expansions of their own. None likely proved more powerful than the Comanches, an assortment of hunter–gatherers from the Rocky Mountains and the Great Basin who took advantage of what the Spanish had introduced. Others came from farther away. The Cheyenne crossed over to the Plains from somewhere north of the Great Lakes, from the Hudson's Bay area in present-day Canada. The Sioux in turn probably originated near Lake Michigan. These people embraced various cultural and economic adaptations when entering the West, the overall trend being from pedestrian farmer-hunters to equestrian buffalo hunters and horse pastoralists.

The impacts of European contacts – disease, fur trade, new weaponry, violence, and slavery – reshuffled relations on all shores of the Great Lakes. The Sioux and the Cheyenne tried to take advantage of the new situation. They, for instance, hunted beaver pelts for French traders, who sold them to Montreal and then onward to Europe, where they were in high demand. When their role as suppliers of the latest European fashion became too precarious due to indigenous competition, and with the Plains in their sights, the Cheyenne moved. They reached the Minnesota River by approximately 1700, gradually making their way to the Sheyenne River in modern-day North Dakota. They concentrated on the Missouri River near the boundary of the Dakotas and touched the Black Hills by century's end. From there, the Cheyenne advanced to the central Plains south of the Black Hills and north of the Arkansas River by the 1820s and 1830s.

It is possible that the Sioux migrations took place in three identifiable stages. The initial movement was during the late seventeenth and early eighteenth centuries onto the prairies east of the Missouri. This was followed by a conquest of the middle Missouri River region during the late eighteenth and early nineteenth centuries as the river villagers, the Mandans, Arikaras, and Hidatsas, were nearly wiped out by epidemics. Lastly, the Sioux headed west and south from the Missouri during the early and mid-nineteenth century. Crossing the Missouri River by 1800, they dominated the horticultural villagers, contested the Pawnees for the hunting grounds of western Nebraska, as well as struck their semisedentary villages and cornfields. In the 1830s, the Sioux took the Black Hills. They were pushing the Crows westward in the Yellowstone and Powder River area at the time when white overland emigrants heading for Oregon and California began crossing their domain regularly.

In the West, the Sioux and Cheyenne traded energetically, formed shifting alliances, and fought plenty when operating in contested transnational migratory landscapes. They shared space with the agents of the French, Spanish, British, and U.S. empires as well as with thousands of more or less sedentary Natives and removed eastern Indians like the Cherokees, Kickapoos, and Shawnees. They also, either individually or in groups, incorporated many peoples. One significant incorporation took place when the Cheyenne, in the late 1700s, encountered the Sutaio, strangers from the north who spoke an Algonquin language similar to theirs, and merged with them.

As the Cheyenne reached the Black Hills and the Sioux crossed the Missouri, the Scottish explorer Mungo Park took his second, fatal expedition in West Africa and the German naturalist Alexander von Humbolt advanced the cause of the Spanish Empire, and his own, in Latin America. Exploration and expansion was fast transforming, from the primarily ocean and coastal ventures that had been characteristic of the eighteenth century to a notable thrust toward the interiors of Africa, Asia, Australia, and the Americas. It was also becoming a worldwide effort by empires to fill the blank spaces on their maps; to know, categorize, and make understandable the world; as well as to instigate new trade relations, extract resources, and scout suitable land for settlement. As historian Dane Kennedy explains, exploration in the 1800s was a key, and perhaps defining, aspect of the encounters white Europeans had with other peoples and lands. It laid the groundwork for imperial expansion, advanced a new phase of globalization, and fostered the rise of modern scientific knowledge and notions of difference (often based on race). Explorers paved the way for the settler colonial advance to the West. They did the same with the settler penetration of the British Wests (Australia, New Zealand, Canada, and South Africa), French thrust in West Africa and Algeria, the British expansion across India, and the Russian settlements in Siberia and the Caucasus. Climaxing with the surge toward the polar regions in the 1900s, explorers gathered intelligence for sponsoring empires and claimed territory on their behalf. They often functioned as celebrated agents of knowledge, courage, and power. Some, like David Livingstone, fought against slavery and strove to spread Christianity, while also promoting himself and the cause of his exploration. Many had their eye on the needs of commerce and industry, and men like Henry Morton Stanley and Richard Francis Burton certainly understood the value of publicity.

An enterprise distinct from travel, exploration developed its own scientific protocols and its unique partnerships with scientific societies, the state, and the public in the 1800s. In short, exploration became a more organized enterprise than ever before. Motivated by rivalry and public's urge for land, Washington, Berlin, Paris, and London, as well as the regional governments in Ottawa, New South Wales, Victoria, and Western Australia, sponsored and conducted a series of expeditions. So did several geographic societies, most famously the Royal Geographic Society, which grew to dominate British exploration after its founding in 1830. Companies like the British East India Company and the HBC were also actively involved. Since the late 1600s, the HBC had already delivered entire collections of natural history specimens and meteorological diaries to Royal Society in London. Later, as historian Ted Binnema writes, the Royal Society, as well as the Royal Navy became dependent on HBC for data and collections relating to geology, ethnography, and hydrography – even craniometry, as company employees shipped Native skulls to London. The HBC was also the single largest provider of natural history and ethnographic collections to the newly founded Smithsonian Institution. Indeed, museums such as the British Museum and the Smithsonian, as well as universities, were active in promoting exploration. So were the armies of France, Russia, and the United States (especially with its Topographical Engineers). Many explorers, including Gustav Nachtigal, a German explorer of Central and West Africa, as well as Burton, Clark, Zebulon Pike, Stephen Long, and John Wesley Powell came from military backgrounds.

Regardless of what empire you played for, it was close to mandatory for explorers to make detailed observations of the land, its natural environment, and its peoples; to collect incredible volumes of botanical specimens, geological samples, and ethnographic artifacts; to produce maps; and to record latitude and longitude. Explorers, as a rule, kept extensive diaries, filled sketchbooks with drawings, and penned pages after pages of reports. Many also took professional painters or photographers along. They required precision instruments such as sextants, chronometers, pedometers, and barometers for scientific observation and measurement. The explorers' gaze also began to more meticulously infiltrate even the most intimate domains in peoples' lives.

This scientific effort impressed in its sheer quantity. Take, for example, the Spanish Malaspina expedition on the Americas and the Pacific from 1789 to 1794. It produced nearly 16,000 plant and seed specimens, 450 albums of astronomical observations, over 300 journals and logbooks, 80 drawings, and 183 charts, among other things. When exploring the great lakes of East Africa, Burton not only kept record of rainfall levels and barometric pressure, prepared maps, gathered geological samples, and shipped botanical specimens (shell, snake, insect, and plant samples) and human artifacts to the Royal Geographic Society in Kew Gardens and the British Museum; he also measured genitals and queried about the sexual and marital arrangements of the locals in the name of science. Claiming scientific authority through standardization and comparability, explorers not only needed to master special skills, but they were also held accountable for their efforts. Funding and reputation depended on results.

Explorers produced massive volumes bursting with scientific data that came off the press with the same regularity as exhilarating stories of adventure. Mungo Park's account of his first outing to the Niger River, *Travels in the Interior Districts of Africa*, proved a best seller in 1799. So did many of Stanley's works, for instance. Targeting diverse audiences, Burton published dozens of books. They ranged in tone from exciting personal accounts to sexually progressive translations of the *Kama Sutra*. He also penned travel writings on the American West and more serious works of exploration, such as *The Lake Regions of Central Africa*, his 1860 volume containing nearly 600 pages. Others were just as productive. In the 1850s, the U.S.–Mexico boundary surveyor William H. Emory penned two thick volumes, over 700 pages, of detailed description of the places, peoples, and nature he encountered. Another boundary surveyor John Bartlett's printed narratives totaled a whopping 1,300 pages. Alexander MacKenzie gained distinction throughout the world by being a daring explorer as well as a successful writer and self-promoter. John C. Fremont gained such fame by penning successful stories of his four 1840s expeditions in the West, and promoting the farming potential of the Plains, that he earned the sobriquet "pathfinder."

Lewis and Clark in turn kept voluminous diaries and wrote numerous reports on the climate, topography, soil fertility, river drainage, and Indian cultures. They also organized enough specimens to fill a small museum: dozens of plants; the hides of several animals, some stuffed; live magpies, sharp-tailed grouses, and prairie dogs; and a variety of embalmed insects. All this and much more they packaged and sent to Washington. In the drive to collect and categorize, Lewis and Clark differed little from Burton in Africa, from the British explorers of Australia, or from what numerous others had done and would do in the West. In fact, they were following an established tradition. Only as self-promoters did Lewis and Clark pale in comparison to Burton, Stanley, and others, as their achievements were largely overlooked in a time when explorers hurried to gain fame by filling the last blank spaces of the world.

Scores of international explorers and scientists touched on the West. These included the Scottish botanist Archibald Menzies, who explored the Pacific Coast in the 1790s, and David Douglas, who reached the region in the 1820s (sending 7,000 species back to Britain). John Bradbury in turn studied areas in and around St. Louis in the 1810s, while his fellow Scot Thomas Drummond botanized through Texas from 1833 to 1835. Aboard the Russian *Rurik* in the 1810s, a Russian expedition lead by Captain Otto von Kotzebue included Adelbert von Chamisso, a French-born, Berlin educated exile, nobleman, poet, and naturalist, as well as the Prussian-Russian painter Louis Choris. Departing Europe in July 1815, the expedition survived Cape Horn, touched land in Chile, and cut across the Pacific to winter in Kamchatka. The next year, the *Rurik* not only scouted the Bering Strait and the Aleutian Islands for the Northwest Passage but also anchored in San Francisco Bay. This offered Choris the opening to paint the Native and Spanish inhabitants before the expedition continued to Hawaii, and actually ended up circumnavigating the globe. In 1819, Choris had his drawings and paintings published in Paris using the comparatively novel technique of lithography. He ended up selling copies of his volume of more than 100 plates to the Russian czar and the kings of France and Prussia, among others (Figure 1.2).

There were numerous other international scientists making their name in the West later in the century as well. Gustaf Nordenskiöld was one of them. This nobleman and scholar of Finnish-Swedish descent, and the eldest son of the polar explorer Baron Adolf Erik Nordenskiöld, landed in New York in May 1891. Applying his scientific training, Nordenskiöld conducted the first archaeological excavation of the Mesa Verde ruins in Colorado. Loading volumes of artifacts onto railroad cars, being arrested by locals angered by this looting, but acquitted by the court for having broken no laws, he eventually headed back home. The bulk of the Mesa Verde items Nordenskiöld plundered were brought back to Sweden, and they ended up in the National Museum of Finland, where they still are.

The close companion of exploration was expansion. Lewis and Clark were in the West to advance the federal government's authority and interests; Choris advocated the Russian cause; Burton spearheaded British authority in Africa;

FIGURE 1.2 *Jeu des habitans de Californe*, painting depicting Native women watching men play a game, possibly related to gambling, at a mission near San Francisco, California.1822 by Louis Choris (1795–1828). Courtesy of the Library of Congress Prints and Photographs Division, LC-DIG-ppmsca-02900.

Nachtigal made local rulers sign treaties acknowledging German rule in Cameroon and Togo; and Stanley worked to expedite the claim of Belgium's King Leopold II in Congo. Many followed established European traditions of claiming dominion over "new" lands through raising flags, making speeches, and putting pen to paper. Lewis and Clark, for instance, performed the change in dominion through voluminous speeches, music, flag ceremonies, saluting, and some more speeches. Whether their Native audience understood or took them seriously is another matter entirely.

In truth, the West remained very much a contested imperial domain. The American explorer Zebulon Pike first found this out as he brushed against the British assertions when in search for the source of the Mississippi River in 1805. Next he explored the western reaches of the Louisiana Purchase. Dubbing much of the Plains the "great American desert," the American Sahara unfit for white futures, Pike and his party studied the Kansas and Arkansas rivers area, reached the Rockies in present-day Colorado, and then crossed the "border" into Spanish territory in New Mexico. Pike ostensibly thought he was on the Red River, while he actually was on the Rio Grande. The Spanish had been searching him already earlier, but now they imprisoned Pike and his party for spying in what essentially amounted to an "illegal" border crossing. Pike was escorted via Santa Fe and Chihuahua to Natchitoches in Spanish Texas before deported as an "illegal." Back in the states, he nevertheless published a popular narrative of his exploits, gaining fame and, as historian Jared Orsi remarks, wanting recognition as a national hero.

But things were changing. In two decades, Missouri merchants would be crossing the U.S.–New Spain/Mexico border, as defined by the Adams–Onís Treaty in 1819, with permission from Mexican authorities. While numerous British, French, and German explorers hurried to all corners of Africa, many American expeditions in turn mapped, described, categorized, and catalogued the West, its physical landscapes, and human populations. The federal government conducted big expeditions in the 1840s and still did so decades later, including those led by Clarence King, Ferdinand V. Hayden, and George M. Wheeler. In 1869, John Wesley Powell took on the Green and Colorado Rivers, becoming the first European to go through the Grand Canyon.

In 1848, the Spanish (Mexican), Russian, and British claims had been eliminated in the West and dominion transferred to the United States. Furs depleted, Russia made treaties with the United States in 1824 and with Britain in 1825 limiting their presence north of the 54th parallel. After the Crimean War, much of Russian focus was on settler colonial projects on the Caucasus and on southward expansion in Central Asia, where it ran the risk of colliding with British India. Russia sold Alaska to the United States in 1867. After some heated negotiations and escalating tensions, Britain and the United States reached a compromise, splitting the Pacific Northwest in 1846. In the same year, the United States waged a short, aggressive, and successful war, gaining half of Mexico as a result. While American on paper, the West would remain very much a crossroads of the Atlantic and Pacific worlds, a place of convergence for different peoples, cultures, and pathogens, as it had been, in one shape or another, for centuries. It also would become perhaps the world's foremost settler colonial space.

Bibliography

Contact Zones

Barman, Jean, and Bruce McIntyre Watson. *Leaving Paradise: Indigenous Hawaiians in the Pacific Northwest, 1787–1898*. Honolulu: University of Hawai'i Press, 2006.

Brooks, James F. *Captives & Cousins: Slavery, Kinship, and Community in the Southwest Borderlands*. Chapel Hill: University of North Carolina Press, 2002.

Calloway, Colin. *One Vast Winter Count: The Native American West before Lewis and Clark*. Lincoln: University of Nebraska Press, 2003.

———. *White People, Indians, and Highlanders: Tribal People and Colonial Encounters in Scotland and America*. Oxford: Oxford University Press, 2010.

Chang, David A. "Borderlands in a World at Sea: Concow Indians, Native Hawaiians, and South Chinese in Indigenous, Global, and National Spaces." *Journal of American History* 98 (September 2011): 384–403.

———. *The World and All the Things upon It: Native Hawaiian Geographies of Exploration.* Minneapolis: University of Minnesota Press, 2016.

Colley, Linda. *Captives: Britain, Empire, and the World, 1600–1850.* New York: Anchor Books, 2002.

Cook, Warren L. *Flood Tide of Empire: Spain and the Pacific Northwest, 1543–1819.* New Haven: Yale University Press, 1973.

Dolin, Eric Jay. *Fur, Fortune, and Empire: The Epic History of the Fur Trade in America.* New York: W. W. Norton, 2010.

DuVal, Kathleen. *The Native Ground: Indians and Colonists in the Heart of the Continent.* Philadelphia: University of Pennsylvania Press, 2006.

Elliott, John Huxtable. *Empires of the Atlantic World: Britain and Spain in America 1492–1830.* New Haven: Yale University Press, 2007.

Fenn, Elizabeth A. *Pox Americana: The Great Smallpox Epidemic of 1775–82.* New York: Hill and Wang, 2001.

———. *Encounters at the Heart of the World: A History of the Mandan People.* New York: Hill and Wang, 2014.

Frost, Alan. *The Global Reach of Empire: Britain's Maritime Expansion in the Indian and Pacific Oceans, 1764–1814.* Melbourne: Melbourne University Publishing, 2003.

Galley, Alan, ed. *Indian Slavery in Colonial America.* Lincoln: University of Nebraska Press, 2010.

Gibson, James R. *Imperial Russia in Frontier America.* Oxford: Oxford University Press, 1976.

———. *Otter Skins, Boston Ships, and China Goods: The Maritime Fur Trade of the Northwest Coast, 1785–1841.* Seattle: University of Washington Press, 1992.

Giraldez, Arturo. *The Age of Trade: The Manila Galleons and the Dawn of the Global Economy.* Lanham: Rowman and Littlefield, 2015.

Gitlin, Jay. *The Bourgeois Frontier: French Towns, French Traders, and American Expansion.* New Haven: Yale University Press, 2010.

Gitlin, Jay, Barbara Berglund, and Adam Arenson, eds. *Frontier Cities: Encounters at the Crossroads of Empire.* Philadelphia: University of Pennsylvania Press, 2012.

Gough, Barry. *Distant Dominion: Britain and the Northwest Coast of North America, 1579–1809.* Vancouver: University of British Columbia Press, 1980.

Hackel, Steven W. *Children of Coyote, Missionaries of Saint Francis: Indian-Spanish Relations in Colonial California, 1769–1850.* Chapel Hill: University of North Carolina Press, 2005.

Hämäläinen, Pekka. "The Rise and Fall of Plains Indian Horse Cultures." *Journal of American History* 90 (December 2003): 833–862.

Hurtado, Albert L. *John Sutter: A Life on the North American Frontier.* Norman: University of Oklahoma Press, 2006.

Hyde, Anne F. *Empires, Nations, and Families: A New History of the American West.* New York: HarperCollins, 2012.

Igler, David. *The Great Ocean: Pacific Worlds from Captain Cook to the Gold Rush.* Oxford: Oxford University Press, 2013.

Jackson, Robert H., and Edward Castillo. *Indians, Franciscans, and Spanish Colonization: The Impact of the Mission System on California Indians.* Albuquerque: University of New Mexico Press, 1996.

Kamen, Henry. *Empire: How Spain Became a World Power, 1492–1763*. New York: HarperCollins, 2004.

Kessell, John L. *Spain in the Southwest: A Narrative History of Colonial New Mexico, Arizona, Texas, and California*. Norman: University of Oklahoma Press, 2002.

Mapp, Paul W. *The Elusive West and the Contest for Empire, 1713–1763*. Chapel Hill: University of North Carolina Press, 2011.

Martin, Bonnie, and James F. Brooks, eds. *Linking the Histories of Slavery: North America and its Borderlands*. Santa Fe: School for Advanced Research Press, 2015.

Matthew, Laura E., and Michel R. Oudijk, eds. *Indian Conquistadors: Indigenous Allies in the Conquest of Mesoamerica*. Norman: University of Oklahoma Press, 2012.

Matsuda, Matt K. *Pacific Worlds: A History of Seas, Peoples, and Cultures*. Cambridge: Cambridge University Press, 2012.

Okihiro, Gary. *Island World: A History of Hawai'i and the United States*. Berkeley: University of California Press, 2008.

Owens, Kenneth. *The Wreck of the Sv. Nikolai*. Lincoln: University of Nebraska Press, 2001.

Perry, Richard J. *Western Apache Heritage: People of the Mountain Corridor*. Austin: University of Texas Press, 1991.

Pethick, Derek. *The Nootka Connection: Europe and the Northwest Coast 1790–1795*. Vancouver: Douglas & McIntyre, 1980.

Reid, Joshua L. *The Sea Is My Country: The Maritime World of the Makahs*. New Haven: Yale University Press, 2015.

Reséndez, Andrés. *A Land So Strange: The Epic Journey of Cabeza de Vaca*. New York: Basic Books, 2007.

———. *The Other Slavery: The Uncovered Story of Indian Enslavement in America*. New York: Houghton Mifflin Harcourt, 2016.

Richards, John F. *The Unending Frontier: An Environmental History of the Early Modern World*. Berkeley: University of California Press, 2003.

Richardson, Brian W. *Longitude and Empire: How Captain Cook's Voyages Changed the World*. Vancouver: University of British Columbia Press, 2005.

Shoemaker, Nancy. *Native American Whalemen and the World: The Contingency of Race*. Chapel Hill: University of North Carolina Press, 2015.

Simmons, Marc. "Tlascalans in the Spanish Borderlands." *New Mexico Historical Review* 39 (April 1964): 100–110.

Starr, Frederick S., ed. *Russia's American Colony*. Durham: Duke University Press, 1987.

Thomas, Hugh. *World Without End: The Global Empire of Philip II*. New York: Allen Lane, 2014.

Thomas, Nicholas. *Cook: The Extraordinary Voyages of Captain James Cook*. New York: Walker, 2003.

Van Dyke, Paul A. *The Canton Trade: Life and Enterprise on the China Coast, 1700–1845*. Hong Kong: Hong Kong University Press, 2005.

Vinkovetsky, Ilya. *Russian America: An Overseas Colony of a Continental Empire, 1804–1867*. Oxford: Oxford University Press, 2011.

Wade, Maria F. *Missions, Missionaries, and Native Americans: Long-Term Processes and Daily Practices*. Gainesville: University of Florida Press, 2008.

Weber, David J. *The Spanish Frontier in North America*. New Haven: Yale University Press, 1992.

Weddle, Robert S. *The Wreck of the Belle, the Ruin of La Salle*. College Station: Texas A & M University Press, 2001.

Williams, Glyn. *Arctic Labyrinth: The Quest for the Northwest Passage*. Berkeley: University of California Press, 2011.

Wishart, David J. *The Fur Trade of the American West, 1807–40: A Geographical Synthesis*. Lincoln: University of Nebraska Press, 1979.

Wood, Peter H. "La Salle: Discovery of a Lost Explorer." *American Historical Review* 89 (April 1984): 294–323.

Exploration and Expansion

Binnema, Ted. *"Enlightened Zeal": The Hudson's Bay Company and Scientific Networks, 1670–1870*. Toronto: University of Toronto Press, 2014.

Bush, Robert D. *The Louisiana Purchase: A Global Context*. New York: Routledge, 2013.

Driver, Felix. *Geography Militant: Cultures of Exploration and Empire*. Oxford: Blackwell, 2001.

Edney, Matthew H. *Mapping an Empire: The Geographical Construction of British India, 1765–1843*. Chicago: University of Chicago Press, 1997.

Fabian, Johannes. *Out of Our Minds: Reason and Madness in the Exploration of Central Africa*. Berkeley: University of California Press, 2000.

Fernandez-Armesto, Felipe. *Pathfinders: A Global History of Exploration*. New York: W. W. Norton and Co., 2006.

Gleijeses, Piero. "Napoleon, Jefferson, and the Louisiana Purchase." *International History Review* 39.2 (2017): 237–255.

Goetzmann, William H. *Exploration and Empire: The Explorer and the Scientist in the Winning of the American West*. New York: Knopf, 1966.

Jeal, Tim. *Explorers of the Nile: The Triumph and Tragedy of a Great Victorian Adventure*. New Haven: Yale University Press, 2011.

Kastor, Peter J. *The Nation's Crucible: The Louisiana Purchase and the Creation of America*. New Haven: Yale University Press, 2004.

Kastor, Peter J., and Francois Weil, eds. *Empires of the Imagination: Transatlantic Histories of the Louisiana Purchase*. Charlottesville: University of Virginia Press, 2009.

Kennedy, Dane. *The Last Blank Spaces: Exploring Africa and Australia*. Cambridge, MA: Harvard University Press, 2013.

———, ed. *Reinterpreting Exploration: The West in the World*. Oxford: Oxford University Press, 2014.

Lavender, David. *The Way to Western Sea: Lewis & Clark across the Continent*. New York: Harper & Row, 1988.

MacKenzie, John M., ed. *David Livingstone and the Victorian Encounter with Africa*. London: National Portrait Gallery, 1996.

Orsi, Jared. *Citizen Explorer: The Life of Zebulon Pike*. Oxford: Oxford University Press, 2014.

Reynolds, Judith, and David B. Reynolds. *Nordenskiöld of Mesa Verde*. Bloomington: Xlibris, 2006.

Riffenburgh, Beau. *The Myth of the Explorer: The Press, Sensationalism, and Geographical Discovery*. Oxford: Oxford University Press, 1994.

Ronda, James. P. *Lewis & Clark among the Indians*. Lincoln: University of Nebraska Press, 1984.

West, Elliott. *The Contested Plains: Indians, Goldseekers, and the Rush to Colorado*. Lawrence: University Press of Kansas, 1998.

————. *The Essential West: Collected Essays.* Norman: University of Oklahoma Press, 2012.

White, Richard. "The Winning of the West: The Expansion of the Western Sioux in the Eighteenth and Nineteenth Centuries." *Journal of American History* 65 (September 1978): 319–343.

————. *The Middle Ground: Indians, Empires, and Republics in the Great Lakes Region, 1650–1815.* Cambridge: Cambridge University Press, 1991.

Williams, Glyn. *Naturalists at Sea: Scientific Travellers from Dampier to Darwin.* New Haven: Yale University Press, 2013.

Worster, Donald. *A River Running West: The Life of John Wesley Powell.* Oxford: Oxford University Press, 2001.

2
SETTLER REVOLUTIONS

In his twenties, Peter Wigen became a transnational settler when he relocated from Selbu, a tiny municipality in Norway, to Minnesota in the 1870s. A decade later, he had married his Selbu sweetheart, Beret "Betsy" Kjosnes, and started a family and a dairy farm. It was 1901 when the Wigens were again on the move. They first caught promotional writings in the Norwegian-American paper *Skandinavien* advertising the prairie lands of La Crosse, Washington State. Learning more about the location through their Norwegian connections, the family sold their Minnesota farm and bought 800 acres of land in the interior Pacific Northwest. Like Minnesota earlier, their destination was land wrestled from indigenous peoples through wars and treaties, in this case the Nez Perce, the Umatilla, and the Walla Walla. Soon, two of Peter's brothers also relocated from Minnesota to La Crosse, as did at least 11 other former Selbu natives from Minnesota, historian Robert Elliott Barkan explains. In 1906, Betsy personally crossed the Atlantic to Selbu on a recruiting trip. The outcome: she prompted some 25 people to proceed to La Crosse. In the meantime, more Norwegians from North America and Europe continued to cluster at La Crosse, changing the face of the area in the process. But some Norwegians, who struggled with the relative scarcity of farming lands, soon moved again; they headed for other ethnic Norwegian communities, this time in Canada and Colorado. Once more these settlers crossed borders and/or settled on lands taken from Natives, joining familiar ethnic surroundings and using their ethnic networks for information and assistance in getting there.

These transregional and transnational circulations to La Crosse and beyond, and millions of other chain, step, and community migrations like it, illustrate the nineteenth-century global "settler revolutions," to use historian James Belich's term. The trans-Mississippi West remained richly multicultural in the late 1800s and early 1900s – meaning it saw ethnic mixing and drew people representing different races, ethnicities, and religions. Yet, this settler colonial West was less the syncretic meeting ground of cultures, communities, and empires the West had been in the past and more a realm where settlers came to stay, take the land, substitute the Natives, and instigate racial hierarchies and policies of exclusion. In short, the early West of shared worlds and middle grounds gradually and unevenly made way for a settler colonial West as the nineteenth century progressed. As a settler colonial space, the West was made into a target for a distinctive form of colonialism, a social formation and project where the settlers destroyed and replaced the Natives and made the land their own. It involved conquest, long-range migration, permanent settlement (or at least intent of such), and the reproduction of one's own society. It took place in various stages and impacted areas unevenly from the Texas Revolution, the Oregon Compromise, and the Mexican–American War to the American Civil War, the Gilded Age, and beyond. The West continues to be settler colonial today: it represents a geographical and cultural space in which white Europeans have invaded and settled on what used to be other peoples' lands, where they and their offspring have become and been/remained politically, economically, and culturally dominant, and where a diverse society has developed in terms of class, ethnicity, and race despite intense racialization and measures to exclude specific, often nonwhite, settler groups.

This settler revolution involved, coincided, spurred, and was a consequence of industrial and transportation revolutions, massive population growth and outward migration from Europe, idealization of yeoman farming cultures, the rise of print culture and intense marketing (boosterism), mining rushes, the spread of market economy, and capital flows in extractive industries and agribusiness that crossed national borders and signified new forms of global integration. It also saw extended state power and nationalization of imperial spaces. And the West was not alone. It had earlier precedents in the national context in the Ohio region, the Kentucky frontier, and in the cotton South where the settler project also involved chattel slavery. The West also shared much in common with parallel settler colonial processes taking place in the British Wests (Australia, New Zealand, South Africa, Canada, and to a lesser extent Rhodesia and Kenya), French Algeria, Russian Caucasus and Siberia, many Latin American countries, and German Southwest Africa and the German–Polish borderlands. These settler revolutions typically linked the local and the global through far-flung networks and circulation of knowledge, ideas, and peoples, and their histories increasingly appear as complex webs of entanglements, crossovers, transfers, and exchanges.

Luring scores of immigrants from Europe and driven by the logic of elimination against the Natives as sovereign polities, by the late nineteenth-century the American West had become the global standard for a successful settler colonial project. Some settler projects proved more effective in their long-term substitution of Natives and positioning of settler cultures than did others. In Australia and New Zealand, the settlers overpowered and outnumbered the Natives and made their presence permanent. In South Africa and Algeria, sizable numbers of European settlers also employed harsh measures targeting the indigenous populations, but in both places settlers remained a minority and their power would not last. Following the genocidal wars against the indigenous Hereros and Namas by the German government, German Southwest Africa still had less than 20,000 white settlers by World War I when Germany lost its formal colonies. The German drive to the East and dreams of living space inside Europe also crumbled with their defeat in World War II. Japanese settler colonialism in Korea and Manchuria also came to an inglorious end by 1945.

Initially the settler colonial West tried to look very much like a "white man's West." The right kind of whites – meaning of northern European ancestry and preferably decent, respectable peoples and families – constituted the ideal settlers. In practice, however, settler projects such as the West attracted a diverse pool of peoples in term of class and race and often needed nonwhite labor. These "non-desirables" included poor whites from eastern and southern Europe, emancipated black slaves from the South, Chinese and other Asians, as well as Mexicans. Their transnational migration and settlement contributed to the setting up of racial hierarchies and policies of exclusion. The West, together with settler projects in Australia, South Africa, and Canada, developed new methods of border enforcement, immigration policies, and racial privilege in an effort to make their settler spaces into "white man's countries." Still, the borders of these settler colonial spaces proved habitually contested and uncontrollable, acting more as avenues of mobility for peoples, industry, and goods rather than as walls separating them.

Chin Lung was one "unwanted" settler who crossed the Pacific Ocean to reach the West. He arrived from China to California in 1882, ten years later than Peter Wigen made his first crossing to Minnesota. Chin claimed status as an agricultural merchant, and his successful operations in Stockton and later Sacramento both cemented his place in the West and enabled his transnational mobility. In 1888, Chin returned to China to marry Leong Shee, and five years later he was even able to sponsor his wife to join him in the West. Eleven years and five kids later, Leong, unhappy in San Francisco, where the Chinese were openly discriminated against, returned to China and converted to Christianity there, Barkan writes. Chin instead remained in the West for the most part. While the aspirations of Chinese settlers often halted at the borders, and while Chin lived on a different continent than his family, he was able to skirt exclusion and make periodic trips to China and back, siring two more sons in the process. Eventually all of his five boys relocated to the West, while his two daughters married in China (some of the latter's offspring entered America in the 1940s). As for Chin, a successful merchant and a settler with family members on two continents, he took his exit and returned to China and his wife in 1932. The two eventually settled in Portuguese Macao and spent the latter years of their transnational lives there.

Age of Mobility

Some 650,000 British and Irish immigrants and some 100,000 Germans had moved to North America before 1780. Less than two million British and Spanish had relocated to the whole of North and Latin America up to that time, compared to the approximately 10–12 million sub-Saharan African slaves who crossed the Atlantic in chains before 1810. However, the floodgates of migration opened in nineteenth-century Europe, as well as Asia, even as they slowed in the black Atlantic. Historian Adam McKeown has identified three major long-distance migratory systems between 1840 and 1940. First is the approximately 55–58 million people to the Americas. These were mostly Europeans who crossed the Atlantic to the settler colonies in North and Latin America. As James Belich claims, approximately 36 million of those engaged in far settlement were "Anglos" – English, Scots, Welsh, and Irish, but also native-born Americans and Germans. In all, some five million immigrants entered the United States from 1820 to 1860, and 30 million more before the restrictions of the mid-1920s. This is the flow most Europeans and Americans know quite well. But its equals in size were the migration of 48–52 million people to Southeast Asia, the Indian Ocean Rims, and the South Pacific, mainly from India and Southern China, but also (some four million) from Europe, Africa, the Middle East, and northeastern Asia. The third major flow saw 46–51 million people move to Manchuria and Siberia, mainly from northern China and European Russia.

If the majority of the people on the move in the world were not Europeans, neither did the majority of Europeans on the move enter America or its West. Instead, they went from the countryside to mushrooming industrial urban spaces within Europe. Many also chose Canada, Australia, Brazil, or Argentina over the United States. Several also crossed borders within Europe. Tens of thousands of Italian workers moved to France in the late 1800s and early 1900s, while Germany, especially the industrial Ruhr Valley and the rural eastern Prussia, drew scores of Polish laborers. Many French, Italians, Spanish, and Greeks crossed the Mediterranean, some 480,000 of them being busy building a settler colonial state in Algeria by 1890. The settler movement also often constituted of several smaller steps. Many Irish first went to Liverpool, Glasgow, or other industrial centers in Britain. Countless stayed, but after a time others moved forward to the Americas or to the British Wests, in which a lot of them kept on moving in irregular intervals. Following their arrival to the eastern seaboard of North America, the settlers changed the face of Boston, New York, and Philadelphia, but others opted for shorter stopovers prior to pushing westward. The Germans, for instance, made their mark in Cincinnati and Chicago, before taking over the northern Plains. Some settlers chose detours via Canada before ending up in the West; others moved from the West to Canada (and possibly back again). In all, it seemed that for the majority of settlers, borders existed just to be crossed over.

Transport Webs

The settler revolutions were enabled by a steam-driven revolution in transport on both sides of the Atlantic. Steamboats and railroads made leaving more fathomable, getting there easier, and staying in touch across national borders and oceans normal. The first commercially viable steam engines were developed in 1807; steamboat traffic started regularly on the Mississippi River from 1817, and ocean steamers started crossing the Atlantic in the 1840s, dominating the traffic in people and freight by the 1860s. The opportunities for a truly global movement improved quickly as boats got bigger, faster, and safer, and as tickets became cheaper and travel more regular. For example, on the Atlantic each of the White Star Line's ships carried an average of 1,000 passengers in the 1870s but by the turn of the century the new liners could fit at least twice that many people. And there grew a fierce rivalry for passengers: the Red Star Line shipped settlers from Antwerp, Liverpool, and Southampton; the Cunard Line and the American Line from Southampton and Liverpool; the Holland America Line from Rotterdam; and the Norddeutscher Lloyd from Bremen.

Intense competition resulted in bigger ships and ship line merges but also expansion to world markets. According to McKeown, just approximately half of the world trans-oceanic migration between the 1840s and 1940s went to the Americas. For example, the Hamburg–Amerika Linie was making weekly passages to New York (via Southampton), but it also reached Baltimore as well as ports in the West Indies, Mexico, Latin America, China, Japan, and Australia. It thus transported goods and settlers across the world, not just between Europe and North America. The Latin American route, for example, included stops at Hamburg, Antwerp, Salvador, Rio de Janeiro, Santos, Buenos Aires, Punta Arenas, Chacabuco, Castro, Puerto Monti, Valparaiso, Antofagasta, Arica, Callao, Guayaquil, and Buenaventura. Regular steamship routes also began to operate between Japan, China, and California, so that by the end of the century six lines in the Pacific were regularly packed with passengers. The trip across the world's biggest ocean took less than 12 days in 1898, while it had lasted some 22 days just a decade earlier. By 1911, there were 14 major shipping companies sharing the oceans, several of them displaying a global reach with operations not only on the Atlantic but also in Asia and Africa.

While the trip across the Atlantic to the United States was cheaper and quicker than to Australia, Asia, or Latin America, reaching the West was far from easy. Often potential settlers, especially if short on economic means, had made preparations for weeks, months, or even years in advance. Europe was teeming with potential settlers without permanent homes as thousands journeyed overland every year from various corners of Europe to reach the seaports of Antwerp, Hamburg, Bremen, Rotterdam, Southampton, and Liverpool where it was possible to catch a ride to America. Bucharest, Vienna, Warsaw, Berlin, Danzig, Stockholm, and other major cities were buzzing with transit people, who came from small villages and rural areas and who yearned to reach the Atlantic port cities. Potential settlers often had to cross several borders and encounter hardships, unfamiliar languages, and government officials and citizens who did not respond to them too kindly or sought to take advantage of them. They also underwent health inspections, disinfections, and harassment (sexual and otherwise) in the process. Sometimes travel funds were spent before reaching even the port of departure, which meant that settlers and their families had to work en route, depend on charity organizations, and beg to obtain food, temporary accommodation, and preferably boat tickets to America. Many individuals and families were stuck in the port cities for weeks or months, subject to unsanitary conditions, diseases, and exploitation. Some never got to the seas.

Heading from the eastern seaboard of North America toward the West, people quickly realized that the West's major waterways, like the Missouri, flow north to south, while those rivers aligned from west to east, like the Platte and Red Rivers, habitually proved unnavigable for steam-powered vessels. At first overland traffic had to be done using wagons, on horseback, and by walking. Settler wagon travel to Oregon and California grew into epic proportions in the 1840s and 1850s. But it was a time-consuming and potentially hazardous endeavor on the account of vast distances and shortages of water on many sections. And there was always the danger of winter catching up on travelers in the Rockies, ruining your trip and possibly costing your life. Although the settlers could hunt along the way if they knew how, and while the U.S. Army had set up a few posts – such as Forts Kearney and Laramie – as stopover stations on the major routes, the migrants from Europe had to haul much of their supplies with them. Traditionally these overland trails and covered wagons have represented historical images strongly linked with the West. Yet, similar migrations took place elsewhere. The Boer trek to Orange and Transvaal in the early 1800s was very much an overland wagon trek, in this case an evasion to put some distance against the British. Images of wagons and settlers also featured heavily in the Australian national imaginary, in the Argentinian Pampas, and in German settler movements in Southwest Africa and in Eastern Europe all the way to World War II.

By the late 1800s, rails also moved settlers, supplies, and labor to the settlers and carried farm produce and natural resources to markets. In Canada, the railways enabled the settlers to reach the prairies and jumped national grain production and exports to Britain. The reach of the British in Australia, Africa, and India was also very much centered on tracks. The South African gold and diamond rushes prompted rail construction, which in turn drew more settlers. In Australia, wool production and mining spread side by side with rails. So did cotton production in India when rails linked the fields with the mills in Bombay and Calcutta. In Southwest Africa, the German settler access to inland pastoral and farming lands relied on the Swakopmund-Windhoek-rail line, while subsequent lines connected the coastal Lüderitz to the booming diamond fields in the interior. Rails also allowed for the rapid deployment of the military. The latter happened, for instance, in the Geronimo campaign of 1885–1886 and in Germany's conflict against the Hereros and Namas in Southwest Africa. The success of British military campaigns against the Boers was also very dependent on the railroads. Railroads were also the iron spine holding together the administrative structures of many colonies, and they would make capitalistic market agriculture possible on the Great Plains, interior reaches of Africa, in the highlands of Kenya, in French Indochina, in the settler enclaves of northern Algeria, on the Moroccan Plains, and in German East Africa. The Chinese immigration to Manchuria and Siberia would also have proven impossible in the scale it took without the railways, and the competing Russian claim and settler expansion in the Siberian-Manchurian borderlands also relied heavily on trans-Siberian railroad networks.

The impacts of the railroads were often as intense as was the growth in the volume of tracks. India had no tracks in 1850. In 1900, it had 25,000 miles of them. Mexico had mere 400 miles of line when Porfirio Diaz took office in 1876, but 12,230 miles when he resigned in 1911. Rails also rapidly replaced other forms of mobility. The number of porters going inland from Dar es Salaam to Lake Tanganyika in German East Africa dropped from 43,000 in 1900 to 193 in 1912 with the advent of the railroad. In 1877, civilian freight contractors operated 19 wagon routes from California and one from Colorado to supply the U.S. Army forts in Arizona, while the garrisons in New Mexico were maintained by eight supply routes from the East. Five years later, the railroads had driven most of these freighters out of business.

The world's first transcontinental railroads crossed the American West in 1869 as the Union Pacific and Central Pacific joined in Utah. This achievement was immediately hailed by numerous European commentators as an extraordinarily effective agent of colonization. By the time of the trans-Siberian link opened in 1904, three more transcontinental lines operated on the northern Plains (of which one was in Canada) and two in the Southwest and the southern Plains. The latter lines spanned across the border and linked to copper mining communities run by multinational corporations in northern Mexico. Other transcontinentals were also in the plans, none more ambitious than the British Cape-Cairo or the French trans-Saharan connections. Despite decades of planning, surveys, and smaller completed track sections, these big lines, unlike the Western transcontinental connections, which had also been in the works decades prior to completion, never materialized in their intended scale.

Heavily subsidized by the federal government, the transcontinental railroad companies gained the right of way and some 20 square miles of land for each mile of track. They ended up transferring millions of acres of land to market appropriation, drawing and moving large masses of settlers from inside the United States and from Europe and Canada, and generating mushrooming, yet sometimes short-lived, communities along the tracks. Together with shipping lines, railroad companies enabled the import of material goods produced in eastern factories and in Europe and the export of Western livestock, grain, timber, and gold, silver, copper, and other minerals in unprecedented quantities to the industries and consumers in urban market places on both shores of the Atlantic and the Pacific. In fact, intersecting rail and ship lines provided the skeleton for global integration. European capital was also often invested in Western railroad construction, as were globe-spanning dreams. The famous Missourian Thomas Hart Benton and many of his contemporaries saw the construction of a travel route across the continent as an American road to China. Indeed, many saw the motive in the Mexican–American War in the potentially lucrative Asian markets achieved in part by transcontinental rails.

The railroads also prepared the Plains for the transnational settler and market invasion by fueling the wholesale slaughter of the bison, animals that were essential for the economy of most Plains Indians. Railroads transported an estimated 5,000 hunters to the Plains and took tongues or hides out to global consumers. The former proved a highly sought-after delicacy among the chic upper classes of Europe, and the latter, when tanned into leather, were in high demand as machine belts throughout the industrializing world. Bones too were gathered and shipped via rail to destinations such as Chicago for processing into industrial carbon and fertilizer. That you could shoot the animals without leaving the comfort of the trains proved enticing for upper-class hunters, many arriving from Britain and continental Europe for these bison-killing extravaganzas. Importantly, bison slaughter made the grass and water available for settlers' livestock, farms, and industries.

Settler Networks

Various push and pull factors have been suggested by scholars to explain settlers' transnational movements. Certainly the rapidly developing transportation systems provided avenues for running away from poverty, unemployment, overpopulation, troubles with the law, personal problems, or oppression such as the Jewish pogroms that hit Europe. Dreams of a more prosperous and respectable life, what can be called "settler utopianism," also proved powerful. One particularly strong notion revolved around the notion of agrarian pioneers as harbingers of civilization and the promise of yeoman freeholds – the owning of one's own piece of farming land, home, and some domestic animals. While many settlers moved to established communities taking place in urban environments, the yeoman ideal attracted the European landless classes as it combined the prospect of dignified labor conditions, the opportunity for social advancement, and economic independence. It also promoted Western lands as ripe for the taking, extremely bountiful, and free of Natives (and the bison). Relocation to the West seemed to promise life free of servitude and class barriers that marred the everyday of masses in Europe. As free individuals, settlers could imagine they were the co-owners of society, nation, and empire, not lowly subjects to undemocratic rulers. These notions lured not only people heading toward the West, but entered the social psyche in various other settler landscapes in the British Wests, Algeria, and Latin America. In fact, one could argue that throughout the settler colonial world it was the agrarian pioneers and the promise of individual freeholds that stirred the imaginations of countless potential settlers. This is made visible in European literature; for example, German publications promoting settler spaces in Brazil, the German–Polish borderlands, Southwest Africa, and the American West alike emphasized individual opportunity, land ownership, and the social advancement that accompanied them. Even in tsarist Russia, peasants were similarly perceived as carriers of the agrarian ideal, the purveyors of modernity, and equal to American pioneers.

While farming had reached the edges of the Great Plains in the 1850s, it is usually the Homestead Act of 1862, and to somewhat lesser extent the Desert Land Act of 1877, that is seen to catapult the rapid change from plains/deserts to fields, from Native lands to settler spaces, in one generation. Although some 700 million acres of land were sold in the market, much of it by the railroads, the Homestead Act's 270 million acres sold and 50% success rate (counted from the more than 1.4 million applications from 1862 to 1900), certainly mattered. Also, for instance, in Nebraska some 45% of all acres sold were distributed under the act, which was the largest percentage in any state. In all, some four million claims were made as homesteading continued until the 1970s, with 1913 being the peak year. The Homestead Act gave European peasants and urban laborers something concrete on which to base their dreams, something that would make the idea of moving seem more fathomable, as practically free land grants were allocated to anyone who could prove "improving" the claim after five years.

By the 1880s, the settler penetration was in full swing on the Plains, including those sections hardly suited for long-term agriculture on the High Plains. The population jumped: Montana's population grew from practically no white people in 1860 to 39,000 in 1880 and to 143,000 by 1890, and North Dakota's increased from 37,000 to 191,000 between 1880 and 1890. Nebraska grew from 28,000 in 1860 to 1.1 million in 1890. And this influx was very much transnational in character. Some 45% of North Dakota residents were recent immigrants in 1890, mainly Germans or Scandinavians, more than anywhere else in the country at the time. Ten years later, North Dakota had 319,000 inhabitants, of whom over 70% were foreign-born. From 1890 to the early 1900s, about half of the population in Nebraska and South Dakota were also foreigners, as were 25% of people in Kansas and Washington State, 18% of Oregonians, and 14% of Texans.

Advancing to the American West or the British Wests, the German, Swedish, Polish, Irish, Czech, and other settlers often practiced community, chain, and step migration. Much like Peter and Betsy Wigen and the other Selbu people, they followed relatives and clustered close to people from the same town, region, or country of origin, forming transnational ethnic settler networks in the process. Finn Hilma Tolonen Salvon revealed the raw reasoning behind these choices: "When somebody sends you a ticket from America – well, you go."[1] In Hilma's case, it had been her father's cousin who had relocated to Astoria, Oregon, while Hilma, her parents, and four siblings followed suit. They left eastern Lapland, where the family was involved in the local lumber industry, for Astoria, where the family also entered the logging business. Opportunity and the chance to move in the footsteps of one's kin and to a familiar profession made for a usual story. Hilma and her family received tickets, borrowed money, and gained all kinds of practical help and advice from their relatives and from the large Finnish community in Astoria. They did the same in turn for those coming in their wake. Ethnic networks also arranged not only jobs and living quarters but also marriages.

If many settlers wanted the opportunities of individual landholding, they preferably did it in familiar ethnically homogenous environments. The Plains were dotted with German, Czech, Swedish, and Norwegian ethnic communities, where people found a familiar social and cultural environment in a new geographical setting. Frequently settlers were kept on their toes and habitually on the move by cycles of agricultural boom and bust. Some of the vulnerable Plains regions in western Kansas and Nebraska were losing population already in the 1890s. More heartache followed as droughts and giant dust storms crushed many settler dreams of yeoman freeholds on the Plains by the 1930s. Numerous European transplants moved on, heading toward urban centers, to California, and back home to Europe. They again moved as individuals but more so as families and kin groups seeking familiar ethnic clusters. Also, as farming communities grew due to immigration and natural increase and therefore experienced shortages of lands, young people, especially married couples, could join together and leave to find a suitable ethnic cluster somewhere else.

All the links in these transnational settler networks typically kept up communications, shared information of new opportunities, and maintained their ties within the migrant-filled multicultural West and beyond. This is how the Wigens behaved throughout their lives, as did Chin Lung and his family. The settlers especially strove to stay in touch and involved with the society they had left behind. They turned into eager consumers of art and popular culture of their former homelands. They also sent home money (cash in letters or in the form of money or postal orders) to ease the lives of relatives and friends. And this was the case not just with European settlers. Asians and immigrants from Latin America commonly used (and still use) their ethnic networks for information and help; they sent remittances back to their families, supported political causes, and traveled back and forth between the West and the locales where their family members lived.

Settlers and their ethnic enclaves circulated multiple cultural practices and traditions across the oceans and between empires. In the settler colonial world from Australia and New Zealand to North America, different groups celebrated

---

1 Quoted from Barkan, *From All Points*, 70.

their own religious and cultural festivals, such as the Scottish Highland games. An array of organizations, religious and secular, were created to enforce the national consciousness of settlers who had left their homes and moved to the West. For example, the Finns in the West had the Knights of Kalevala and the Finnish Socialist Club; the Swedes put together the Valhalla Lodge; and the Norwegians met at the Norse Club and the Ancient Order of Vikings, among many other examples. The Sons of Malta, the Sons of St. George, and the Albion Society were all active in bringing Englishmen together in the West, although such organizations were less prevalent among the English than with the Irish, Scots, or Germans. There were also dozens of foreign-language newspapers in the settler colonial West, among them numerous German papers such as the *San Antonio Zeitung, New Braunfels Zeitung, Minnesota Staats-Zeitung, Omaha Taegliche Tribuene,* and *Nebraska Deutsche Zeitung.*

Religious membership and organizations further linked the settlers in the West to transnational networks. Not only the larger nominations, but also smaller groups, such as Mormons and the Mennonites, made their homes in the West. Mennonites were Anabaptists, products of the Protestant Reformation in the 1500s, and many had migrated to the United States or Russia in response to persecution. Thrown out of the Russian Empire in the 1870s, they journeyed to North America, entering Kansas and Missouri as well as Mexico and Canada. They were drawn by the Santa Fe Railroad that sent recruiters to Russia. From the Plains some Mennonites continued to northern Mexico during World War I, again escaping maltreatment. For the Mennonites, their prime allegiance continued to be their religious group, not any particular nation-state. With their strong commitment to pacifism, their diaspora spanned several empires and dodged calls to arms in Russia, Prussia, and the United States. Mormons also took their brand of religion overseas, sending thousands of recruiters to gather converts from the industrial centers of Britain and from Sweden, Denmark, and Norway. Even Brigham Young conducted missionary work in Liverpool in the 1840s. Europeans flocked to join the church and its Western settlements, centered on Utah and dotting much of the Rocky Mountains and Great Basin but also spread past the Canadian and Mexican borders.

All these organizations, newspapers, and church denominations enabled a heightened awareness of ethnicity and national origin. Many immigrants, who previously had identified with multilayered webs of localized villages, broader regions, or linguistic and religious identities in Europe that poorly fit national designations, now increasingly saw themselves as "Poles," "Germans," "Czechs", or some other specific nationality. Thus, transnational mobility played a key role, not only in cultural exchanges but also in forging more tightly defined understanding of nations and ethnicities. Wanting a stable identity, and on guard against rootlessness, many settlers retained their foreign nationality even after years of living in the West, Canada, or Australia. Some nations responded in turn. The *Kaiserreich* sought to preserve the Germanness among its emigrants, being especially fearful of losing Germans in what was seen as the melting pot of the West. In the mid-1800s, Germans replaced the term *Auswanderer*, emigrants, with *Auslandsdeutsche*, Germans abroad, and extended it to cover the German diaspora in and outside of Europe. New terminology functioned as part of the Reich's *Weltpolitik*, representing a mental shift and serving as basis for imagining a global Germanness, a shared ethnic and cultural connection not confined by the borders of the *Kaiserreich*. As historian Stefan Manz writes, pockets of Germanness existed in places as varied as the American West, Shanghai, Samoa, New Zealand, Brazil, and Russia, demonstrating a collective commitment to the old homeland, including the notion of contributing actively to its trade and colonial ambitions. In short, there were strong claims that there existed a people identified as Germans, that these people remained Germans, and that they shared a membership in a global community of Germans, wherever they went.

These notions of *Auslandsdeutsche* also reflected very concrete desires for German colonies in the American West. The earliest border-crossing white mass settler migrations in the West targeted Texas. The American businessman Moses Austin secured a land grant from Mexico, and his son Stephen Austin catapulted an Anglo settler invasion in the 1820s. Others soon followed, swelling the non-Spanish speaking population and leading to a shift in allegiance away from Mexico that culminated in rebellion and independence in the mid-1830s. As an attempt to lure Anglo settlers and redirect their loyalties to a non-Anglo state, Texas proved a costly and embarrassing mistake from Mexico's viewpoint. No other settler colony would try such a project. Desiring the whitening of their population, Latin American countries like Brazil and Argentina would focus on attracting Europeans from many different countries, preferring settlers from northern Europe but managing to lure large numbers not only of Germans but also of Portuguese, Italians, and Spanish. Mexico in turn would attract very few European settlers of any kind after Texas.

Texas also offers an early example of transnational settler movement from Europe to the West and of the aspirations to build German colonies in the West. Having heard of the Austin land grant, settler-promoter and eager marketer of Texas Johann Friedrich Ernst from Lower Saxony, applied and in 1831 received a grant of more than 4,000 acres in today's Austin County. This would be the basis of "New Germania," where Ernst soon established the Teutonic Order of Texas, a German Catholic military society. Drawing settlers from Holstein, Westphalia, and Oldenburg in what became a chain migration, Ernst's Texas project was widely publicized in Germany. This attracted others dreaming of German colonies in the West. Among those interested was a group of noblemen that included Prince Frederick of Prussia as one of its founding members. Spearheaded by Prince Carl of Solms-Braunfels, who toured Texas in 1844 promoting immigration and establishing New Braunfels,

FIGURE 2.1   Logo of the Mainzer Adelsverein. Courtesy of Paul Fearn/Alamy stock photo.

this group set up an organization on the Rhine called the *Mainzer Adelsverein*, or the *Verein zum Schutze Deutscher Einwanderer*. These noblemen felt that German colonization in Texas would bring them wealth, power, and prestige. It could also, they thought, alleviate overpopulation in rural Germany. This project managed to draw thousands of Germans to Texas from 1842 onward, even negotiating a private treaty with the Comanches on the account that one of the Germans' land grants stood on Comanche lands (Figure 2.1).

Although many Irish figured in the development of Texas independence and statehood, the Germans – historian Terry Jordan, among others, shows – formed the largest white ethnic group in Texas (and they still do). What was referred to as the German Belt stretched from Houston to the west of San Antonio. "German customs of life still hold sway" in this "most thoroughly Germanized portion of the United States," a 1907 report stated.[2] German communities differed from each other in many ways. Some had Protestants, while others consisted of Catholics, Jews, Slavic Wends, or atheists. People also came from a variety of German provinces, although old neighbors who had lived close together in Germany tended to do the same in Texas. In the 1880s, 60% of the residents of Dallas were German. By 1910, one-third of the 60,000 people in the Spanish-established San Antonio had German roots, numerous enough that many African Americans and Mexicans in the city also spoke German. Still, the German immigration slowed down by the turn of the century and ended by the time of the two World Wars and the anti-German sentiment that

2 Quote from Barkan, *From all Points*, 77.

accompanied these conflicts. In many places, intermarriage, rural depopulation, the move to the suburbs, the breakup of old German neighborhoods, and the closure of German papers and schools eroded German cultural basis and directed the Germans toward the Anglo mainstream by the mid-1900s.

The British also sought to establish ethnic communities in the West. According to historian Peter Pagnamenta, one enclave of Britishness, Runnymede, Iowa, was complete with polo fields, football clubs, tennis courts, and private social clubs. But the harshness of farming and an unfamiliar environment, including tornados, sent most settlers packing. By 1892, Runnymede met a humiliating end after the railway was routed two miles away from the town, and the prosperity it might have brought never materialized. Another British effort in 1873 saw an enterprising Scottish nobleman named George Grant coming up with an idea of a settlement in western Kansas inhabited solely by the British upper classes. By demanding that the residents had to have at least £2,000 in assets and would each get at least a square mile of land, Grant kept out the working-class settlers. Instead of the mud-brick and grass-roof dwellings that many other Europeans on the Plains built, here the settlers lived in English-style brick villas with gardens and hedges. They even erected a limestone church with donations from Britain. Victoria, as the settlement was patriotically called, was talked of back home as a second Eden, but the new arrivals – an estimated 200 people, most of whom had zero farming experience – quickly realized that the Plains was a difficult environment in which to be a landed gentleman. Following Grant's death in 1879, the settlement also died, and it was overshadowed by scores of ethnic Germans arriving from Russia. It had been aggressive and far-reaching advertising campaigns that attracted these Germans from the Volga River region to the West. They soon planted wheat on the Kansas Plains, helping to break the myth of the "great American desert," at least until recurrent drought and explosive dust storms proved their optimism wrong. The Germans also renamed Victoria as Herzog (after their township in Russia) although the new name did not stick (the community was renamed Victoria in 1913).

Although they formed ethnic clusters, settlers were distributed in the West very unevenly. In addition to Germans, nineteenth-century Texas had significant minorities of Austrian, Bohemian, Scot, and Swiss immigrants. The Swedish community in Texas was larger than in any other southern state, yet still small when compared to Swedish presence on the Plains or the Pacific Northwest. Texas had only a few Italians before 1880, but after that their numbers increased somewhat. Typical Italians in the West, in Denver and Los Angeles, for instance, included unskilled urban laborers and miners. For their part, the Basques (from Spain and France) remained closely associated with shepherding and clustered on appropriate locations in Oregon, California, Nevada, and Idaho. The Finnish presence in turn concentrated on the timber- and farming-intense lakes region of Minnesota, as well as such places as

Astoria, Oregon, which was also a logging, farming, and fishing center. In fact, concentrations of Finns and Swedes controlled much of logging and milling operations in the Pacific Northwest, while numerous Scandinavians such as the Wigens engaged in agricultural endeavors across the West. Many Finns, as well as Cornish and Irish, were also found in mining centers such as Bisbee, Arizona and Butte, Montana. In the latter place, where one-fourth of the world's copper came from, the population, just below 30,000 people in 1900, included at least 12,000 Irish, many of them originating from Cork and with previous work experience in copper mines. The city's principal business, the Anaconda Copper Company, was also Irish owned. Yet Butte also had a sizable Finntown and a big Cornish and Italian presence.

In the late 1800s and early 1900s, a sizable percentage of settlers kept on crossing borders, using their networks for relocating or for heading back to their country of origin. Waves of repatriation typically accompanied economic downturns, but the estimates of how many actually went back differ quite a bit. Tracking down all the exchanges, scholars have said that, for instance, around 20% of Swedes or as many as 40% of all English emigrants returned, but that not many Irish went back. Going back home was of course a quite logical choice for those who started out as seasonal workers or with the intent to work abroad for just a few years, which became more common as transportation fares got cheaper and travel time quicker. Numerous people also returned temporarily, to marry, to attend funerals, or to visit family and friends, each arriving with firsthand knowledge and connections to the place he/she had settled into, which, in turn, impacted others contemplating on becoming transnational settlers. But many also returned for good after their dreams were smashed by the realities of the West, the economic failures, and other adversities in everyday life.

Information Flows

Settler revolutions promised not merely unprecedented transnational mobility for common people, or overlapped with the transportation revolution, but also coincided with a spectacular growth in literacy rates, mechanized paper-making, steam-powered printing presses, the rise of international postal services, and the targeting of mass audiences by publishers and promoters. Booster and travel literature, newspapers – including numerous ethnic papers – and letter-writing gained immense popularity. While the United States had 200 newspapers in 1800, the figure for 1860 stood at 3,000. Practically everybody in Europe knew somebody who had gone to America, and most settlers in America had some relative, sweetheart, or friend back Europe. Thus correspondence between the West and Europe was intense, and in many households and communities, nothing was expected as much or speculated on as excitedly as the arrival of the mail, both national and international. Post offices multiplied and prior to the transcontinental railroads, high-volume mail services like the famous Pony Express and Butterfield Overland Mail, a stagecoach service running the southern overland "oxbow" route between San Francisco and St. Louis and Memphis via Fort Smith, Arkansas, already linked people across national borders and delivered information in unprecedented fashion. Butterfield, essentially an international line in itself – as it crossed some 115 miles in Mexican Baja California and had several of its stations in Mexico – connected the Pacific and the Atlantic worlds through the West. The short-lived Pony Express did much the same. It delivered British home dispatches from China during the Second Opium War. Advancing the rapid surge in the flow of information, telegraph wires crossed the Atlantic in 1858, wired the North American continent 1861, and spanned the Pacific in 1902.

Exploding after 1815, boosterism was practiced by government agencies, charities, cultural organizations, pressure groups, labor unions, newspapers, and shipping, land, and railroad companies. They printed millions of copies of books, pamphlets, brochures, fliers, and ads in a global recruitment drive for settlers. The Northern Pacific Railroad alone mailed over 600,000 pieces of literature in numerous languages to Britain, Germany, Switzerland, the Netherlands, and the Scandinavian countries. The transatlantic shipping lines in turn sent over 3,000 booking agents as passage brokers in the British Isles alone. These efforts encouraging settler mobility targeted moneyed people as well as common folk. And the texts were shamelessly partisan and polemical. They were still hugely influential, although displaying a paradise complex. The West just abounded with Gardens of Eden, El Dorados, and all kinds of promised lands, to use David Wrobel's book title. The texts were filled with religious or earthly escapes, singular guarantees of brighter, more prosperous futures. Many marketers also catered to people with urban angst when promising getaways to simpler and more genuine times lost to industrialization.

Also at work was an armada of lecturers. From 1845, 33 states and territories sent emigration agents and publications to New York and to Europe in their hunt for potential settlers. The Northern Pacific Railroad forwarded 831 representatives to Britain and another 124 to northern Europe in the late 1880s. One speaker, James Erwin, an agent for the Southern Pacific Railroad, by 1914 had delivered his presentation "Wonders of the Western Country" 3,357 times, reaching an estimated audience of more than 1.5 million people.

Marketing settler spaces was never solely about the West. Ever since taking over the coastal enclaves of Algeria in the early 1830s, the French government actively promoted settler possibilities – highlighting farming, land ownership, and respectable family life – for Europeans in northern Africa. In the early 1900s, the New Guinea Colonization Society targeted Dutchmen, especially mixed-blood Indo-Europeans (offspring of European men and indigenous women), to create a new Netherlands in New Guinea.

Drawing inspiration from Mormons in the West and the Boers in South Africa, the organization called for a space where the nearly 200,000 Indo-Europeans (1930) could remain European, own land, and become yeoman farmers. This fantasy, which mixed notions of racial purity and awaiting virgin lands, drew plenty of attention and hundreds of colonizers. It did not, however, last.

In the 1870s, Australia and New Zealand outstripped both the United States and Canada in promotional activity. New Zealand had 73 agents in Scotland alone, and it advertised in 288 Scottish papers. The booster literature titles describing New Zealand include such stereotypical gems as "The Land of Plenty" and "An Earthly Paradise." Not all governments were pleased, and by the mid-1800s some British and German politicians already feared that settler trails that led to the West and other settler colonies would sap from their country its youngest and brightest, its energy and strength.

Removing the authority of the Hudson's Bay Company in western Canada during the Fraser River gold rush in the 1850s, the British government formally extended its imperial control to the Pacific. With the setting up of Native reserves, the 1870s and 1880s saw scores of new settlers. They were drawn by the Canadian Dominion Lands Act of 1872, which was similar to the U.S. Homestead Act of 1862. Both offered 160 acres, used the grid, and charged a small fee. Canada required a three-year residency against the five years in the United States. Still, it was the early 1900s that witnessed the bigger boom. The population of Western Canada tripled, the growth centering on urban centers of Winnipeg, Calgary, and Edmonton. There was also a huge increase in wheat exports to Britain. From 1896 to 1906, the Canadian government and the transcontinental railroad spent four million dollars publicizing the opportunities for settlement in what was called the "last, best West." The Canadian Minister of the Interior, Clifford Sifton, began a vigorous effort to recruit experienced farmers from Europe and especially from the American West. His invitation applied to whites only; no blacks or Chinese were welcome, much like in the policies of the United States and Australia. What Sifton got was a significant number of Germans, Scandinavians, Ukrainians, Russians, and Poles: some directly from Europe, others via the American West. In addition to an aggressive and widespread advertising campaign, Sifton's men invited American journalists to visit and write about the Canadian West. They also set up nine Canadian agencies south of the border in 1897. By 1914, there were already 21 of them. The agencies produced a mass of supporting literature on the Canadian West, including pamphlets, books, maps, and circulars. The titles of such publications included "The Wondrous West," "Canada, the Land of Opportunity," and many others. The best seller, which was in the press year after year, however, was "The Last Best West." In short, Canada represented a fresh and dynamic West, the finest of what might prove a limited supply (Figure 2.2).

FIGURE 2.2 *The Last Best West.* Advertisement of the Canadian government in the Christmas edition of *The Globe* encouraging the settlement of Western Canada, December 25, 1907. Courtesy Library and Archives Canada/Wikimedia Commons.

Rushes and Markets

Stressing their shared causes, characteristics, and results, historian Douglas Fetherling claims the gold rushes in the United States, Canada, Australia, New Zealand, and South Africa, while not identical, were part of a single discontinuous event essential to settler revolutions worldwide. Much like agricultural expansions, rushes flooded what used to be Native lands with thousands of people. Yet they did it in a shorter time and pulled fewer families and more young, single, ambitious, or restless men, hit hard by economic slumps. The literature covering settler colonial exchanges across the world is full of references to "fevers," "manias," and "rushes," suggesting that people could be swept up by a sense of belief that a particular movement was their life calling or would solve all their prevailing problems. Take, for instance, the peak in global immigration as news of gold in California and in Victoria, Australia drew people from across the world from the late 1840s to the 1850s. In both cases, the crowd was as big as it was varied. Both California and Victoria pulled in some 100,000 people a year at their peaks, and both had a gross inflow of 500,000 people, Belich notices. Melbourne quickly rivaled

San Francisco as a major boomtown, and in the 1880s it boomed again and actually outgrew San Francisco.

In California, an international cast arrived by land from the East, crossed the border from Mexico, or took maritime routes via the Panama isthmus. The crowd included native-born Anglo men, Mormons, and both slave and free African Americans. Some 40%, says the 1860 census, were foreign-born, from several dozen counties. This was, historian Walter Nugent writes, three times the U.S. average at the time. The biggest groups included 35,000 Chinese, 33,000 Irishmen, 21,000 Germans, and 17,000 British. There were also some 9,000 Mexicans – some of them escaping the cross-border Apache and Comanche raids that peaked in the 1840s and emptied the countryside in northern Sonora. There were also Chilean merchants, Indians from across California, and Indians from India. While it is often noted how France was the one major global power whose people did not move to the American West or to the British Wests in large numbers, the California gold rush actually drew thousands of Frenchmen. Many of them were escaping the political turmoil of 1848, which had ended the Orleans monarchy and initiated the Second Republic in France.

Many British, Australians, and others who flocked first to California in 1849 next headed to Victoria. Among them was an Australian named Edward Hargraves. He left America empty-handed, only to find gold in his own backyard. A South African named Pieter Jacob Marais had departed to California merely a week after the news reached his native Cape Town. The arduous journey via England only increased his desire for panning gold. He got enough to open a small business, which burned in late 1850 in what was one in a series of fires that almost destroyed San Francisco several times over between 1849 and 1851. Marais next headed for the mining areas in Australia, returning home poorer than ever. Then he worked on copper mines and prospected in the Transvaal on the slopes of Witwatersrand. There Marais found specks of gold, hurried to tell the world, and aroused a general interest in gold prospecting. The big rush would not occur until 1886 at Rand, with fortune-seekers from across the globe congregating there and leading to the establishment of Johannesburg. The Kimberley diamond rush to the south in Cape Colony had already preceded it by nearly two decades.

Many veterans of the California and/or Victoria rushes also headed to New Zealand's Otago rush in the 1860s. In the American West, rushes followed in quick succession, including the first Comstock boom in Virginia City, Nevada, in 1859 and near Denver in 1859 ("Pike's Peak or Bust"). Then came the 1863 rush to Virginia City, Montana, the 1864 boom at Helena, Montana, the second Comstock strike in 1873, the Black Hills gold rush in 1874, the Tombstone silver boom in 1878, and many more. There was also the Fraser River strike of 1858 in British Columbia and the Klondike rush in 1897. In all these cases, national boundaries proved no deterrent for people on the move. In fact, the Klondike boom not only drew men across the world; the through traffic in peoples, supplies, and other goods practically made modern Seattle, then a burgeoning town which was over 30% Scandinavian in the early 1900s. While people moved from one rush to the next, they grew older but not necessary any richer in the process. Being male-dominated societies, the best chance of earning in all these rushes was typically in mining the miners: providing food, booze, gambling, prostitutes, accommodation, picks and shovels, and all sorts of other supplies.

These rushes also proved representative of the global settler revolutions, as they linked settler exchanges with transnational circulations in extractive industries and corporate capitalism. These were aggressive intrusions to Native domains: for example, the California rush leading to genocide of numerous local indigenous communities, the Black Hills rush replacing the Sioux and Cheyenne claims through bloody conflicts, and the Tombstone boom occupying the Chiricahua Apache domains. Taking over indigenous space, many rushes left ghost towns and a terrain punctuated with tunnels and debris in their wake. But the land was seldom, if ever, returned to the Natives. Rushes also spurred the growth of major modern urban settler communities such as Victoria, Johannesburg, San Francisco, and Seattle. It also happened that most strikes that lived past the initial rush quickly developed into corporate businesses that called for capital, investments, machines, workers, and technical know-how necessary for underground mining. Over time what had started as rush of the masses was dominated by fewer and fewer men. Yet this did not mean an end to mobility.

Techniques and capital circulated in the global mining sector as did qualified professionals who took their "Western" mining skills abroad in the service of multinational businesses and foreign empires. Fitting the new professional type was Herbert Hoover. Before the presidency, he took advantage of British capital and worked for the British mining interests. He served in a number of locations, including Western Australia, New South Wales, and in China as an engineer building a railroad from Peking to the Mongolian border. There were several other Westerners as well who became prominent in the global mining industry using their Western know-how from South Africa to Australia in the late 1800s. They worked: for instance, for Cecil Rhodes and became caught in the notorious Jameson Raid in 1895 and the Boer War.

These kinds of global exchanges extended from mining to livestock and agribusiness. A recent study by Edward Melillo shows how Chilean migrant workers and mining techniques as well as crops and fertilizers shaped California during the gold rush and the subsequent rise of agribusiness. The turn-of-the-century Miles City, Montana, in turn, was a livestock center from which horses were shipped around the world, especially to the Boer War in South Africa where the Boers were able to escape the British infantry on their Western mounts. One young cowboy working himself into the horse business in Montana, Fred Barton, was invited by a visiting Russian delegate to build massive horse ranches for the Czar. Barton arrived in Vladivostok, Russia, in 1911. When World War I interfered and the Russian Empire collapsed, he went to work for the Chinese commanders. In 1917, he organized and partook in an epic horse drive from Mongolia to northern China. To please his Mongolian hosts, Barton and his fellow Montanan wranglers put on a Wild West show with roping, shooting, and riding exhibitions. He also set up a massive ranch in the Shansi province and bred a new stock combining Mongol ponies; Russian Orlov mounts from Khabarovsk, Siberia; and American Morgan horses. After he returned to Los Angeles, Barton married himself into a prominent family and became part of the Hollywood social scene.

Another career that linked the West and the world by joining settler activities with capital flows was that of the Frenchman Marquis de Morés. In the 1890s, de Morés hoped for a reputation as a dashing figure in service of the French Empire in North Africa. But before that he had an unpredictable career as an army officer in Algeria, a rancher in the Dakota Territory, a railroad promoter in French Indochina, an anti-Semitic politician in his native France, and an explorer of the Sahara. In 1883 he established Medora along the Northern Pacific rail line, naming the community after his new bride Medora von Hoffman, who was a daughter of a wealthy New York banker. De Morés purchased 45,000 acres of land for ranching, had a 26-room house known as the Chateau de Morés built for his family, opened a stagecoach business, and erected a meatpacking plant for shipping refrigerated meat via the railroad. His efforts toward becoming a big businessman crumbled as de Morés quickly made enemies due to his fierce temper – he was possibly arrested twice and suspected of murder in Dakota but acquitted – and by stepping on the toes of the big and powerful in the meatpacking industry of the Chicago stockyards, who had little toleration for competition.

The family returning to France, de Morés claimed that Chicago and its livestock operations were run by vicious Jews. Openly anti-Semitic and a growing favorite of the far right in France, he traveled across Asia and lived for a while in French Indochina. In the mid-1890s, de Morés tried to recruit the Tuareg, the famed desert warriors, against the Jews in French Algeria. Known to dress in a cowboy hat and a buckskin jacket with a revolver in the hip, and being an ardent and famous duelist, de Morés was raided and killed by the Tuareg in 1897 in Sahara. After the death of her husband, Medora never returned to Medora, North Dakota, but died in France in 1921, allegedly of a disease she had first caught in India.

The mobility of European, predominantly British, capital also characterized mining, the livestock industry, and corporate agriculture in the West, as well as in Canada, New Zealand, Australia, southern Africa, and much of Latin America, a sphere of informal British, and later American, imperialism since gaining independence from Spain. As British money brought millions of acres under cultivation worldwide, the cheaper farm exports drove many peasant farmers in Europe out of the market. Many made the move to cities, and many headed as settlers for the American and British Wests. Some well-born Britons who crossed North America to see the Indians and hunt buffalo in turn used their wealth to invest in cattle ranching, mining, and urban development, buying up vast tracts of land in the West. A 1884 report by the federal government estimated that foreign businessmen, most of them British, owned 21 million acres of America, the equivalent of a ten-mile wide strip running from the Atlantic to the Pacific. While the Alien Land Bill of 1887 barred non-Americans from buying land, it was seldom stringently enforced.

European corporate agriculturalists operated factory-type systems in the West using a sizable multinational labor force. The large-scale British-invested wheat operations in the Red River Valley of the North provide one example that involved absentee ownership, strictly market-oriented production and specialization, and seasonal work forces drawn from both sides of the U.S.–Canadian border and from Europe. These ventures were the object of much public interest. A delegation of members of the British Parliament visited the Red River farms in 1879, and newsmen described the undertakings in the London *Times*. But even these bigger operations were vulnerable to dropping wheat prices around the world and to cycles of drought, which culminated in parceling off many of the biggest estates.

The global shifts in demand and prices and the local shifts in weather were very much evident in the cattle business as well. Rising beef prices in Britain had prompted a royal commission to support investing in the American cattle business. The number of investors interested in placing cattle across the Plains multiplied in the 1880s, and soon too many cattle overgrazed too many ecologically vulnerable ranges. Drought-filled summers and the winter storms of 1886–1887 decimated the herds amassed by British investment companies. This "big die-up" on the Plains led to restructuring of the industry, yet it did not diminish the role of British money. For instance, the Scottish-owned Swan Land and Cattle Company and the Matador Land and Cattle Company reduced stocking the herds and began to move the cattle in a systematic fashion, while also installing wells and reservoirs. Set up in 1885, the famed XIT ranch in the Texas Panhandle was owned by the Capitol Freehold Land and Investment Company of London, a syndicate of mostly British investors, including the Earl of Aberdeen and Henry Seton-Karr, a Member of Parliament. The operations started with the equivalent of roughly $5 million invested. Comprising over 3,000,000 acres and run like a corporation, the ranch had at its peak some 150,000 cows, 325 windmills, 100 dams, and 1,500 miles of fence.

The transnational networks and exchanges in cattle ranching and agriculture were not limited to foreign money, ownership, the use of multiethnic work forces, or even the rise of settler societies. They ran much deeper in the colonization of the Americas. According to Terry Jordan, the practices of Western cattle ranching can be traced to livestock areas spanning from equatorial west Africa north to the Shetland Islands, with main contributions stemming from the interplay of British and Iberian (especially Andalusian) influences. Distinctively, Iberian ranching practices were first transferred to the Caribbean by the Spanish in the 1500s. There they encountered new environments and soon merged with British and African herding practices before moving to the mainland. There more merges took place, primarily with British husbandry traditions, to form a hybridized Anglo-Mexican cattle culture. It shot north and west from Texas after the Civil War, reaching the Pacific Coast and the Canadian Plains. After the big cattle die-up in 1880s, Midwestern Anglo cattle raising techniques from Iowa and Missouri in turn gained more hold in the West, on the Great Plains and beyond toward the Pacific and Canada.

Exchanges, of course, did not mean the straightforward transplanting of Spanish or British practices to new settler-occupied settings. Lassoing, for instance, although closely connected with the Spanish cattle culture in the Americas, was not an Iberian practice but an innovation of African cowboys in seventeenth-century Mexico. If the variations in ranching cultures from Patagonia to the Yukon were grounded on a vivid Spanish influence, they also shared much in common with each other. The lives of Western and Canadian cowboys, Mexican vaqueros, Venezuelan llaneros, Argentinian gauchos, and Chilean huasos shared much in key values and characteristics; in their social status; professional pride and sense of superiority; values of everyday lives (emphasis on humble, simple lives); and in work and leisure practices, as historian Richard Slatta writes. Furthermore, these exchanges did not hit a brick wall as they reached the Pacific. Recently historian John Ryan Fischer has shown how Hawaii and California became major linked nodes in the livestock economy of the Pacific world through the circulation of labor and trade in livestock products, such as hide and tallow. In the 1830s, Hispanic California cowboys had already started working in Hawaii, at approximately the same time as the Hudson's Bay Company was bringing Hawaiian and other Pacific Islander trappers to the Pacific Northwest.

Borders and Exclusion

Asian Transfers

Certain types of transnational mobility were not welcome in the settler revolutions in the American West or in settler colonies elsewhere. Since the Jacksonian Era, doubts and protests had regularly surfaced among the native-born white Americans against the migration of Irish and other Catholic settlers. Even after the mid-century, the whiteness of Jews, Mormons, Eastern and Southern Europeans, as well as the Irish remained in doubt. Strong anti-German feelings also erupted by World War I, as did protests against the Mexicans, especially in the 1930s and again in the late 1900s. But the main focus in the pre-World War II West was on curtailing the migrations of the Chinese and other Asians, who were on the move as much as or more so than the Europeans. While a relatively small number of Chinese were drawn to their own "far west" of Tibet, Mongolia, and Xinjiang, some 30 million Chinese, mainly from north China, made the move to the Manchurian frontier. Some migrated, and still do today, to Siberia, the vast East-Uralian expanse that was also a principal target for those Russians engaged in far settlement. Another approximately 20 million people, many from southern China, moved to Southeast Asia, to the countries around the Indian Ocean, and to the southern Pacific. The third big migratory flow took some 2.5 million Chinese workers, chiefly from the rural and urban underclasses, to the west coasts of North and Latin America, as well as to the Caribbean, Australia, and southern and eastern Africa.

This third form of Chinese mobility, often referred to as the "coolie trade," ostensibly signified a return to slavery. It represented a form of contract labor and settlement that bordered on kidnapping and was characterized by inhuman transport conditions, petty wages, tight discipline, and cruel treatment. In reality, most of those involved emigrated more or less voluntarily, although countless went to fill the labor gaps left by the abolition of slavery around the world. It was the growing labor demands of expanding colonial powers, the surge in sugar and cotton plantations, building of transportation networks, and booming extractive industries like mining that called for a reliable, cheap, and mobile workforce. The Chinese seemed to offer the answer, but they were not the kind of answer white settler societies cared to embrace. Measures targeting Chinese exclusion connected the white settler societies across the Pacific. But some Chinese, like Chin Lung and his family, found ways to negotiate and overcome the boundaries set up against their movement.

From the late 1840s onward, this coolie settler immigration, historian Madeline Hsu shows, originated predominantly from the five small regions in the southern Chinese provinces of Fujian and Guangdong. Natural catastrophes, population pressure, the loss of Canton's monopoly on foreign trade and the subsequent unemployment, the secession of Hong Kong to Britain, and the devastation and political and religious oppression caused by the Taiping Rebellion made people in southern China consider emigrating. Often passing through Singapore, the hotspot of international labor recruitment in Asia, the Chinese spread to plantations and other workplaces from Hawaii and Fiji to Cuba, Trinidad, and Peru. By the end of the century, over 100,000 Chinese were employed in the tobacco plantations in Deli, on the eastern coast of Sumatra on the Dutch East Indies. They also went to work in wool production in Australia after the deportation of British convicts there ended in 1840. Many also made it to German East Africa and Germany's colonies in Guinea and Samoa, becoming the principal labor force in these Pacific colonies. There were even talks of importing Chinese workers to Germany itself in the late 1800s to replace the Polish seasonal workforce in Germany's eastern provinces. Nothing came of this plan, however, and the Prussian agriculture continued to rely on Polish and Ruthenian (Ukrainian) migrant laborers (many of whom continued their border crossings by emigrating to the West).

Many Chinese also followed the gold trails to California as well as to Victoria, Fraser River, South Africa, and Klondike. In 1852, there were some 30,000 Chinese in California, while some 40,000 Chinese had reached Australia by the late 1850s. In South Africa, the Boer War resulted in difficult times for the gold mines, and one way of cutting costs was to hire Chinese laborers. From 1904 to 1906, some 63,000 "coolies" were brought to Transvaal. In the West, Chinese workers were employed in railroad construction, most famously on the Central Pacific line. To get through the Rockies, the Canadian Pacific Railway also used thousands of Chinese workers in the 1880s. They were brought north on the initiative of an American contractor. In the early 1880s, over 28,000 Chinese comprised the principal labor force in the burgeoning California agriculture. They worked as laborers for Anglo landowners or on their own as tenant farmers, leasing land, growing their own crops and often hiring their countrymen to work at their sides. Many also were active in marketing their crops or partnered with Chinese merchants like Chin Lung. Some, prior to the enactment of the Alien Land Law of 1913, were even able to own the land they farmed. Furthermore, as many as 78,000 Chinese worked on commercial ships traversing the Pacific. The Chinese in fact constituted a sizable percentage of "American" seamen.

As the numbers of Chinese climbed, so did alarmed writings that circulated widely across the American West, British Wests, and beyond. Beginning in the 1850s, the racial character of "John Chinaman" was created, and reinforced images of the Chinese in songs, plays, fiction, newspapers, and minstrel shows. It depicted the Chinese as unassimilable pollutants who endangered the futures of white settler societies and as laborers who threatened to replace white workers. Their dress, customs, language, and ethnic clustering, together with their secret societies, made the Chinese appear more than suspicious in the eyes of numerous whites who systematically dehumanized them. The Chinese were seen as the lowest kind of beasts of burden, animal-like inventive torturers, prone to predatory cruelty, opium, and vice. Comparisons to various other nonwhite groups were also made: for instance, the Chinese were seen as Jews of the East. They were also depicted as sexually aggressive and mischievous and thus as a severe threat to white women.

Fears of racial mixing were coupled with notions that the Asian settlers would replace and destroy whites, who were at that time in the process of substituting and destroying the indigenous peoples. Historian Kornel Chang writes about how fears over massive Asian settler flood helped various European ethnicities to find a common ground across the Pacific. Labor unions and writers in Washington as well as in British Columbia took their cues from Australia and commonly used Natal as a warning of what could happen. In Natal, as its economy moved to sugar production and needed cheap labor, some 150,000 Asian (Indian and Chinese) workers entered the province from 1860s onward. By 1902, Asians outnumbered the whites, although restrictions to Asian immigration had been adopted in the Natal Acts of 1896–1897. Also, the neighboring Cape Colony passed an Immigration Restriction Act targeting Asians in 1902. By then the British Empire had transported more than one million contract workers from Asia to Mauritius, the Caribbean, East Africa, and the Pacific Islands.

It was the Chinese who, as a racial group, were first barred from entering the settler societies. State policies curtailed Asian immigration from the

1860s onward and created a global color line by World War I. The Chinese Exclusion Act of 1882 (repealed in 1943), and the preceding Page Act of 1875, which targeted "undesirable" immigrants (Asian forced laborers, prostitutes, and convicts), limited Chinese immigration to the West. While the 1882 act targeted laborers only, and denied the Chinese the right of naturalization, the law was very broadly interpreted. It was also followed by a succession of acts targeting other Chinese groups, which made female migration, for instance, very difficult. With no women, there were no Chinese families and no offspring, and thus no Chinese settler futures in the West. Thousands of Chinese had also entered the West by first relocating to Hawaii, where they constituted the second largest ethnic group and the principal farm workers in the 1880s after Native Hawaiians. In 1900, the Chinese entry to the West via Hawaii was barred after its U.S. annexation, as American exclusion laws were extended to the islands.

The first Chinese exclusion act from 1882 had been closely followed in Europe, and it was soon emulated in various parts of the world. After 1888, ships with Chinese passengers were not allowed in Australian ports, and by the time of the "White Australia Act" of 1901, the reaction against Chinese migration had become one of the central components in the nascent Australian nationalism. British Columbia took various discriminatory measures from 1898 to 1908, as Asian immigrants kept coming to the Canadian western provinces as well as using Canada as back door for reaching the American West. While Canada allowed Chinese entry for a fee, Mexico actively encouraged Chinese migration since it had failed in attracting white settlers during the Porfiriato (1876–1911).

The prevention of Chinese settlers from entering the West became a contested issue on both the southern and northern land borders in the early 1900s. Active smuggling networks developed around the Chinese, who were provided local guides for the crossings as well as American money, dictionaries, railroad maps, guidebooks, fraudulent immigration documents, and Chinese American newspapers. They were also provided appropriate disguises to hide their ethnicity, and many Chinese entered the West dressed as Mexicans or as Indians. Historian Erika Lee notes how American officials pressured Canada and Mexico to assist in enforcing U.S. exclusion laws, sought moving the immigration control from the U.S. border to Canadian and Mexican ports of entry, and encouraged its neighbors to adopt immigration laws that were compatible with American goals. While U.S. immigration officers conducted inspections on Canada's sea border, Mexico refused such cooperation. And while the 1923 Exclusion Act (revoked in 1947) forbid all people of Chinese origin or descent from entering Canada, Mexico, despite strong anti-Chinese protests in the country and U.S. pressure, passed no such legislation. On the other hand, the Chinese also remained hated outsiders in Mexico, where they easily became victims of nationalistic xenophobia, historian Elliott Young writes (Figure 2.3).

FIGURE 2.3   Chinese immigrants at the San Francisco customhouse. Courtesy Library of Congress Prints and Photographs Division, LC-USZ62–93673.

Asian settlers kept coming legally to the West in the form of the Japanese, until their entry was restricted by the so-called gentlemen's agreement between the United States and Japan in 1908 and by the Alien Land Laws that spread like wildfire: California in 1913, Arizona and Washington in 1921, Idaho, Montana, and Oregon in 1923, Kansas in 1925, and several other Western states such as Utah and Wyoming up to 1943. This type of legislation was meant to keep the Asians out, to prevent their settlement by restricting their ability to own land and property. Like the Chinese, the Japanese would-be settlers frequently carved exceedingly transnational lives while negotiating the long shadows of exclusion and racial prejudice in the West. They included people like Hiroka Maeda, whose grandparents had emigrated from Japan to Oregon in the 1890s.

Maeda was not only a native-born Westerner, born in The Dalles, Oregon, in 1918, but also a member of immigrant networks that spanned several continents. She was adopted by a Japanese family after her mother succumbed to influenza, renamed Suma, and raised on a small truck farm outside Portland. She attended a local community college and went to Japan to study in 1938. There she married a Norwegian pilot who had fled Nazi occupation in his homeland and who had reached Japan via Russia. Meanwhile, her brother had relocated to Canada and her biological father had remarried, ventured back to Japan, joined the flow of Japanese emigrants to Latin America, and settled in Brazil. Back in The Dalles in the early 1940s, Suma, a native-born American with a European husband fighting the Nazis and with family on three different continents, became a suspected enemy alien, a Japanese infiltrator, in the eyes of the U.S. Federal Bureau of Investigation. She was ordered to Pinedale Assembly Center near Fresno. Like thousands of other Japanese immigrants and their offspring, Suma spent much of the war interned in California. She was a prisoner while her Norwegian husband was shot down over England. After being released, Suma remarried in Chicago and returned to The Dalles. This time she – a woman with more than 50 relatives in the settler colonies of Canada and Brazil, and probably many more in the United States – faced what was open racist discrimination from local whites who simply saw her as a Japanese turncoat. After being treated as a potential traitor by her government, she became a social outcast in her place of birth.

Borderlands Crossings

Ever since they were drawn and surveyed, the southern and northern land borders of the American West proved mobile spaces. These borders were at first mere lines in the woods or sand, with border markers few and far between and even those decaying and destroyed. Certainly boundaries were meant to establish national sovereignty and political control, assert state claims to natural resources and inhabitants' loyalty, establish (closed) zones of economic activity, and, in myriad ways, determine who was in and who was out of the settler project in the West. But by the late 1800s, Western land borders were not the zones of increased anxiety they became in the second half of the twentieth century.

Borders enabled crossings of various kinds. There were the Anglo filibusters seeking expansion in Mexico and engaged in violent turmoil in the 1850s and the Apaches and Comanches who raided deep into Mexico (see Chapter 3). Then there were the European settlers who crossed from the West to Canada and back. In the 1840s and 1850s, the Mexican government, with the intention of establishing a buffer zone between Mexican settlements and the Comanche and Anglo threat stemming from the north, invited eastern Indians who had relocated to the Indian Territory to settle in Coahuila. Many Kickapoos and Seminoles as well as some Cherokees, Shawnees, and Delawares answered the call. Disappointed with their treatment and violence in Mexico, many soon returned to the Indian Territory.

After the bitter defeat in the Civil War, people from different social classes in the Confederate South moved across the border to Mexico, while many others journeyed to Venezuela, British Honduras, and Brazil. Their settler visions and experiences in Mexico, historian Todd Wahlstrom comments, proved quite complex and multifaceted. Many sought to transplant the Dixie to Latin America, others accepted integration to their new host societies, and most simply wanted to improve their standing in life. There were also those who thought in global terms, exhibiting broad commercial and hemispheric visions.

Exiles' efforts to rebuild plantation lives at the colony of Carlota in central Mexico, for instance, mostly failed. While high-profile immigrants such as Jubal Early and Sterling Price rather easily drew close to the administration of Emperor Maximilian von Hapsburg, the French-backed "puppet" ruler, most ambitions for the colonization of northern Mexico faltered in the violent maelstrom that spanned the Texas–Coahuila–Nuevo Leon–Tamaulipas borderlands and involved Comanches, Apaches, and Kickapoos as well as French troops and Mexican ranchers and bandits. Some Southerners also tried to make a name for themselves in railroad construction, while less well-to-do settlers found headway in mining, which often involved Chinese labor at San Louis Potosi and in the Tuxpan-Tampico region on the Gulf of Mexico. While some better accustomed themselves to Mexican Catholicism and culture and fitted into the political climate of the Porfiriato, many southerners soon returned back north across the border after the downfall of Maximilian and the French in 1867.

Borderlands were also places that railways and mining and ranching operations crossed in volume. Two years after the Southern Pacific Railroad made its way through Arizona and New Mexico, it branched south across the border to Guaymas, Sonora, in 1883. Soon more American railroads linked the Southwest and northern Mexico. This was at a time when no tracks led from northern Mexico to the interior of the country. While more people arrived into the borderlands, significant quantities of copper and cattle were shipped out. Mining was the centerpiece of economic growth, and venture capitalists, both American and European, invested in smelters and livestock production on both sides of the border. The demands of mining for skilled and unskilled labor created new communities such as Bisbee, Globe, Clifton, and Jerome in Arizona and Nacozari and Cananea in Sonora. These became destinations for workers arriving from established mining areas in Germany, Scotland, Ireland, and Cornwall. The latter especially had earned a special reputation as mineworkers of colonial empires.

Miners made up most of the 250,000–300,000 Cornish who moved abroad before World War I. You could find skilled Cornish in the U.S.–Mexico borderlands as well as in the mines of Australia, South Africa, Brazil, Cuba, and Chile. As British money financed much of the mines, the Cornish directors of these operations preferred hiring proven Cornish workers, some of whom lived for the better part of their adult lives moving internationally from one job to the next, with fixed contracts and return tickets bought in advance. But whether transient or permanent, the Cornish, like so many other settlers, formed tight-knit communities and did not lose contact with either the people or the customs of their homeland. Wrestling competitions took place in the new settlements, Cornish Methodist chapels were constructed, and pasties and saffron cakes became well-known, as did the sound of brass bands and Cornish carols.

The majority of the European settlers who made it over the Mississippi had not reached the Southwest borderlands in the mid-1800s. Short on farming lands, lacking manufacturing and industrial foundation, these areas offered little immediate economic promise for the potential settlers. These areas also had few white women, high percentages of nonwhites (New Mexico), or lacked the familiar ethnic communities where the immigrants could move in and feel at home. Still, Arizona and New Mexico had a few thousand Irish, Germans, Scots, and Swiss settlers by the 1880s, while several Jewish immigrants made their name as businessmen. Many Irish and Germans originally arrived to the borderlands as soldiers fighting the Apaches. In fact, the late- 1800s roster of the Indian-fighting U.S. Army throughout the West carried a very cosmopolitan tone and included men from practically every European country plus the British Wests. Military service proved a suitable way for these potential settlers to acquaint themselves to the land and the English language. When their army contracts (usually five year stints) ran out, many immigrant soldiers stayed in the West to make their permanent homes there.

It was the copper mining boom that drew not only larger numbers of Cornish but also numerous Mexicans, Italians, Spanish, Czechs, Serbs, Montenegrins, Finns, and Bohemians to the borderlands communities dominated by Phelps Dodge. In borderlands mining towns, like in the mining regions of southern Africa, visible racial hierarchies existed. Campsites, for instance, were segregated into different European nationalities, Anglos, and Mexicans. Better paying and more skilled jobs went to Anglos, while the Mexicans occupied the lower tiers. Until World War II, when the huge infusions of federal investment altered conditions on the U.S. side, the copper industry provided an important attraction for potential settlers as well the number one source of personal income and tax revenue on the borderlands. Yet it was a precarious world. World mineral prices and mining investments or disinvestment determined how the borderlands operations grew or did not. A rise in the price in Paris or the opening of a new mine in Chile impacted life in the mines of the borderlands and throughout the West. In 1893, the information that the British government ceased the practice of coining silver rupees in India brought immediate chaos to the mining and smelting centers in Colorado (Leadville, Aspen), Utah, Montana (Butte, Helena), and Idaho's Coeur d'Alene area. Unemployment threatened close to a third of the workforce in many places.

The crossings of some nonwhite laborers caused tensions on the borderlands early on. Global cotton trade linked Texas and the South with the British Empire, but also linked them with Mexico as black slaves escaped across the border. Indeed, prior to and in the aftermath of the Treaty of Guadalupe Hidalgo (1848), runaway slaves from Texas, aware that the border separated two sovereignties, sought refuge on the other side, historian James David Nichols writes. And so did the peons from northern Mexico crossing in the opposite direction. These border-crossing Mexican workers proved important in filling labor shortages in Texas. Stuck in debt and violent repression, neither the Mexican peons nor the American blacks saw the border as a limit, but rather as a gateway to freedom and the opportunity for settler life as free people. Thus a line intended to seal off one side from the other and keep people bound in their place served the contrary function of increasing mobility.

In the late 1800s and early 1900s, whites and Mexicans could typically cross the land borders of the West relatively easily. There were the custom officials on both sides of the line, arriving in the 1880s as railroads crossed the borderlands and new towns sprang up along the lines. They were, at least at first, less interested in peoples and more inclined to collect a duty on the growing stream of cross-border commerce. They also designated a few points of the boundary line as ports of entry and in theory sealed off the rest to traffic. Enforcement of regulations proved typically flexible, yet duties and crossing regulations still made it more difficult to move a wide range of goods, commodities, and animals across the border. Ranchers used to operating on both sides of the line could now face considerable payments for the border crossings of their own livestock. Cross-border traffic involved disputed realms and plenty of smuggling, from cattle and horse thieving on the southern border by Apaches, Mexicans, and whites to opium transport in the Puget Sound area. In the latter area, there even existed something we can call "contraband salmon," as fishermen ignored the border and instead sold their catch to the highest offer on either side of the U.S.–Canadian line, as historian Lissa Wadewitz has shown. In the south, the Mexican revolutionary unrest in the 1910s led to new emphasis on smuggling weaponry, drugs, and alcohol.

It was still the Chinese that caused the biggest alarm and saw the largely unguarded U.S.–Canadian and U.S.–Mexican borders gradually develop into sites of state policing and deterrence. Surveillance included a network of custom officers, train employees, diplomats, and civilian informants. Immigrant inspectors began to include "line riders" and "Chinese catchers" in the late 1800s, and they extended their reach from the border into interior cities, striving to institute a vigorous policy of arrests and deportations. A new type of immigrant, the "illegal immigrant" was coined with the Chinese in mind by the American public, and by the 1920s, the borders were effectively closed against "illegal" Chinese. In hindsight, one can say that the Chinese exclusion functioned as a "trial run" for the turning of the U.S.–Mexico border into the militarized zone it is today. Designed to deter immigration from Mexico and Latin America, the present border is a space of fences; 24-hour, high-tech surveillance; civilian volunteers; and of course the U.S. Border Patrol, today's small army that has grown from much humbler beginnings since it was first established to stop the Chinese in 1924.

It was in 1924 that the Johnson–Reed Immigration Act restricted and brought national quotas to European immigration, thus a year that marked a shift in the settler revolution that tied the West and the world together. As settler flow from Europe rescinded, entanglements with Mexico and the larger Latin America grew from a stream into a torrent as the twentieth century progressed. Approximately 1.5 million Mexicans (or 10% of Mexico's population) crossed the border from 1900 to 1930 compared to the 17,000 Chinese "illegals." American businesses eagerly lobbied for Mexican labor, arguing that there was not enough (or it was not cheap enough) of a white settler workforce, so it was necessary to hire Mexicans for the growing mining and agricultural sector. They also believed that the Mexicans would return back home once their jobs were done. The boom in irrigation, the industrialization of California and Texas agriculture, and the shift from cattle ranching to agribusiness quickly grew to rely on the Mexican workforce, as did much of the borderland mining operations. The literacy test and head tax imposed on the Mexicans in 1917 went actively unenforced by U.S. border officials and the American railroad companies. Agricultural enterprises from the Plains to California sent recruiters and promotional material to and across the border in order to attract more Mexican laborers. In Salt River Valley, Arizona, cotton growers even organized special trains to move whole families directly from Mexico. Together with Filipinos, emigrating from the recently acquired U.S. overseas colony, Mexican workers became the leading agricultural labor group in the West. For instance, the 120,000 acres of intensive crop farming operations in California's Imperial Valley, close to the border, depended on irrigation and Mexicans, who made over 30% of the labor force in 1920.

The driving factors of the increase in Mexican border crossings stemmed from the rise of debt peonage among Mexican workers. This in turn represented a result of land policies during Porfiriato that encouraged the setting up of large haciendas and a move from maize, the all-important staple of ordinary Mexicans, to export crops. Transnational passages also overlapped with a population boom in Mexico and its accompanying labor surplus and reduction of wages. The revolutions and political unrest in Mexico also shoved refugees across the border. Most border-crossing Mexicans originated from northern Mexico or close to the railways further south. In the 1890s and 1900s, new rail lines linked northern Mexico efficiently with the population centers of central Mexico, thus making transnational mobility much easier.

Mexicans often practiced step migration, meaning that most of those who ended up in the West normally first moved, and only intended to move, within Mexico. They frequently went from small villages to urban centers such as Mexico City, which saw its population multiply threefold between 1900 and 1930. Furthermore, it was often older sons from rural areas who sought income in Mexican urban or mining centers, while younger men journeyed to the West. Many migrants, especially families, who eventually settled in the West first made the move to border communities, such as Tijuana, Baja California; Nogales, Sonora; Ciudad Juárez, Chihuahua; and Piedras Negras, Coahuila. Together with their American counterparts such as El Paso, Texas, these locales developed into bustling ports for cross-border labor and economic mobility and exchange. Many also frequently moved within the West. Before ending up in Los Angeles in 1919, Zeferino Velázquez, a native of León, Guanajuato, had seen many places. He first crossed the border to El Paso with his brother-in-law. From El Paso, historian George J. Sánchez writes, the two men were instantly recruited for railroad work in Kansas, an occupation from which Zeferino soon switched to meatpacking. To avoid the Kansas draft for World War I, he skipped to California and found farm work in the Imperial Valley. In 1918, he went to Ciudad Juárez to help his father, his sister, and her children to cross the border, before the whole extended family settled in Los Angeles.

Mexicans also characteristically practiced circular migration. They exhibited a pattern of back-and-forth mobility that would continue for several years. In short, many of those Mexicans who started to move stayed on the move, sometimes for much of their lives, while also staying in touch with their place of origin. Also, most men who crossed into the West believed their stay was only temporary, but upon their return to their local villages, these men actively disseminated knowledge of the West among the residents. In all likelihood they increased the number of potential settlers contemplating on leaving.

Legally white for the most part, Mexicans were not white enough in the eyes of most Anglos and European settlers in the West. Capitalistic agribusiness proved an exploitative economy, a dual labor system often defined by Jim Crow-type segregation and disparities in labor conditions. Social isolation of the Mexican migrants, ethnic hierarchies that placed native-born Anglos on top, what seemed like a permanent and universal working-class status, poor labor conditions, and the tensions between corporate control and unionization led to frequent bouts of labor violence, all of which further reinforced the ethnic Mexican identity. Yet, from the perspective of the Mexicans the pay was better north of the international line. There were also more jobs, less political unrest, and brighter prospects for the future. While the continued need for Mexican workers north of the border and the continued need of Mexicans to find jobs in the north led to mounting cross-border mobility, it also turned many of the newcomers into settlers.

When the U.S. economy collapsed in 1929, the appetite for Mexican migrant labor also collapsed, only to rise again with the start of World War II. In the 1930s, Mexicans workers turned from desirable to expendable. Massive repatriations, deportations, and voluntary return migration saw one-third of them, an estimated one million people, leave the American West. Two-thirds, however, stayed put, many of them establishing permanent settler roots in Western communities such as San Antonio and Los Angeles. Then the Bracero Program brought some 4.5 million Mexican guest agricultural workers north of the border between 1942 and 1964. These people, who were supposed to be participants in a short-term work program, also eventually stayed, while countless others also practiced circular migration. World War II had stimulated massive economic growth in the West, fueling its agricultural and industrial sectors. In the process, many employers grew more and more dependent on Mexican labor. Coinciding with the braceros, there was also a rising number of illegal Mexicans entering the West, which prompted protests from the Anglo populace and led to mass deportations, like Operation Wetback in 1954. Still, by the mid-century Mexican immigrants vastly outnumbered all other settler newcomers in the West and had in fact done that for quite some time already.

The settler revolutions in the West linked the local and the global and carried people, capital, goods, and ideas across maritime and terrestrial spaces and revolved around the contested dynamics of exclusion and inclusion. As the twentieth century progressed, the settler projects of the world moved toward increased multiculturalism. More and more Asians arrived to Australia, Canada, and the American West, while the latter continues to draw millions of workers from Mexico, many of whom become settlers over time. Today, several areas in the settler colonial West, such as California, New Mexico, and Texas, have, or will soon have, noticeable nonwhite majorities. In all likelihood, the transnational networks that have connected the settler West and the world continue to take fresh trajectories that are bound to further undermine any notions of the West as a "white man's country." The West was, is, and will in all likelihood remain an ongoing and constantly changing settler project drawing potential arrivals from all corners of the world.

Bibliography

Age of Mobility

Barkan, Elliott Robert. *From All Points: America's Immigrant West, 1870s–1952.* Bloomington: Indiana University Press, 2007.

Belich, James. *Replenishing the Earth: The Settler Revolution and the Rise of the Angloworld.* Oxford: Oxford University Press, 2011.

Brands, H. W. *The Age of Gold: The California Gold Rush and the New American Dream.* New York: Anchor, 2003.

Cravens, Craig, and David Zersen, eds. *Transcontinental Encounters: Central Europe Meets the American Heartland.* Austin: Concordia University Press, 2005.

Dresden, Donald. *Marquis de Morés: Emperor of the Bad Lands.* Norman: University of Oklahoma Press, 1970.

Emmons, David M. *Beyond the American Pale: The Irish in the West, 1845–1910.* Norman: University of Oklahoma Press, 2010.

Evans, Simon, Sarah Carter, and Bill Yeo, eds. *Cowboys, Ranchers and the Cattle Business: Cross-Border Perspectives on Ranching History.* Calgary: University of Calgary Press, 2000.

Fetherling, Douglas. *The Gold Crusades: A Social History of Gold Rushes, 1849–1929.* Toronto: University of Toronto Press, 1997.

Findlay, John M., and Ken S. Coates. *Parallel Destinies: Canadian-American Relations West of the Rockies.* Seattle: University of Washington Press, 2002.

Fischer, John Ryan. *Cattle Colonialism: An Environmental History of the Conquest of California and Hawai'i.* Chapel Hill: University of North Carolina Press, 2015.

Francis, R. Douglas, and Howard Palmer, eds. *The Prairie West: Historical Readings*, 2nd ed. Edmonton: Pica Pica Press, 1995.

Goodman, David. *Gold Seeking: Victoria and California in the 1850's.* Stanford: Stanford University Press, 1994.

Hansen, Karen V. *Encounter on the Great Plains: Scandinavian Settlers and the Dispossession of Dakota Indians, 1890–1930.* Oxford: Oxford University Press, 2013.

Harper, Marjory, and Stephen Constantine. *Migration and Empire.* Oxford: Oxford University Press, 2010.

Hixson, Walter L. *American Settler Colonialism: A History.* New York: Palgrave Macmillan, 2013.

Hoerder, Dirk, and Jörg Nagel, eds. *People in Transit: German Migrations in Comparative Perspective, 1820–1930.* Cambridge: Cambridge University Press, 1995.

Holliday, J. S. *The World Rushed In: The California Gold Rush Experience.* New York: Simon & Schuster, 1981.

Isenberg, Andrew C. *The Destruction of the Bison: An Environmental History, 1750–1920.* Cambridge: Cambridge University Press, 2000.

_____. *Mining California: An Ecological History.* New York: Hill and Wang, 2006.

_____. "Mercurial Nature: The California Gold Country and the Coal Fields of the Ruhr Basin, 1850–1900." In Ursula Lehmkuhl and Hermann Wellenreuther, eds. *Historians and Nature: Comparative Approaches to Environmental History.* Oxford: Berg, 2007: 125–145.

Jones, David C. *Empire of Dust: Settling and Abandoning the Prairie Dry Belt.* Edmonton: University of Alberta Press, 1987.

Jordan, Terry G. *German Seed in Texas Soil: Immigrant Farmers in Nineteenth-Century Texas.* Austin: University of Texas Press, 1975.

_____. *North American Cattle Ranching Frontiers: Origins, Diffusion, and Differentiation.* Albuquerque: University of New Mexico Press, 1993.

Khodarkovsky, Michael. *Russia's Steppe Frontier: The Making of a Colonial Empire, 1500–1800.* Bloomington: Indiana University Press, 2002.

Knowles, Valerie. *Strangers at Our Gates: Canadian Immigration and Immigration Policy, 1540–2015,* 4th ed. Toronto: Dundurn, 2016.

Loewen, Royden. *Family, Church, and Market: A Mennonite Community in the Old and New Worlds, 1850–1930.* Urbana: University of Illinois Press, 1993.

Luebke, Frederick C. *Ethnicity of Great Plains.* Lincoln: University of Nebraska Press, 1980.

_____. *Germans in the New World: Essays in the History of Immigration.* Urbana: University of Illinois Press, 1990.

_____, ed. *European Immigrants in the American West: Community Histories.* Albuquerque: University of New Mexico Press, 1998.

MacDonald, Norbert. *Distant Neighbors: A Comparative History of Seattle and Vancouver.* Lincoln: University of Nebraska Press, 1987.

Manz, Stefan. *Constructing a German Diaspora: The "Greater German Empire," 1871–1914.* New York: Routledge, 2014.

McCarthy, Angela, ed. *A Global Clan: Scottish Migrant Networks and Identities since the Eighteenth Century.* London: I. B. Tauris, 2006.

McKeown, Adam M. "Global Migration, 1846–1940." *Journal of World History* 15 (June 2004): 155–189.

McManus, Sheila. *The Line Which Separates: Race, Gender, and the Making of the Alberta-Montana Borderlands.* Lincoln: University of Nebraska Press, 2005.

Melillo, Edward Dallam. *Strangers on Familiar Soil: Rediscovering the Chile-California Connection.* New Haven: Yale University Press, 2015.

Mulder, William. *Homeward to Zion: The Mormon Migration from Scandinavia.* 1957; reprint, Minneapolis: University of Minnesota Press, 2000.

North, Douglas C. "International Capital Flows and the Development of the American West." *Journal of Economic History* 16 (December 1956): 493–505.

Nugent, Walter. *Crossings: The Great Transatlantic Migrations, 1870–1914*. Bloomington: Indiana University Press, 1992.

_____. *Into the West: The Story of Its People*. New York: Knopf, 1999.

Owens, Kenneth N., ed. *Riches for All: The California Gold Rush and the World*. Lincoln: University of Nebraska Press, 2002.

Pagnamenta, Peter. *Prairie Fever: British Aristocrats in the American West 1830–1890*. New York: W. W. Norton and Co., 2013.

Paul, Rodman Wilson. *Mining Frontiers of the Far West, 1848–1880*. New York: Holt, Rinehart and Winston, 1963.

Robbins, William G. *Colony and Empire: The Capitalist Transformation of the American West*. Lawrence: University Press of Kansas, 1994.

Rohrbough, Malcolm J. *Days of Gold: The California Gold Rush and the American Nation*. Berkeley: University of California Press, 1997.

_____. *Rush to Gold: The French and the California Gold Rush, 1848–1854*. New Haven: Yale University Press, 2013.

Russell, Lynette, eds., *Colonial Frontiers: Indigenous-European Encounters in Settler Societies*. Manchester: Manchester University Press, 2001.

Schulz, Charles S. *Forty-Niners 'Round the Horn*. Columbia: University of South Carolina Press, 1999.

Sharp, Paul F. "When Our West Moved North." *American Historical Review* 55 (January 1950): 286–300.

Sisson, Kelly J. "Bound for California: Chilean Contract Laborers and 'Patrones' in the California Gold Rush, 1848–1852." *Southern California Quarterly* 90.3 (2008): 259–305

Spence, Clark C. *British Investments and the American Mining Frontier, 1860–1901*. Ithaca: Cornell University Press, 1958.

Slatta, Richard W. *Cowboys of the Americas*. New Haven: Yale University Press, 1994.

_____. *Comparing Cowboys & Frontiers: New Perspectives on the History of the Americas*. Norman: University of Oklahoma Press, 1997.

Sunderland, Willard. *Taming the Wild Field: Colonization and Empire on the Russian Steppe*. Ithaca: Cornell University Press, 2004.

Szasz, Ferenc Morton. *Scots in the North American West, 1790–1917*. Norman: University of Oklahoma Press, 2000.

Tate, Michael L. *Indians and Emigrants: Encounters on the Overland Trails*. Norman: University of Oklahoma Press, 2006.

Teisch, Jessica B. *Engineering Nature: Water, Development, and the Global Spread of American Environmental Expertise*. Chapel Hill: University of North Carolina Press, 2011.

Veracini, Lorenzo. *Settler Colonialism: A Theoretical Overview*. New York: Palgrave Macmillan, 2010.

Weaver, John C. *The Great Land Rush and the Making of the Modern World, 1650–1900*. Montreal: McGill-Queen's University Press, 2003.

Weirather, Larry. *Fred Barton and the Warlords' Horses of China: How an American Cowboy Brought the Old West to the Far East*. Jefferson, NC: McFarland, 2016.

White, Richard. *Railroaded: The Transcontinentals and the Making of Modern America*. New York: W. W. Norton, 2012.

Winther, Oscar O. "Promoting the American West in England, 1865–1890." *Journal of Economic History* 16 (December 1956): 506–513.

Wrobel, David M. *Promised Lands: Promotion, Memory, and the Creation of the American West*. Lawrence: University Press of Kansas, 1992.

Borders and Exclusion

Almaguer, Tomas. *Racial Fault Lines: The Historical Origins of White Supremacy in California*. Berkeley: University of California Press, 1995.

Atkinson, David C. *The Burden of White Supremacy: Containing Asian Migration in the British Empire and the United States*. Chapel Hill: University of North Carolina Press, 2016.

Azuma, Eiichiro. *Between Two Empires: Race, History, and Transnationalism in Japanese America*. Oxford: Oxford University Press, 2005.

Bowman, Timothy P. *Blood Oranges: Colonialism and Agriculture in the South Texas Borderlands*. College Station: Texas A &M University Press, 2016.

Bright, Rachel. *Chinese Labour in South Africa, 1902–10: Race, Violence, and Global Spectacle*. New York: Palgrave Macmillan, 2013.

Bryce, Benjamin, and Alexander Freund, eds. *Entangling Migration History: Borderlands and Transnationalism in the United States and Canada*. Gainesville: University Press of Florida, 2015.

Carey, Elaine, and Andrae M. Marak, eds. *Smugglers, Brothels, and Twine: Historical Perspectives on Contraband and Vice in North America's Borderlands*. Tucson: University of Arizona Press, 2011.

Carey, Jane, and Claire McLisky, eds. *Creating White Australia*. Sydney: Sydney University Press, 2009.

Chan, Sucheng. *This Bittersweet Soil: The Chinese in California Agriculture, 1860–1910*. Berkeley: University of California Press, 1986.

Chang, Gordon H. *Fateful Ties: A History of America's Preoccupation with China*. Cambridge: Cambridge University Press, 2015.

Chang, Kornel S. *Pacific Connections: The Making of the Western U.S.-Canadian Borderlands*. Berkeley: University of California Press, 2012.

Cohen, Deborah. *Braceros: Migrant Citizens and Transnational Subjects in the Postwar United States and Mexico*. Chapel Hill: University of North Carolina Press, 2011.

Deutsch, Sarah. *No Separate Refuge: Culture, Class, and Gender on an Anglo-Hispanic Frontier in the American Southwest, 1880–1940*. Oxford: Oxford University Press, 1987.

Díaz, George T. *Border Contraband: A History of Smuggling across the Rio Grande*. Austin: University of Texas Press, 2015.

Foley, Neil. *The White Scourge: Mexicans, Blacks, and Poor Whites in Texas Cotton Culture*. Berkeley: University of California Press, 1997.

Geiger, Andrea. *Subverting Exclusion: Transpacific Encounters with Race, Caste, and Borders, 1885–1928*. New Haven: Yale University Press, 2015.

Gibson, Arrell Morgan. *The Kickapoos: Lords of the Middle Border*. Norman: University of Oklahoma Press, 1963.

Hernandez, Kelly Lytle. *Migra!: A History of the U.S. Border Patrol*. Berkeley: University of California Press, 2010.

Hsu, Madeline. *Dreaming of Gold, Dreaming of Home: Transnationalism and Migration between the United States and South China, 1882–1943*. Stanford: Stanford University Press, 2000.

Jacobson, Matthew Frye. *Whiteness of a Different Color: European Immigrants and the Alchemy of Race*. Cambridge, MA: Harvard University Press, 1998.

Jung, Moon-Ho, ed. *The Rising Tide of Color: Race, State Violence, and Radical Movements across the Pacific*. Seattle: University of Washington Press, 2014.

Lahti, Janne, ed. *Soldiers in the Southwest Borderlands, 1848–1886*. Norman: University of Oklahoma Press, 2017.

Lake, Marilyn, and Harry Reynolds. *Drawing the Global Colour Line: White Men's Countries and the International Challenge of Racial Equality.* Cambridge: Cambridge University Press, 2008.

Lee, Erika. *At America's Gates: Chinese Immigration During the Exclusion Era, 1882–1943.* Chapel Hill: University of North Carolina Press, 2003.

Marak, Andrae, Clarissa Confer, and Laura Tuennerman, eds. *Transnational Indians in the North American West.* College Station: Texas A & M University Press, 2015.

McGrady, David G. *Living with Strangers: The Nineteenth-Century Sioux and the Canadian-American Borderlands.* Lincoln: University of Nebraska Press, 2006.

McKeown, Adam M. *Chinese Migrant Networks and Cultural Change: Peru, Chicago, Hawaii, 1900–1936.* Chicago: University of Chicago Press, 2001.

_____. *Melancholy Order: Asian Migration and the Globalization of Borders.* New York: Columbia University Press, 2008.

Montejano, David. *Anglos and Mexicans in the Making of Texas, 1836–1986.* Austin: University of Texas Press, 1987.

Mulroy, Kevin. *Freedom on the Border: The Seminole Maroons in Florida, the Indian Territory, Coahuila, and Texas.* Lubbock: Texas Tech University Press, 1993.

Ngai, Mae M. *Impossible Subjects: Illegal Aliens and the Making of Modern America.* Princeton: Princeton University Press, 2004.

Nichols, James David. "The Line of Liberty: Runaway Slaves and Fugitive Peons in the Texas-Mexico Borderlands." *Western Historical Quarterly* 45 (Winter 2013): 413–433.

Northrup, David. *Indentured Labour in the Age of Imperialism, 1834–1922.* Cambridge: Cambridge University Press, 1995.

Oharazeki, Kazuhiro. "Anti-prostitution Campaigns in Japan and the American West, 1890–1920: A Transpacific Comparison." *Pacific Historical Review* 82 (May 2013): 175–214.

Payton, Philip. *The Cornish Overseas.* Fowey: Alexander Associates, 1999.

Peck, Gunther. *Reinventing Free Labor: Padrones and Immigrant Workers in the North American West, 1880–1930.* Cambridge: Cambridge University Press, 2000.

Rosas, Ana Elizabeth. *Abrazando el Espíritu: Bracero Families Confront the U.S.-Mexico Border.* Berkeley: University of California Press, 2014.

Sánchez, George J. *Becoming Mexican American: Ethnicity, Culture, and Identity in Chicano Los Angeles, 1900–1945.* Oxford: Oxford University Press, 1993.

St. John, Rachel. *Line in the Sand: A History of the Western U.S.-Mexico Border.* Princeton: Princeton University Press, 2011.

Torget, Andrew J. *Seeds of Empire: Cotton, Slavery, and the Transformation of the Texas Borderlands, 1800–1850.* Chapel Hill: University of North Carolina Press, 2015.

Truett, Samuel. *Fugitive Landscapes: The Forgotten History of the U.S.-Mexico Borderlands.* New Haven: Yale University Press, 2006.

Young, Elliott. *Alien Nation: Chinese Migration in the Americas from the Coolie Era through World War II.* Chapel Hill: University of North Carolina Press, 2014.

Wadewitz, Lissa. *The Nature of Borders: Salmon, Boundaries, and Bandits on the Salish Sea.* Seattle: University of Washington Press, 2012.

Wahlstrom, Todd W. *The Southern Exodus to Mexico: Migration across the Borderlands after the American Civil War.* Lincoln: University of Nebraska Press, 2015.

PART II
Global Circulations

3
VIOLENCE

Emilio Kosterlitzky was a transnational warrior, one man among many who specialized in violence while crossing empires and borderlands. Historian Samuel Truett writes that Kosterlitzky was born to a Russian, or possibly Cossack, father and a German mother in Moscow in 1853. Raised in Russia and Germany, Kosterlitzky trained at a military academy in St. Petersburg before joining the Russian navy. In 1872, he deserted a Russian training vessel for the coast of Venezuela. He took one ship to New York and boarded another heading for San Francisco, making it no further than Guaymas, Sonora, on Mexico's Pacific coast. Soon he joined the Mexican Army and rose in their ranks while fighting in northern Mexico against the *indios barbaros*, the Apaches, in the 1870s and early 1880s. Sometimes he worked in cooperation with the U.S. troops, while on other occasions, he thought that he was protecting the Mexican peasant communities against the U.S. Army Apache scouts who operated south of the international line. In 1886, Kosterlitzky was chasing Geronimo and the independent Chiricahua Apaches. By then he had also worked for the Mexican customs guards. He would continue to serve the borderlands corporate and national elite against bandits and organized labor on both sides of the border. In 1906, the cosmopolite, who purportedly spoke Russian, German, Spanish, French, Polish, Italian, Danish, Swedish, and English, became Colonel Emilio Kosterlitzky in the Mexican Army.

When the Mexican Revolution spread to the borderlands, Kosterlitzky was caught between U.S. troops and revolutionaries in a fight in Nogales in 1913. He surrendered to U.S. authorities. Next he joined hundreds of other Mexican refugees at Fort Rosecrans in San Diego. Authorities released him in September 1914. Instead of returning to Mexico, Kosterlitzky remained in California and Los Angeles, where he had vacationed previously. Now the Russian-German youth, Mexican/Indian fighter, and customs policeman became a spy for the

United States in the borderlands. Kosterlitzky first worked for the Bureau of Investigation (a precursor of the Federal Bureau of Investigation) and then as a permanent agent for the Department of Justice until 1927. By the time of his death, in 1928, he was a legend in the violent folklore of the borderlands. As a transnational man, Kosterlitzky's identity aroused speculation among those who tried to fix him to a single nationality. He has been variously described as a Russian or German immigrant and a Mexican patriot. There exist claims that he was ethnically Mexican, an American-born soldier of fortune from Maine, or an ex-U.S. Army officer. There was, however, no debate on whether or not Kosterlitzky had been a transnational warrior, a fighter who crossed multiple national spaces and touched on several nineteenth-century wars for empires.

As Kosterlitzky's story illustrates, histories of violence seldom come in neat packages or with internal coherence and clear beginnings and endings. Nor do they follow the boundaries of the nation-state. Instead, in its different shapes and formations, violence connects the West with the world. It operates on different scales and with gradated intensities blending individual, local, national, and global concerns and flows in those Western spaces where rival peoples, communities, groups, nations, and empires competed for military advantage, economic gain, resources, land, and cultural and social supremacy. Works exposing the many subtle facets of violence in the West in comparative and transnational contexts include those of William Carrigan, Brian DeLay, James Gump, Benjamin Madley, Robert Utley, Bruce Vandervort, David Weber, and others. They make the world of empires and borderlands – their networks, circulations, and parallels – their frame of reference alongside the nation-state. They offer mappings of violence from individual acts of murder, mob lynching, and labor conflicts to raiding, wars, and genocide and show how violence originated from and involved private individuals, corporate mercenaries, organized labor, indigenous polities, and federal and state forces. This chapter outlines a sampling of these diverse practices of violence and their cross-border ramifications and transnational associations.

Social Conflict

If you ask the public in the United States, Europe, or pretty much anywhere in the world about violence in the American West, they most likely answer the gunfighters and shootouts first and the Indian wars second, or vice versa. Much historians' ink has also been spilled describing the violent doings of cowboys and gunslingers in "rowdy" settler communities such as Dodge City, Kansas or Deadwood, South Dakota. No less attention grabbing have been epic gunfights such as the one at the O.K. Corrall in Tombstone, Arizona. Plenty has also been written of men like William H. Bonney (Billy the Kid) or Wyatt Earp, the two being frequently depicted by authors as symbols of American individualism. Explaining violence in the West through the personal is not only common but tempting for both the public and for historians as it makes for vivid stories that underpin notions of American national exceptionalism. It makes possible claims of extraordinary staying power, such as the assertion that American individualism is rooted on a rugged frontier ethos. It has also advanced arguments that democratic and moral society is somehow grounded on the purifying and justice-bringing impacts of interpersonal violence. But what is much less appealing is acknowledging that the mythic force of inter-personal violence in Western history allows us to sidestep painful questions about social conflict springing from racialization, class divides, and cultures of masculinity and femininity that accompanied settler colonialism. Emphasis on interpersonal violence can camouflage these things and the global connections they carry.

It can also make domestic violence invisible. As in most places around the world, the majority of interpersonal violence in the West took place inside ordinary people's homes. In the late nineteenth- and early twentieth-century borderlands communities in British Columbia and Washington, as suggested by historian David Peterson del Mar, wife beating, rape, and child abuse proved all too common. So did frequent feuding and brawling among working-class men. Both were linked to complex notions of manliness, to the need to prove one's worth at home and in front of other men. They could derive from men's fears of losing their standing as men, of being disgraced in front of other men, women, or family, and of being controlled by more formidable men. Significantly, these forms of violence were usually nonlethal.

However, the main comparative aspect and the central dispute in Western histories of interpersonal violence have traditionally concerned homicidal gun violence. Historians such as Richard Maxwell Brown, Robert Dykstra, Roger McGrath, and Randolph Roth have used cattle towns and mining camps – select social environments that suffered from an excess of young, single men – as their principal foci. They have for decades tried to assess how deadly the West actually was but have yet to reach a consensus. Many have pointed out that epic shootouts were few and far between, and cattle towns were actually much safer (at least in number of homicides) than one would think, because many of them enforced gun control and recruited organized police forces. For instance, Dodge City at the height of its overland cattle drive activity had less than two reported murders annually. Also, in mining and timber camps – as well as at military posts, railroad construction sites, and other places occupied by a high percentage of single men prone to compensate for their hard work and loneliness with even harder drinking and reckless brawling – corporate regula-tion and communal pressures often tempered lethal interpersonal feuding. Fear of serious sanctions and punishments reduced whatever homicidal tendencies there surfaced.

So was the West not so lethal after all? As scholars have contrasted Western violence with other regions in the United States, they have come up with provocative results. Preferring homicide rates to raw numbers, some have placed side by side today's cities – populations in the hundreds of thousands or in millions – and the nineteenth-century Western cattle towns and mining camps – that usually had from one to five thousand residents. Looked at this way, Dodge City comes out as highly lethal. The town's homicide rate between 1876 and 1885 amounts to 129, which is twice that of violence-plagued St. Louis's 60 in 2016, which topped U.S. cities for that year. And Dodge City is not an anomaly in the West. In the nineteenth-century California mining camp of Bodie, the murder rate soared to 116 between 1877 and 1883, while Globe, Arizona, topped this with a homicide rate of 152 between 1880 and 1884. Still, there were "just" 29 killings total in Bodie and 17 in Dodge City during all these years combined.

While comparison of murder rates by applying the "adult homicides per 100,000 population" formula to very small human aggregations can lead to contested conclusions, one could imagine that more suitable comparative perspectives into homicidal interpersonal violence could be offered by situating Western cattle towns and mining camps alongside similar "frontier communities" in other parts of the world: the Australian, South African, Algerian, or Argentinian settler frontiers, for example. Still, hardly any transnational comparisons exist outside the works of social science historian Randolph Roth. Relying on quantitative analysis, Roth linked the West with nineteenth-century Canada and Western Europe and produced cross-regional analyses within the United States. In Roth's reading, the West was an exceptionally violent region. Its adult homicide rates were consistently far greater than those of Europe and comparable with the extreme conditions that afflicted communities in the South where political or racial violence spiraled out of control during the Civil War and Reconstruction era.

With his eyes set on individuals rather than numbers, the veteran military historian Robert Utley modified the scholarship of Western gun fighters to incorporate global outlooks when discussing the parallel lives of Billy the Kid and Ned Kelly. Connecting outlaw life in the American Southwest with the bushranger experience in Australia, Utley shows how two disadvantaged and disgruntled outcasts graduated from petty crimes to killers on the perilous margins of settler societies. Both joined gangs of misfits, took up armed robbery as a way of life, got arrested, and escaped. Both also witnessed personal injustice and lived on the run, preoccupied with survival and escape from those hot on their tails. Both also died violently at the hands of authorities. And both were transformed by writers and filmmakers into legends postmortem. Both also became prototypes of "social bandits," untamed everymen pushed to violence: men who represented the common people against greedy big business and government bullies.

Outlaw biographies can tell us something about what drove individuals to violence in different settler societies. When investigated closely, much of what looks like interpersonal violence was typically part of larger, often complex social struggles linked to nationalization of colonial spaces, industrialization, and the global integration of markets. New Mexico's Lincoln County War, where Billy the Kid made much of his name in 1878, was a business rivalry, a clash for the economic upper hand between two rival circles. Disputes over land use and ownership, class gulf, and ethnic tensions (Irish against British) among settlers also drove Ned Kelly to arms in Victoria in 1878. Both New Mexico and Victoria witnessed distrust and antagonism against the powerful economic and political factions, whether it was the Australian "squattocracy" of established grazers or the American merchants of the "Santa Fe ring." In both situations, social distrust exploded into a series of violent confrontations in which governments – while ostensibly neutral – sided with the "law and order" and the economically powerful, contributing to the villanizing and squashing of the rebellious "outlaws."

It is this context that the stories of Billy the Kid and Ned Kelly tie in with the wider world of social conflict stemming from economic rivalries, class divisions, and racial hierarchies that came in many shapes and sizes in the West and the world being remade and penetrated by colonial powers. There is no reason why, for example, the Pleasant Valley War, a violent feud between two ranching families in Arizona's rim country in the 1880s; the Johnson County War, a clash between ranchers of various pedigrees in 1890s Wyoming; or the mining clashes in Colorado in the early 1900s should not be discussed on the same plane with similar disputes over land use, access to resources, and control over labor in other colonies and empires. Many social conflicts in the West seemingly carry quite explicit transnational characteristics relating to industrialization, class warfare, and racial tensions, the heated questions surrounding the development of the modern world.

Usually viewed as a prime Western example of the kind of open class warfare that characterized much the industrial relations in nineteenth-century Europe, the Ludlow Massacre in Colorado echoed the expanding global hierarchies of whiteness. Before their camp was demolished in the attack by the Colorado National Guard on April 20, 1914, which left 20 people dead, the community of 1,200 striking miners at Ludlow spoke over 20 languages. Indeed, the majority of the community consisted of immigrant Greeks, Italians, Slavs, and others from southern and eastern Europe. Arguably, the strike and the massacre demonstrated a growing gulf between the wealthy, often native-born Anglos, and the largely immigrant workers. This show of corporate power was also a chapter in an ethnic warfare that sought to limit access to the privileges of whiteness. If eastern and southern Europeans were shunned, the Chinese and the Mexicans were straightforwardly excluded from the "white man's" West and from other "white man's" countries (Figure 3.1).

As discussed in the previous chapter, anti-Chinese agitation, racial fears of being swamped by a flood of Chinese settlers, and exclusive measures in legislation drew from transnational circuits straddling the various settler colonial communities of the Pacific and beyond. So did anti-Chinese violence. In the

FIGURE 3.1   The anti-Chinese wall in North America goes up as the Chinese original goes down. A cartoon showing laborers, among whom are Irishmen, an African American, a Civil War veteran, Italian, Frenchman, and a Jew, building a wall against the Chinese. Congressional mortar is used to mount blocks of prejudice, nonreciprocity, law against race, fear, etc. Across the sea, a ship flying the American flag enters China as the Chinese knock down their own wall and permit trade of goods such as rice, tea, and silk. 1882, Cartoon by Friedrich Graetz (c. 1840–c. 1913). Courtesy of the Library of Congress Prints and Photographs Division, LC-USZC4–4138.

West and in Australia, antagonistic whites set up anticoolie clubs or other social alliances and political pressure groups with a knack for racist propaganda and tolerance for mob violence. Such whites blamed unemployment, poor pay, and other difficulties related to labor conditions and economics on the Chinese. In the goldfields of Victoria, New South Wales, and Queensland, the Chinese were regularly targeted for violence over several decades. For example, in 1860 and 1861, a series of violent acts in New South Wales flamed into what is known as the Lambing Flat Riots. Dreading Chinese competition, a mob of white workers looted and sacked Chinese dwellings and camps and beat and forcefully evicted Chinese miners. It all climaxed when white miners stormed the police force sent to quell the disturbances. Some two-thirds of the 55 anti-Chinese riots in the West between 1871 and 1887 took place in California. In 1871 Los Angeles, a mob consisting of hundreds of white men entered the local Chinatown to attack, rob, and murder its residents. The outcome: 18 dead Chinese. In the mid-1880s, waves of violence rocked Chinese communities from California to

British Columbia to the Plains. Chinatowns were burned to the ground and the Chinese were murdered and evicted from many communities: for example, in Vancouver, Seattle, and in Rock Springs, Wyoming. In the latter, 28 Chinese were beheaded, scalped, mutilated, and hanged by the white coal miners.

Social conflicts carrying transnational implications also revolved around Anglo-Mexican relations. In the Southwest borderlands, disputes over land and the commercialization of agriculture and mining created rigid racial hierarchies and violence that crossed borders. Already in 1859, in the overwhelmingly Hispanic region of South Texas, Juan Cortina, a large ranch operator, came into conflict with an influential group of lawyers and judges of Brownsville, whom he accused of expropriating land from its Hispanic owners. According to historian Jerry Thompson, Cortina, fed up with Anglo harassment and discrimination, shot and wounded a local sheriff whom he witnessed mishandling an elderly ranch hand. Then Cortina went into exile and gathered a paramilitary following. He and his men stormed Brownsville, looting and executing four Anglos known for their crimes against Hispanics but who had previously gone unpunished. A war of sorts broke out between Cortina's followers and Texas Rangers, Cortina evading and crossing the border, and the Rangers attacking ethnic Mexicans in the region indiscriminately.

In 1877, Anglo attempts to curtail access to the salt beds at the base of Guadalupe Mountains in San Elizario in the vicinity of El Paso exploded into a "salt war." What the local Hispanic populace had used as a communal resource, Anglo businessmen saw as a valuable commodity, historian Paul Cool explains. After years of arguments and deliberations among politicians and speculators, an Anglo banker from Austin made a claim on the salt in 1877 and tried to enforce it. This sparked a violent insurgency as local, mainly Hispanic, residents challenged the claim. The situation climaxed with the intervention of U.S. troops, which further empowered the local Anglos while eroding the power of the area's Hispanics.

In the early 1900s, countless more ethnic Mexicans were killed and made to leave the United States. Perhaps the most notorious and violent cross-border deportation took place in Bisbee, Arizona, in 1917. The mining corporation Phelps Dodge attacked workers who demanded better working conditions and who had organized a peaceful strike to achieve them. If the unions as such represented radical leftist ideas and dangerous "un-American" activity, the heavy Mexican presence among the strikers challenged the prevalent racial order. When the U.S. Army refused to help, Phelps Dodge organized a posse of "loyal Americans" that swept through the town, arresting, harassing, and knocking workers around. They drove some 1,300 people into railroad boxcars and drove them out to the border. Rather than solely ethnic Mexicans, the deportees proved in fact to be an international bunch, representing some 20 different nationalities. There were over 200 Mexicans but also some 140 Brits, 80 Serbs, dozens of Irishmen, and over 70 Finnish workers.

Bisbee forms an episode of cross-border social conflict where class tensions and ethnic prejudice intersected, targeting the workers and the unprivileged. Other violent outbursts drew from Mexico's inner political turmoil that spilled across the international line. On September 15, 1891, Catarino Garza, a Mexican journalist and political activist, led a band of Mexican rebels out of South Texas and across the Rio Grande. Garza, historian Elliott Young remarks, declared a revolution against Mexico's dictator, Porfirio Díaz. Drawing support from a broad cross-border coalition of ranchers, merchants, peasants, and discontented military men, Garza's insurgency was the biggest and longest lasting threat to the Díaz regime up to that point. It took two years of sporadic fighting and the combined efforts of the U.S. and Mexican troops, Texas Rangers, and local law enforcement to subdue the uprising. Forced into exile, Garza was killed in Panama in 1895.

In 1915 and 1916, a revolutionary fervor of transnational proportions again gripped South Texas. Drawing from global ideological currents and calls for a socialist revolution, Plan de San Diego provided for the formation of a "Liberating Army of Races and Peoples," to be made up of ethnic Mexicans, African Americans, and Asians. The plan, seriously understudied prior to historian Benjamin Johnson's work, aimed to carry out the "freeing" of Texas, New Mexico, Arizona, California, and Colorado from U.S. control. The liberated states would be organized into an independent republic, which might later seek annexation to Mexico. Soon a revised plan emphasized the liberation of the proletariat and focused on Texas. It called for a social republic to serve as a base for spreading the revolution throughout the Southwest borderlands. Native Americans should also be enlisted to fight for the cause of the oppressed and the workers. Texas Rangers, law and order leagues, and private mobs responded with a far bloodier campaign that killed an unknown number (between 300 and 5,000) of ethnic Mexicans. The worst killing spree ended when the U.S. Army intervened to reclaim control from lynch mobs. But after the war, an anti-Mexican Ku Klux Klan revived local vigilantism in a region that shared a similarly volatile commercial agriculture system with the South. And, as in the South, vigilantism worked to install a system of harsh racial segregation and tightly managed labor.

It is little surprise that many of the social conflicts involving the Chinese or ethnic Mexicans shared a particular form of violence: lynching. Although usually seen as predominantly Southern and Jim Crow practice, lynching represented a transnational subset of violence. Blending ethnic suppression and interpersonal violence, it has been used for defending structures of power or to implement them and for affirming racial hierarchies and otherness in the West and the world. Ethnic Mexican, Native American, and Chinese men were frequently targeted for lynching in the West. Unlike African Americans in the South, who were vilified as sexual predators bent on raping white women, most Mexicans were not lynched for fears of their uncontrollable sexuality, arguably because Anglo stereotypes frequently conceived them as a nonthreatening race. Much like the lynching of blacks in the South, however, Western lynching targeting racialized groups served as a form of social control. But Western lynching was also a method of ethnic cleansing, of driving the racial minorities away.

Older accounts, like those penned by historian Richard Maxwell Brown, applied clearer boundaries between vigilantism (organized) and lynching (unorganized), but modern interpretations see the lines between legal/state-sanctioned and community-driven/extralegal actions as increasingly blurred. A case in point is the San Francisco Vigilance Committee of the 1850s, which went after Irish, Chinese, Mexican, and other immigrants. As the committee grew to more than 10,000 members and after its members won several positions of public office, it held immense social influence and actually became synonymous with law and order. The line between state power and vigilante violence was muddled also in the Arizona mining communities of Clifton and Morenci half a century later as ethnic Mexican workers were lynched in order to keep this essential labor source cheap, docile, and available. According to historians William Carrigan and Clive Webb, the men responsible for lynching in the Southwest borderlands from Texas and California often acted in open disobedience of the law and with the approval of the majority of their communities.

Lynching was made visible and rested on public performances and spectacles. It also gained acceptability and visibility in postcards, souvenir cards, and published photographs of mob violence that were widely circulated and collected in the United States up to the 1930s. Interestingly, at the same time, similar images of colonial violence – for example, of the German-Herero conflict in 1904–1907 – were also made into popular trading cards series in Europe, as historian Benjamin Madley has shown. The author and artist Ken Gonzales-Day's analysis confirms that these often-romanticized visual celebrations of "frontier justice" in the West were of public killings "guided by anti-immigration sentiments, the fear of miscegenation, a deep frustration with the judicial system, or in combination with white supremacy."[1]

Lynching operated in a global context, and it carries a long history from the ancient Middle East to twentieth-century South Africa, the late Ottoman Empire, Brazil, and Northern Ireland. Furthermore, British, Russians, Japanese, and others proved keen observers of American lynching in the late 1800s and early 1900s. Historian Gregory Smithers identifies lynching as a ritualistic affirmation of white unity in Australia and the United States. In its twin roles as a real and a rhetorical threat, lynching served to discipline racialized male bodies and enforce the social order and hierarchies of races in both Australia and the American West. In both settler societies, lynching of racial others was

---

1 Gonzales-Day, *Lynching in the West*, 3.

usually socially acceptable for the sake of order and to guard white women against miscegenation. Historian Robert Thurston takes a different approach. He suggests that lynching was too random and that it was too often used against whites to qualify as systematic form of racial control in the colonial world. Instead, Thurston sees lynching primarily as a collective response based on local circumstances of political instability: lynching constituted of reactions to immediate social threats caused by a lack of legitimate and effective authority.

Wars for Empires

When historians write of "Indian wars" in the West, they ordinarily refer to clashes pitting communities of indigenous residents against the U.S. Army, white settlers, or other Indian groups. Often these histories, which typically take place on the Great Plains or in the Southwest, have taken the nation-state, or the territory or state, as their principal frame of analysis, positioning the wars in relation to the master narrative of U.S. frontier expansion. In recent years, borderlands scholars have been in the forefront in rethinking wars in the West. Their revisionist works have taken indigenous power seriously and have examined both smaller, more intimate, threads of conflicts involving families and communities while mixing these investigations with explorations of transnational, even hemispheric, trends. Borderlands scholars have examined different shapes and different temporal and geographical spaces of violence – transcending the early West with the settler colonial period – that intersected with the paradigm of imperial rivalries or later settler colonial and national expansion but did not necessarily confine themselves to either.

Spain relied on violence throughout its American empire. Violence was instrumental in toppling the Aztecs, subduing the Incas, and in establishing and maintaining exploitative mining and plantation economies built upon forced indigenous and African labor. Violence was also crucial in Spain's attempts to bring under its control the indigenous peoples from New Mexico and Texas through the northeast coast of Venezuela and the Andes all the way into Patagonia. Culturally, violence drew from an active root system. Many Spanish men in the Americas carried deeply implanted family legacies from the generations-long reconquest of the Iberian Peninsula from Muslim rule. They not only brought deadly diseases to the Americas but also made demands for forced labor and farm produce, abused indigenous women, and interfered with Native belief systems and social practices. As a consequence, fierce indigenous resistance flamed in the 1600s. The Pueblos revolted in New Mexico in 1680, as did the Zuaques (1600) and the Tehuecos (1611) in Sinaloa and the Acaxees (1601) and the Xiximes (1610) in Durango. In 1616, the Tepehuán of Nueva Vizcaya (Chihuahua) drew widespread indigenous support to their rebellion in the mining towns on the Sierra Madre. Then in 1640, it was the Tobosos, and in 1648–1652, the Tarahumaras and the Conchos who challenged Spanish rule in northern New Spain. These uprisings then spread to Nuevo León (including modern-day south Texas) in the 1660s and to present Arizona as the O'odham rebelled in 1695 and again in 1751. After the initial shock, the Spanish response was typically fierce everywhere, and it involved killing, mauling, and publicly executing scores of people suspected of defying its authority.

According to historian David Weber, in the 1700s, Bourbon Spain's imperial dreams and efforts throughout its American empire relied heavily on violence coupled with diplomacy. Military campaigns, slave raids, deportations, and bodily mutilations were common across Spanish America. But the Spanish met their match as indigenous polities ranging from the Araucanians in the south to the Yaquis, Comanches, and Apaches in the north adopted and invented practices of violence – including lighting raids for plunder and slaves, ambushes, and their own bodily mutilations. Several indigenous raiders made the Spanish pay tribute to them and recognize indigenous autonomy and superiority, thus inverting the relationships of power that Europeans since Columbus and the conquistadors had imagined as proper and normal.

In northern New Spain (the Southwest borderlands), Spanish violence resonated far beyond the immediate reach of the Spanish whose principal settlements lined the upper Rio Grande in New Mexico. Spanish demands for labor and human captives coexisted with the diseases, horses, crops, and manufactured goods they introduced. Both dispersed throughout the West, prompting a maelstrom of exchanges where violence became the lifeline of survival and power. It, historian Ned Blackhawk asserts, recalibrated indigenous lives toward cutthroat competition and caused much Indian pain in the Great Basin. In the "interior world" of the Colorado River basin, historian Natale Zappia points out, the Quechans, Mojaves, and Cocopahs quite successfully thwarted and challenged the power and the impacts of the Spanish yet adapted and incorporated their goods, tools, and markets. These Indians used trading and violence to harness economic and political power through the formation and expansion of a captive and livestock raiding economy that operated within transnational systems ranging from the California coast and the Pacific Ocean far to the desert interior of New Mexico, Sonora, Chihuahua, and beyond.

Some independent Indians dominated outsiders in the transnational vortex of borderlands violence. The Comanches, an assortment of hunter-gatherers from the Rocky Mountains and the Great Basin, made themselves into bison hunters and horse pastoralists and engaged in an expansion of their own on the southern Plains and northern New Spain in the 1700s. Historian Pekka Hämäläinen showcases how the Comanches controlled wide trade networks between northern New Spain and French Louisiana and incorporated subject peoples as kin and slaves. They also pushed the Apaches off the southern Plains in decades-long wars and confronted, and often bested, the Spanish, Osages, Cherokees, and Cheyennes on the violent edges of their realm.

In many borderlands communities, violence became an instrumental part of ordinary life. It was practiced for economic reasons. Raiding smoothened inequalities of individual wealth. It furthered social status and solidified group unity. It created and maintained cultures that centered the warrior and male accomplishment. Men typically became to identify themselves as specialists in violence. In Hispanic borderlands communities, a man's worth was equally determined by his record in Apache and Comanche killing. This vibrant militant ethos then spilled over to the period of Mexican Revolution in the early 1900s. Youngsters in Comanche villages, as well as in Apache communities occupying both sides of the present U.S.–Mexico border, participated in meticulous and systematic warrior-training programs expected of them by their communities and designed to produce superior fighters. Feeding a perilous dependency on products available only from others, violence was, as historian Brian DeLay suggests, also a goal in its own right, a method for revenge, for upholding individual and communal honor and reputation, and for creating fear in subject or tributary peoples.

Violence recalibrated manliness and became a tool that borderlands communities, marked by cultural and ethnic mixing, used to make sense of themselves and their world. According to historian Lance Blyth, for the Chiricahua Apaches and the Hispanic community of Janos, Chihuahua – the jurisdiction of which originally bridged both sides of the current U.S.–Mexico border – violence built cultural identity, social cohesion, and networks of economic and social relations for multiple generations. And it was not just Janos and the Chiricahuas who expressed their power and need for intimacy though violence. Violence and gender proved the glue of the relational field of captivity, kinship, ethnicity, and community in the world of rival and inter-reliant Spanish and indigenous peoples throughout the borderlands and southern Plains.

Historian Karl Jacoby tells four parallel stories of borderlands communities, relations, and violence – that of the O'odham, Mexicans, Anglos, and Aravaipa Apaches – that culminated in a bloody massacre at Aravaipa Canyon, near U.S. Army base Camp Grant, Arizona, in 1871. There a posse of O'odham, Mexicans, and Anglos whose lives and interests traversed both sides of the border smashed an unsuspecting camp of Aravaipa Apaches, who thought they were under protection of the U.S. Army. More than one hundred Apaches died, mostly women and children, and the attackers took numerous children as captives. The attackers shared long (O'odham and Mexicans) or shorter (Anglos) histories with the Apaches where wars, raids, vigilantism, and intimacies blended and coexisted and where violence denoted relations between neighbors sharing transnational spaces. Their intergroup relations comprised of cycles of raiding and reprisals, private, temporary, peace pacts, contraband trade, and the mutual stealing of material property and captive-taking and adoption, as well as voluntary migration of peoples between groups.

In the 1820s, the international boundary between United States and New Spain/Mexico, as stipulated by the Adams-Onís Treaty of 1819, ran along the Red and Arkansas Rivers and the 42nd parallel to the disputed (with Britain) Oregon. During that era, traders and trappers from the United States also penetrated the borderlands via the Santa Fe Trail. When introducing new trade goods manufactured in eastern United States and in Europe and through their demand for animal skins, sent to market in Eastern United States and to Europe, they reshaped the environment and further tilted communal relations toward intense competition. While the United States expanded into worlds shaped by generations of European disruptions, it remade these spaces through its own violent agents of empire. Transnational violence both preceded and became central to American settler colonial expansion to the trans-Mississippi West.

In the 1830s and 1840s, violence, De Lay describes, transformed the Southwest borderlands into "a vast theater of hatred, terror, and staggering loss for independent Indians and Mexicans alike."[2] Outfits of scalp hunters were led by Anglos such as James Kirker and John Joe Glanton, and comprised of white, Hispanic, and indigenous men, including Shawnees, Delawares, and other eastern transplants. Tempted by the reward Sonora and Chihuahua promised on Apache scalps, they murdered sleeping Apaches, "friendly" Indians, and sometimes anyone they could get their hands on, caring very little about any kind of boundaries. Meanwhile, Comanches and Apaches, as well as Kiowas and Navajos, became full-fledged transnational raiders whose campaigns stretched far toward the distant, resource-rich, and vulnerable reaches spanning from Tamaulipas to Sonora and from New Mexico to San Louis Potosí. These indigenous raiders from deep within the continental interior of plains and deserts reached the oceans and visited the lands of rain forests. Their violence created manmade raiding deserts of wrecked economies, empty landscapes, and streams of Mexican refugees, many of whom headed for the California goldfields. It ate away Mexican's fragile sense of national unity and made Mexico look both weak and ripe for the taking in the eyes of U.S. citizens. Many Americans felt Mexico reversed the proper arc of history by retreating in face of indigenous powers. In this transnational reading of violence, indigenous raiding enabled and intertwined with the settler rebellion in Texas and with the aggressive war of conquest by the United States from 1846 to 1848.

During the war with Mexico, U.S. soldiers penetrated deep into Mexico, occupying its capital and claiming half of its territory. As invaders, they brought Anglo and Spanish America into a violent and intimate contact. Historian Amy Greenberg argues that the racist and licentious behavior of U.S. soldiers provoked outrages among the Mexican locals, terrible publicity in the eastern United States, and antiwar protests throughout the Americas. Anglo filibusters

2 DeLay, *War of a Thousand Deserts*, xv.

and indigenous raiders, in turn, took advantage of the new international border, thus continuing to link the violence in the West to violence in northern Mexico for several decades.

As violence flowed across the new border, the international line complicated the matters for the U.S. and Mexican armies, who refused to tolerate any independent Indians. The border also offered considerable advantage to the Apache and Comanche raiders once they realized U.S. troops were forbidden to follow them south and Mexican forces could not reach north. Transnational raiders created much resentment between Mexico and the United States, as officials in both countries tended to protest vocally if any Indians or troops crossed the border. For instance, in the mid-1870s, U.S. soldiers from Texas pursued raiding Lipan and Mescalero Apaches and Kickapoos deep into Coahuila and thus raised a fury of diplomatic protests from Mexico.

In the 1880s, the Chiricahua Apaches, in turn, made the Sierra Madre in northern Mexico their base from where they launched sweeping and destructive raids across northern Sonora and Chihuahua as well as southern New Mexico and Arizona. As a result, in July 1882, the United States and Mexico signed an agreement giving each other the right to cross the boundary when in close pursuit of "savage Indians." The bulk of the last U.S.–Apache wars was actually fought in Mexico. In 1883, U.S. troops invaded the Chiricahua homes in the Sierra Madre, while in 1885 and 1886, they chased the Chiricahuas under Geronimo across northern Mexico. Finally, U.S. troops escorted the Chiricahuas back to the United States, where they surrendered and were sent into exile in Florida as prisoners of war. During these last war years, U.S. Army Apache soldiers got drunk in Mexican villages or were fired at by locals south of the borderline, causing international incidents. U.S. officers also found themselves questioned, arrested, and even shot at by Mexican officials.

In many ways, borderlands histories provide inside views of unsettling, but also empowering, spaces of violence that spanned multiple communities and nations. Although whites used violence to capture indigenous lands and destroy their economies, violence was nuanced. It came with different purposes and meanings, and it often did not fit the kind of dichotomous readings of history that depict indigenous victimization and European mastery. Violence operated on differing scales, from the most intimate levels of individuals and families to grander historical scales involving nations and empires. Obviously, wars for empire and settler colonial spaces, indigenous power, and transnational raiding were not limited to the Americas. The age of global empires and settler colonialism in the 1800s and early 1900s witnessed numerous conflicts as imperial powers used armies to seek access to lands, resources, and labor, as they sought to eliminate the Natives and impose their will on local communities ranging from Algeria to South Africa, from Australia to the Russian Caucasus, and in most spaces in between.

According to historian Bruce Vandervort, the Plains and Southwest wars, the Metis confrontations with Canadian authorities, Yaqui resistance in Sonora, and the Yucatan Caste War produced differing trajectories but also revealed continental linkages on several levels. For one, Indians used cross-border sanctuaries located on the many edges of empires: the Apaches in Mexico, the Lakota Sioux in Canada, the Yaquis in Arizona, and the Mayas in British Honduras. Thus wars did not tidily follow national boundaries, but instead crossed those boundaries, and used the potentially neutral grounds on the other side in search for safety and strategic advantage. Wars of conquest against indigenous peoples also stirred international cooperation, including American diplomatic pressure on Canada to discourage giving asylum to the Sioux and the reciprocal border crossing agreement in the Southwest as both United States and Mexico targeted a common enemy. On the flip side, both Mexico and Canada feared that the United States would use the border area turmoil as a pretext for an invasion, that the conflicts against the Apaches, or the Sioux could prompt accompanying demands on Canada and Mexico.

Much like the U.S.–indigenous wars, the nineteenth-century European invasion of Asia, Africa, and Latin America saw prolonged violence, the targeting of whole societies and their material base, guerrilla war, powerful and expansionist indigenous polities, and brutal killing by multiple actors. For example, post-independence wars against indigenous peoples started in Argentina in the 1830s, expanding white settlement south of Buenos Aires and killing thousands of Indians. More wars followed in the 1870s and 1880s, while sporadic attacks in the far reaches of the Pampas continued until the 1930s. Meanwhile, while settlers took over new indigenous lands in Argentina, those in Chile engaged the Araucanians in a 20-year struggle. Thousands of Indians were killed, and the survivors left abandoned in scattered reservations. In many instances, indigenous peoples rose up against the invasion of their homelands.

Another potential canvas of comparison for the U.S.–indigenous wars lies with the French overseas expansion. Western historians know well that in the 1860s, Mexico was occupied by the expansionist France of Napoleon III. While French cotton merchants and manufacturers urged their country to recognize the Confederacy, many Frenchmen dreamed of reviving past glory and of building a greater France in the Americas and around the world. Although its Mexican venture failed, and France never challenged the United States in the Southwest borderlands, in the mid-1800s, the French empire in Asia and Africa sprang forward. It gained a foothold in Indochina (Laos, Cambodia, and Vietnam, from where France would not leave until forced to do so in the 1950s) and penetrated deeper inland in Algeria and on the Senegal coast in West Africa.

In Algeria, General Thomas-Robert Bugeaud developed the concept of the *razzia*, or raid. Modifying the indigenous raids that targeted booty and showcased enemy vulnerability, in the 1840s, Bugeaud's flying columns ousted the

Arabs by killing their livestock, destroying crops and orchards, and burning villages. The troops also built military bastions to claim and control land, to help draw European settlers to it, and to secure existing European settlements in a "hostile country." Personally encouraging conquest by the sword and the plow, Bugeaud worked on a theory, according to historian Douglas Porch, that if the Algerians could not eat, they could not fight. In the Southwest, among other places, a similar approach – operated from more or less fixed garrisons and never referred to as raids (in the West Native Americans conducted "raids," not the whites) – was applied to end Apache and Navajo autonomy. The plan was to bring about their extermination/submission by targeting material property and the land and to vacate real estate for white miners and settlers. General James Carleton applied a version of this method against the Mescalero Apaches and Navajos in 1862–1864, and General George Crook against the Western Apaches and Yavapais in 1872–1874. In 1863, troops led by Kit Carson burned everything on their path as they invaded the Navajo homelands. With few battles or skirmishes, they destroyed Navajos livelihood before removing the survivors and forcing them to take the "Long Walk" to the utterly miserable Bosque Redondo, a camp/reservation on the Pecos River. Crook utilized mobile flying columns and strived for a campaign that was short, sharp, and decisive. He worked to empty central Arizona lands – where rich deposits were found – of Indians and forcing the survivors to reservations. Much like Bugeaud's men, Crook's troops mercilessly attacked Apache and Yavapais villages, usually making surprise strikes at dawn and destroying everything they could get their hands on, from camp equipment to crops, livestock, and people. On the Plains, General Philip Sheridan envisioned related tactics, albeit on a larger scale, by sending converging columns against the Sioux–Cheyenne alliance in 1876 in an effort to claim the Black Hills country for whites and when seeking to keep the Comanches and Kiowas out of the way of the mushrooming Plain settlements in the Red River War in 1873. On the Caucasus, the Russians also applied their version of this method as they destroyed villages, initiated forceful raids, and used scorched earth tactics and forced removals against the Circassians, replacing them with Russian and Cossack settlers.

Much like Carleton, Crook, Sheridan, and the Russians, Bugeaud saw the *razzia* as the only means at his disposal for quickly and effectively vacating land for settler use when confronting an enemy that was supposedly warlike, understood only force, but would not stand and fight. Similarities do not end here. Bugeaud also understood *razzia* as a way of communicating: he felt it was the kind of warfare that the locals understood and respected. He also saw it as a means of demonstrating to the locals that the French troops – poorly acclimatized, cumbersome, and out of their element, and thus much like the U.S. troops in the West – had now mastered their new environment. Working toward Native elimination, Bugeaud was at least as certain as Crook, Carleton, or Sheridan that the Natives needed a lesson and that only decisive immoderate forms of violence would make their long-term subjugation and administration as subject peoples possible. They also viewed these kinds of methods as acceptable to prevent a more protracted struggle and tolerated the extreme brutality because they felt that in fighting Natives, the rules of "civilized warfare" did not always apply.

In West Africa, the eastward thrust of the French in the 1850s Senegal, ran smack into the Tukolors, a multiethnic Muslim empire of expansionist traders, farmers, and fighters controlling some 400 miles of the Senegal River. This river functioned as a highway of power and as a corridor in transporting trade goods, soldiers, and influence deep into the interior. In some ways it had functioned similarly to the Missouri River system as the United States sought to project its influence on the northern Plains controlled by the Lakota Sioux. By the late 1850s, several U.S. posts already dotted the river, and together with the forts on the Oregon Trail, they practically surrounded the Sioux. But the Sioux sought expansion as well, combatting the Pawnees in northwestern Nebraska and the Crows for the control of the Powder River country. When the U.S. Army built a line of forts linking the Oregon Trail with Montana on the Bozeman Trail, the Lakotas under Red Cloud drove the army back and burned the forts. The Tukulors also challenged the French invasion, launching a jihad in 1853 under the charismatic leadership of al-Haji Umar. The French fort on Medina, situated near the outermost navigable spot of the Senegal River and on an important communication route, was subjected to a vigorous Tukolor siege in 1857. While the French were saved as reinforcements arrived, they, like the U.S. troops on the Bozeman Trail, were badly shaken. In both places the dreams of quick expansion were placed on temporary hold, and peace agreements favorable to the Sioux and the Tukolors were made. Next the Sioux refocused their military muscle on the Pawnees and the Crowns, while the Tukolors conquered the neighboring Bambara Empire (in today's Mali).

The Zulus of South Africa represented another sovereign and dynamic indigenous power with strong expansionist tendencies. They had modified their heterogeneous society and military through conquest and centralization, empowering themselves through the creation of an age-set labor force and a "standing" military. They had also absorbed numerous chiefdoms. The Sioux, in turn, had made themselves more powerful by embracing the equestrian, bison-hunting economy and the opportunities that the Missouri River fur trade offered. They had also made their social structure flexible and decentralized, so as to better suit the needs of conquest and their new lifestyle. Powerful and assertive, the Sioux experienced population growth and carved space at the expense of their more horticultural neighbors, such as the Mandans and the Pawnees, weakened by deadly epidemics. Both the Sioux and Zulus, historian James Gump describes, accumulated prosperity and power through their ability to control and crush others militarily and through their capacity to exploit others economically. As white overland trekkers, traders, missionaries, prospectors, farmers, and government officials made increased inroads into Sioux and Zulu lands, uneasy collaboration and diplomatic openings were accompanied by spouts of violence and increased demands targeting the curtailing of Sioux and Zulu autonomy. By the 1870s, both the Sioux and the Zulus had become barriers to the exploitation of natural resources and the spread of white settlement.

While the Sioux and the Zulus won major fights and often eluded the troops hot on their tail, their triumph was transient and they lost their respective wars. The two epic battles, Little Bighorn – the Sioux-Cheyenne annihilation of Colonel George Custer and sections of his Seventh Cavalry in Montana – and Isandlwana – the crushing defeat of the British forces in Zulu hands in Natal – mattered, but mostly as signs of the frailty of colonial power. Pouring more manpower and resources to the Plains and South Africa, the United States and Britain dissolved and reduced Sioux and Zulu homelands, destroyed their military autonomy, attempted to wipe out their cultures, largely crippled their traditional leadership and social structures, and energetically promoted factionalism. In a generation, the Zulus became a major source of wage laborers in South Africa, while the Sioux endured cultural loss and poverty in their reduced reservations.

In the nineteenth century, several military thinkers in Europe already were situating the U.S.–indigenous wars firmly in the framework of global imperial expansion. Charles E. Calwell, a British colonial war theorist, lumped the wars of the American West together with his analysis of European wars "against nature" in Africa and elsewhere. He suggested that in these wars, the indigenous fighters were not the principal adversary but the unforgiving climate, the heat, scorching deserts, diseases, and vast distances. Also, victories were achieved through mobility and perseverance. While Calwell's analysis downplayed indigenous power, it is useful as a reminder of the linkages between the West and the world. Calwell emphasizes how long distances and problems in acclimatizing characterized many colonial wars from Sahara to the Southwest borderlands. As did wars against whole societies, their material base, and the environment. Equally common were arduous chases against an indigenous enemy who seldom allowed decisive battles. Steeped in their Napoleonic, Prussian, and earlier traditions of "western way of war," standing battles were the one thing many Euro-Americans hoped to achieve but seldom did.

Nineteenth-century imperial warfare also shared ground in logistics and compositions of colonial armies. Whether they were penetrating the vast reaches of the Southwest borderlands, the Great Plains, the Caucasus, the Sahara, Australia, the highlands and deserts of German Southwest Africa, or the dense rain forests of tropical Africa, getting there – the task of transporting troops, supplies, and animals to places distant from the centers of production and short on suitable transportation corridors – proved challenging for any colonial military force. Quite frequently there existed few roads that a large force could follow and many armies welcomed river routes and the railroads in enabling them to relocate to the war zone. Still, much arduous marching was nearly always in the cards. Worse still, many armies had to haul their own food and supplies to the scene of operations and in the field, or they relied on porters to ease the task of white soldiers. For instance, the 1894 plans for the French invasion force in Madagascar included 18,000–20,000 porters and mule drivers for 12,000 soldiers. Much of what came was also unsuited for use; food spoiled, clothing in tatters and incompatible for the terrain and climate, horses were poorly acclimatized, and men inadequately trained and in terrible physical condition. Many soldiers were often sick, with malaria and other diseases taking their toll especially in the humid sections of Asia and Africa but also in the deserts of Sahara or the Southwest borderlands.

Despite the popular image of white soldiers penetrating distant and exotic locales, colonial armies were typically multiethnic assemblages of men with varied geographical and cultural backgrounds, multiple understandings of violence, and different motivations. The top-rung typically consisted of whites from upper- or middle-class backgrounds, while in the lower tiers a mixture of working-class and/or immigrant whites shared space with nonwhite recruits. Often, local recruits proved crucial to the success of imperial armies, even in places you would not expect. According to historian Jonathan Richards, the native police played a prominent role in the conquest of Queensland. They formed the shock troops in a conflict widely understood as a war of extermination. The countless "martial races" the British employed included the Punjabi Muslims, Sikhs, and Gurkhas in India, the Wakamba in eastern Africa, the Sudanese in Egypt, Kaffir Corps and Malay Corps in Sri Lanka, and various units comprised of former slaves in the West Indies. From 1857, the Senegalese light infantry, or *Tirailleurs Sénégalais*, gained a global reputation as the enforcer of French imperial ambitions in Africa. The French preferred Sudanese recruits in Mexico, while King Leopold's rule in the Congo was grounded on a mercenary force made up mostly of Sudanese and local conscripts. Except for Southwest Africa, the Germans enlisted African troopers into their colonial force, the *Schutztruppe*.

Empires typically did not confront unified peoples or singular nations and took advantage of existing grievances and power struggles, offering tempting rewards and lifestyles for conscripts. The *askari* recruited in German East Africa, for instance, hailed from diverse backgrounds and multiple vibrant military cultures. Many were Muslims from Sudan with a background in the Anglo-Egyptian army; others came from the tribes of southern Africa. Historian Michelle Moyd explains that they joined the German *Schutztruppe* to advance their own notions of manhood and to extend their social and material circumstances often destabilized by colonialism. What mattered was closely linked to everyday life; large households, acquisition of livestock, and the ability to act as patrons and power brokers. During the occupation of German East Africa, the *askari* enabled German rule as the executive arm of a violent conquest. Yet the *askari* also carried diverse roles in state-making as tax collectors, police, executioners, etc. So did many other indigenous recruits in other colonial forces.

In the American West, indigenous recruits were usually home-grown talent recruited for specific purposes. After the Civil War, the U.S. Army was allowed to enlist no more than 1,000 indigenous men. While officially labeled "scouts," these indigenous recruits were still often used in full combat duties. This was particularly true with the Pawnees who engaged the Sioux on army payroll several times in the 1860s and 1870s and in the Southwest where General George Crook in the early 1870s and then again in the mid-1880s was an enthusiastic supporter of using Apaches against Apaches. As men recruited for specific operations, Pawnees, Apaches, and other indigenous enlistees balanced between inclusion and exclusion as colonizer labor. They received equal pay with other troops, but their enlistment periods proved random and their membership in the military community appeared uncertain at best. They were typically ostracized by their white peers, and they did not have to do much manual labor or to behave, dress, and fight like other troops. Instead, the indigenous recruits were expected to use their individual skills and home-based training to the army's advantage in combat operations, as spies, during negotiations, and as reservation police. Yet they also found opportunities for advancing their personal and community interests in the service. They could use military service to advance their notions of manliness, to gain economic benefits in times of poverty, and forward family, clan, and community interests against their enemies.

If indigenous enlistees "hired out" to work in "foreign" armies, so did white soldiers of fortune. Anglo filibusters and mercenaries were involved in the Yucatan Caste War; the enlisted personnel of the U.S. Army, while generally having little military experience, included several veterans whom had served in European armies. The global imperial arena also offered opportunities for officers, who had fought in the U.S.–indigenous wars and the Civil War. Among them was John Y. F. Blake, who fought as a lieutenant against the Chiricahua Apaches before ending up in South Africa and commanding the Irish Brigade in the Boer War. As many as 50 Union and Confederate officers made new careers in Khedivi Ismail's Egyptian Army. One such man was William Loring, a South Carolinian with experience in the Mexican–American War, the California gold rush, the Apache conflicts in New Mexico, and the Civil War. He was also a veteran of the invasion of Abyssinia in the mid-1870s. Loring rose to the rank of colonel in the U.S. Army, major general in the Confederate Army, and a major general (*fereek pasha*) in the Egyptian Army. Another ex-Confederate in Egypt was Henry Hopkins Sibley. He had tried to create a Confederate empire stretching to the Colorado mines and the Pacific, but his advance was cut short in New Mexico in 1862. He had also clashed against the Seminoles in Florida, participated in the Mexican–American War, fought over the spread of slavery in the Bleeding Kansas in the 1850s, and taken part in the near war against the Mormons in Utah. A major in the U.S. Army, Sibley was a brigadier general in both the Confederate and the Egyptian armies.

And then there were men like Custer, who carried little personal experience abroad, but whose character and career demonstrated several parallels with other white military "heroes" of empires. While it seems that Colonel George Armstrong Custer and his demise at the Battle of Little Bighorn has been studied inside out, it has not been seriously connected to the world. We are yet to see the global Custer: his life compared, for instance, with Charles Gordon, the flamboyant, reckless, and much publicized British general whose death at Khartoum in the hands of Islamist fighters both shocked the world and was made into a legend, not unlike Custer's fall in the hands of the Sioux. Or how about Garnet Wolseley, another stalwart of the British Empire. Ambitious, snobbish, and an unapologetic and glory-hungry opportunist, Wolseley, much like Custer, practiced rampant favoritism. He also served in the North American West, leading British troops in Canada against the Metis when Custer was fighting the Indians further south on the Great Plains.

Genocide

For anyone interested in discussing the global linkages of Western violence, histories of genocide are at the same time one of the more interesting, polarizing, and, until recently, strangely absent issues in the field. Considering how much scholarship there has been written on violence in North America's borderlands and frontiers over the years, there exists relatively little directly assessing genocide in the American West. Recently, historians Benjamin Madley, Brendan Lindsay, and Gary Clayton Anderson have, however, flamed the interest, although Anderson prefers the term "ethnic cleansing" to genocide. While these discussions should not trump the vast diversity and multifaceted power dynamics that often characterized relations between peoples of various races, ethnicities, and nationalities in the West, historians might do well to ask if genocide and/or ethnic cleansing offer meaningful ways for establishing linkages between cases of extreme violence and mass killings in the American West and elsewhere.

While refusing to go away, genocide has traditionally been sidelined in Western history, irritating some and beckoning others. Many just refuse to believe in it, claiming the shoe does not fit or that it is anachronistic to use such a modern term to describe past incidents. But why is it such a volatile subject? Perhaps it is the idea of discussing U.S. and Western history on the same plane with the Nazis and the Holocaust. But if that is the main line of argument against genocide, then the debate has already been sidetracked. Instead we should look at the bigger picture: what are we actually talking about when we refer to genocide? What exactly can genocide mean?

The Holocaust should not be synonymous with genocide, nor is it exclusively representative of the phenomenon in world history if you consider the range of historical cases including Darfur, Rwanda, Bosnia, Cambodia, or the Armenian genocide, not to mention the colonial genocides that took place in King Leopold's Congo, British Tasmania, and German Southwest Africa. The Holocaust constitutes an extreme form of genocide not only because of its scale, well-documented plans, and industrial efficiency but also because few legitimate parties today contest it.

To understand genocide in the American West and elsewhere, it is crucial to have an agreed-upon definition and one logical starting point is the 1948 United Nations (UN) Convention on the Prevention and Punishment of Genocide. It states that genocide includes

> any of the following acts committed with intent to destroy, in whole or in part, a national, ethnical, racial or religious group, as such:
>
> a   Killing members of the group;
> b   Causing serious bodily or mental harm to members of the group;
> c   Deliberately inflicting on the group conditions of life calculated to bring about its physical destruction in whole or in part;
> d   Imposing measures intended to prevent births within group;
> e   Forcibly transferring children of the group to another group.

The Convention also specifies that these acts shall be punishable as (a) genocide, (b) conspiracy to commit genocide, (c) direct or public incitement to commit genocide, (d) attempt to commit genocide, and (e) complicity to genocide.[3]

This definition is the most commonly used one and is followed in this chapter. It needs to be said that while the UN definition has often proved unenforceable in a legal sense, it offers an internationally recognized rubric, a starting point and an analytical tool for scholars from different disciplines investigating potential cases of genocide across time.

For understanding the nature of genocide, we can go to the source, in a manner of speaking. The man responsible for coining the term "genocide" was a Polish legal scholar of Jewish parentage, Raphael Lemkin. It seems that he actually had both colonialism and the United States very much in mind. For Lemkin, genocide consisted of two phases: one, destruction of the national pattern of the oppressed group, and the other, the imposition of the national pattern of the oppressor. He did see mass killing as intrinsic to genocide, but emphasized that genocide can occur without massacres and executions. He also

---

3 United Nations, *Resolution 260 (III) Prevention and punishment of the crime of genocide, the United Nations General Assembly on 9 December 1948*, www.un.org/ga/search/view_doc.asp?symbol=A/RES/260%28III%29 (Accessed Oct. 4, 2017).

saw the Holocaust – a term he apparently did not use – as a consequence of Nazi colonialism coveting living space for German settlers in Eastern Europe and as the outcome of colonialism across the world, including in North America. Rather than viewing the Holocaust as a representative of genocide, he saw in the extra-European cases of colonial genocide the concept's generic attributes. Projecting a global history of genocide in his unpublished writings, Lemkin wrote of cases involving, among others, the Maoris of New Zealand, the Australian Aborigines, the Herero and Nama in German Southwest Africa, and the Natives of North America. His note cards reveal that he had plans to write, for instance, on the 1890 Wounded Knee Massacre, where the U.S. Army slaughtered a group of Sioux practicing religious revivalism of "ghost dance."

Historians of Native America have commonly downplayed the role of violence while highlighting disease as the principal engine of demographic decline. Encouraging scholars to ask questions about genocidal violence, the anthropologist Russell Thornton published the first scholarly overview in the mid-1980s arguing that genocide was one of the main causes in Native American demographic downfall. He also emphasized that it rarely resulted in total extermination of groups. Going a step further, American Indian Studies scholar Ward Churchill and American Studies scholar David Stannard make genocide a central factor in Native American population fall. Taking a hemispheric approach, Stannard follows a genocidal path from the late fifteenth-century West Indies to Mexico, across Latin America, and then from Virginia and New England to the Plains, the Southwest, and the Pacific states. The destruction of the indigenous peoples was everywhere in the Americas. It amounted to a holy war and the most massive and sustained act of genocide in world history. Churchill shares this idea, proposing that the genocide of Native Americans is unparalleled in its size, ferocity, numbers of perpetrators, and the degree to which its goals were met.

Gold rush California and its wholesale murder, rape, and enslavement of California Indians by white settlers in the mid-1800s occupies much space in discussions of genocide in the West. In his reading of genocidal violence experienced by the Yuki Indians of California, the Aboriginal Tasmanians and the Herero of German Southwest Africa, Benjamin Madley identified three broad phases: invasion, state-sponsored mass murder, and lethal incarceration. First, the settlers, spurred by notions of empty lands and vanishing indigenous peoples, sought to grasp natural resources and lands for themselves, which led to intense conflicts of interest and rivalries between the settlers and the Natives. In Tasmania, the settler boom came in 1828, in California in 1849, and in Southwest Africa a smaller influx commenced in the late 1890s. This also catalyzed the sexual abuse of indigenous women and killings of Natives by settlers. Driven into the corner, the indigenous peoples responded in kind. They organized violent uprisings against injustices in an effort to protect what was left of their economies and autonomy, regain access to vital resources, and reclaim lost land. The Hereros revolted, California Indians robbed, and the Tasmanian Aborigines made small-scale raids. Colonizers responded with disproportionate violence, including lynchings, massacres, and prolonged military expeditions. Unable to quickly crush indigenous uprisings, some settlers began calling for extermination and sought to accomplish theirs aims either through vigilante, militia, or regular military operations. In the final phase, the surviving Natives were locked up in camps and reservations, or they were removed (as in Tasmania, to Flinders Island, where systematic malnutrition, inadequate medical attention, exposure, violence, overwork, and poor sanitary conditions continued the genocide). In all three cases, whites explained genocide as inevitable and natural.

Historian Gary Clayton Anderson opts for an alternate interpretation for linking Western violence against Native Americans to an international context. Using the Rome Statute of the International Criminal Court – crafted between 1998 and 2002 to establish the Court – as his guideline, he sees ethnic cleansing (which is not a separately listed crime in the Statute) not genocide as fitting for the experiences of Native Americans under the United States and its colonial antecedents. His studies address the history of Indian removal in the East, South, Minnesota, Texas, California, and elsewhere. In the nineteenth century, Texas, for example, state authorities, settlers, and Texas Rangers systematically sought to drive out the Comanches, Kiowas, Apaches, and other indigenous peoples. Ethnic cleansing means a forcible transfer or expulsion of population, a method for displacement rather than extermination. While it involves killing, murder is not the primary goal, but rather ethnic cleansing often carries moral restraint that stops people from executing genocide.

One of the key problems in the study of genocide in the United States is the focus on judging the entire history of the continent from 1492 to the present on a single stroke. Applied as a collective brand, one-size-fits-all Native American genocide – or Holocaust, as Churchill, Stannard, and Thornton also call it – makes for splashy headlines. But when used in that manner, it falls short as an analytical tool for understanding place- and time-specific configurations of extreme violence. Proposing that all indigenous peoples throughout the United States and the hemisphere experienced a homogenous genocide post-1492 poses a real danger, not only of overgeneralizing whites as all-powerful and wicked but also of casting all indigenous peoples as more or less victims. Neither proposition sits well with modern scholars, who underline entangled forms of power and differentiated forms of rule and who stress Native American clout, persistence, and continuity. Hundreds of different indigenous powers resisted, from various positions of power, the Spanish, the British, the French, the Russians, and the Americans, and neither the whites nor the Natives formed harmonious, unified entities. Thus it is no great surprise that oversized collective definitions of genocide tend to make historians wary of using the term. At worst genocide suggests a meticulously planned and executed killing spree that lasted for several generations and united people over national, class, and partisan lines across time and space in a shared murderous plot. It causes historians to think that the concept of genocide has the potential to flatten out the complexities of the past by casting violence in the West, and elsewhere, in a singular mold, rather than taking into account its rich diversity of forms and meanings.

The dark cloud of genocide has the potential to cast a shadow over all of Western history and reduce the multiple shapes of violence under a totalizing formula. Instead of producing broad collective arguments over genocide, we, Madley insists, need detailed case studies, tribe-by-tribe, covering particular interactions at particular times and places. He has suggested following four specific methods of inquiry – statements of genocidal intent, massacres, state-sponsored body-part bounties, and mass death in government custody – when evaluating, or ruling out, possible historical cases of genocide in the West. Basically, we should first study the trees and only after that make assessments of what the forest looks like.

The debate on what counts as genocide in the West and in the world and what does not will likely continue. Some of the more pertinent questions without solid answers include, but are not limited to: what constitutes a group and who gets to define it? Does it have to be destroyed in its entirety (after all, millions of Jews survived the Holocaust)? Does scale, the number of casualties, matter, and if so, how? Should we count genocide rates for different communities and areas in the manner quantitative historians count homicide rates? Does genocide require government planning, organizing, and implementation? If so, then at what level of government: federal, state, provincial, or local? Does it have to be a government action, or government-sanctioned action, at all? Do we need a paper trail, written statements to ascertain intent, or do actions speak louder than words? Did genocide not happen if diseases destroyed the bulk of a certain group, while only some were killed deliberately either before the diseases finished the job or after the microbes left some people alive?

How about genocide in the early West? Lemkin already had plans to study Spanish genocide in the Americas. Do Spanish missions in California, where indigenous death rates proved staggering, or their massacre of the Tiguex in 1540, their mass murder at Acoma in 1599, and the whole period in New Mexico up to the 1680 Pueblo uprising qualify as genocide? Furthermore, do the perpetrators of genocide in Western history always need to be whites? This is certainly not the case elsewhere in the world. Just think of Rwanda, Darfur, or the Khmers in Cambodia, for instance. While scholarship today underscores indigenous power, does it make any sense to take this trend so far as to examine whether the Comanches might have been genocidal against the Apaches in the 1700s or the Sioux against the Pawnees and the Crows during the next century? I am not suggesting that they were, but perhaps we ought to ask even these kinds of questions when making sense of the scope and role of genocide in Western history.

In many ways, violence seems integral for grasping Western history in the world. It took many shapes, factoring in personal, group, national, and imperial empowerment and loss. It blended interpersonal violence, vigilantism, raiding, total war, and genocide and involved conquest, taking of land, extermination of groups, control over resources and labor, as well as ethnic suppression. Violence contributed to strong military cultures and to the building of settler societies in the West and around the world. Violence could make local communities and relations – both conflictive and cooperative – within and between groups. It could also split peoples and communities apart, marking and escalating divisions. Used for stability, violence often caused instability. Used for controlling people, violence often proved uncontrollable. In the end, Western violence spilled across national boundaries and came with multidirectional global connections and parallels.

Bibliography

Social Conflict

Benton-Cohen, Katherine. *Borderline Americans: Racial Division and Labor War in the Arizona Borderlands*. Cambridge, MA: Harvard University Press, 2011.

Berg, Manfred, and Simon Wendt, eds. *Globalizing Lynching History: Vigilantism and Extralegal Punishment from an International Perspective*. New York: Palgrave Macmillan, 2011.

Brown, Richard Maxwell. *Strain of Violence: Historical Studies of American Violence and Vigilantism*. Oxford: Oxford University Press, 1975.

_____. *No Duty to Retreat: Violence and Values in American History and Society*. Oxford: Oxford University Press, 1991.

Carrigan, William D., and Clive Webb. *Forgotten Dead: Mob Violence against Mexicans in the United States, 1848–1928*. Oxford: Oxford University Press, 2013.

Carrigan, William D., and Christopher Waldrep, eds. *Swift to Wrath: Lynching in Global Perspective*. Chartlottesville: University of Virginia Press, 2013.

Cool, Paul. *Salt Warriors: Insurgency on the Border*. College Station: Texas A & M University Press, 2008.

Cronin, Kathryn. *Colonial Causalities: The Chinese in Early Victoria*. Carlton, VIC: Melbourne University Press, 1982.

Dykstra, Robert R. *The Cattle Towns*. New York: Knopf, 1968.

Dykstra, Robert R. "Quantifying the Wild West: The Problematic Statistics of Frontier Violence." *Western Historical Quarterly* 40 (Autumn 2009): 321–347.

Faragher, John Mack. *Eternity Street: Violence and Justice in Frontier Los Angeles*. New York: W. W. Norton, 2016.

Gonzales-Day, Ken. *Lynching in the West, 1850–1935*. Durham: Duke University Press, 2006.

Gordon, Linda. *The Great Arizona Orphan Abduction*. Cambridge, MA: Harvard University Press, 1999.

Gump, James O. "Civil Wars in South Dakota and South Africa: The Role of the 'Third Force'." *Western Historical Quarterly* 34 (Winter 2003): 427–444.

Johnson, Benjamin Heber. *Revolution in Texas: How a Forgotten Rebellion and Its Bloody Suppression Turned Mexicans into Americans*. New Haven: Yale University Press, 2005.

Markus, Andrew. *Fear and Hatred: Purifying Australia and California, 1850–1901.* Sydney: Hale and Iremonger, 1979.

McGrath, Roger D. *Gunfighters, Highwaymen &, Vigilantes: Violence on the Frontier.* Berkeley: University of California Press, 1984.

Peterson del Maar, David. *Beaten Down: A History of Interpersonal Violence in the West.* Seattle: University of Washington Press, 2002.

Pfaelzer, Jean. *Driven Out: The Forgotten War against Chinese Americans.* Berkeley: University of California Press, 2008.

Pfeifer, Michael J. *Rough Justice: Lynching and American Society, 1874–1947.* Urbana: University of Illinois Press, 2004.

Roth, Randolph. *American Homicide.* Cambridge, MA: Belknap Press, 2009.

Roth, Randolph, Michael D. Maltz and Douglas L. Eckberg. "Homicide Rates in the Old West." *Western Historical Quarterly* 42 (Summer 2011): 173–195.

Smithers, Gregory D. "Frontier Justice: Lynching and Racial Violence in the United States and Australia." In Manfred Berg and Simon Wendt, eds. *Globalizing Lynching History: Vigilantism and Extralegal Punishment from an International Perspective.* New York: Palgrave Macmillan, 2011: 101–118.

Thompson, Jerry D. *Cortina: Defending the Mexican Name in Texas.* College Station: Texas A & M University Press, 2007.

Thurston, Robert W. *Lynching: American Mob Murder in Global Perspective.* Burlington, VT: Ashgate, 2011.

Utley, Robert M. *Wanted: The Outlaw Lives of Billy the Kid and Ned Kelly.* New Haven: Yale University Press, 2015.

Waldrep, Christopher. *The Many Faces of Judge Lynch: Punishment and Extralegal Violence in America.* New York: Palgrave Macmillan, 2002.

Wood, Amy Louise. *Lynching and Spectacle: Witnessing Racial Violence in America, 1890–1940.* Chapel Hill: University of North Carolina Press, 2009.

Young, Elliott. *Catarino Garza's Revolution on the Texas-Mexico Border.* Durham: Duke University Press, 2004.

Zesch, Scott. *The Chinatown War: Chinese Los Angeles and the Massacre of 1871.* Oxford: Oxford University Press, 2012.

Wars for Empires

Alonso, Ana Maria. *Thread of Blood: Colonialism, Revolution, and Gender on Mexico's Northern Frontier.* Tucson: University of Arizona Press, 1995.

Arielli, Nir, and Bruce Collins, eds. *Transnational Soldiers: Foreign Military Enlistment in the Modern Era.* New York: Palgrave Macmillan, 2013.

Barr, Juliana. *Peace Came in the Form of a Woman: Indians and Spaniards in the Texas Borderlands.* Chapel Hill: University of North Carolina Press, 2007.

Belich, James. *The New Zealand Wars and the Victorian Interpretation of Racial Conflict.* 1986; reprint, Auckland: Auckland University Press, 2015.

Blackhawk, Ned. *Violence Over the Land: Indians and Empires in the Early American West.* Cambridge, MA: Harvard University Press, 2006.

Blyth, Lance R. *Chiricahua and Janos: Communities of Violence in the Southwest Borderlands, 1680–1880.* Lincoln: University of Nebraska Press, 2012.

Bowen-Hatfield, Shelley. *Chasing Shadows: Apaches and Yaquis along the United States-Mexico Border, 1876–1911.* Albuquerque: University of New Mexico Press, 1998.

Brower, Benjamin Claude. *A Desert Named Peace: The Violence of France's Empire in the Algerian Sahara, 1844–1902*. New York: Columbia University Press, 2009.

Callwell, Charles Edward. *Small Wars: Their Principles and Practice*. 1896; reprint Lincoln: University of Nebraska Press, 1996.

Clayton, Anthony. *France, Soldiers, and Africa*. New York: Brassey's Defence Publishers, 1988.

Clayton, Anthony, and David Killingray. *Khaki and Blue: Military and Police in British Colonial Africa*. Athens: Ohio University Press, 1987.

DeLay, Brian. *War of a Thousand Deserts: Indian Raids and the U.S.-Mexican War*. New Haven: Yale University Press, 2008.

Dunlay, Thomas W. "Indian Allies in the Armies of New Spain and the United States: A Comparative Study." *New Mexico Historical Review* 56 (July 1981): 239–258.

Dunn, John Petrie. *Khedivi Ismail's Army*. New York: Routledge, 2005.

Ehrenberg, Myron J. *Colonial Conscripts: The Tirailleurs Sénégalais in French West Africa, 1857–1960*. London: J. Currey, 1991.

Ferguson, R. Brian, and Neil L. Whitehead, eds. *War in the Tribal Zone: Expanding States and Indigenous Warfare*. Santa Fe: School of American Research Press, 2000.

Folsom, Raphael Brewster. *The Yaquis and the Empire: Violence, Spanish Imperial Power, and Native Resilience in Colonial Mexico*. New Haven: Yale University Press, 2014.

Foos, Paul. *A Short, Offhand, Killing Affair: Soldiers and Social Conflict during the Mexican-American War*. Chapel Hill: University of North Carolina Press, 2002.

Gershovich, Moshe. *French Military Rule in Morocco: Colonialism and Its Consequences*. London: F. Cass, 2000.

Giese, Toby. *The Saga of John Fillmore Blake: The Last Missouri Rouge*. Independence: Herald House, 1994.

Graybill, Andrew R. *Policing the Great Plains: Rangers, Mounties, and the North American Frontier, 1875–1910*. Lincoln: University of Nebraska Press, 2007.

Greenberg, Amy S. *Manifest Manhood and the Antebellum American Empire*. Cambridge: Cambridge University Press, 2005.

_____. *Wicked War: Polk, Clay, Lincoln, and the 1846 U.S. Invasion of Mexico*. New York: Knopf, 2012.

Guidotti-Hernández, Nicole M. *Unspeakable Violence: Remapping U.S. and Mexican National Imaginaries*. Durham: Duke University Press, 2011.

Gump, James O. *The Dust Rose Like Smoke: The Subjugation of the Zulu and the Sioux*. Lincoln: University of Nebraska Press, 1994.

Hämäläinen, Pekka. *The Comanche Empire*. New Haven: Yale University Press, 2008.

Hanson, Victor Davis. *The Western Way of War: Infantry Battle in Classical Greece*. New York: Knopf, 1989.

_____. *Carnage and Culture: Landmark Battles in the Rise of Western Power*. New York: Doubleday, 2001.

Hesseltine, William B., and Wolf C. Hazel. *The Blue and the Gray on the Nile*. Chicago: University of Chicago Press, 1961.

Hill, Richard, and Peter Hogg. *A Black Corps d'Elite: An Egyptian Sudanese Conscript Battalion with the French Army in Mexico, 1863–1867, and its Survivors in Subsequent African History*. East Lansing: Michigan State University Press, 1995.

Jacoby, Karl. *Shadows at Dawn: An Apache Massacre and the Violence of History*. New York: Penguin, 2008.

Jones, Kristine L. "Comparative Raiding Economies: North and South." In Donna J. Guy and Thomas E. Sheridan, eds. *Contested Ground: Comparative Frontiers on the*

Northern and Southern Edges of the Spanish Empire. Tucson: University of Arizona Press, 1998: 97–114.

Kiernan, V. G. *Colonial Empires and Armies, 1815–1960.* Montreal: McGill-Queen's University Press, 1982.

Killingray, David, and David Omissi, eds., *Guardians of Empire: The Armed Forces of the Colonial Powers, c. 1700–1964.* Manchester: Manchester University Press, 1999.

Lahti, Janne. "Colonized Labor: Apaches and Pawnees as Army Workers." *Western Historical Quarterly* 39 (Autumn 2008): 283–302.

———. *Wars for Empire: Apaches, the United States, and the Southwest Borderlands.* Norman: University of Oklahoma Press, 2017.

McGrath, Ann, ed. *Contested Ground: Australian Aborigines under the British Crown.* Sydney: Allen & Unwin, 1995.

Moyd, Michelle R. *Violent Intermediaries: African Soldiers, Conquest, and Everyday Colonialism in German East Africa.* Athens: Ohio University Press, 2014.

Nettelbeck, Amanda. "'On the Side of Law & Order': Indigenous Aides to Mounted Police on the Settler Frontiers of Australia and Canada." *Journal of Colonialism and Colonial History* 15.2 (2014) DOI: 10.1353/cch.2014.0031.

Omissi, David. *The Sepoy and the Raj: The Indian Army, 1860–1940.* Basingstoke: Palgrave Macmillan, 1994.

Parsons, Timothy H. "'Wakamba Warriors Are Soldiers of the Queen': The Evolution of the Kamba as a Martial Race, 1890–1970." *Ethnohistory* 46 (Autumn 1999): 671–701.

Peers, Douglas M. *Between Mars and Mammon: Colonial Armies and the Garrison State in India, 1819–1835.* New York: Tauris, 1995.

———. *Wars of Empire.* London: Cassell, 2000.

Rettig, Tobias, and Karl Hack, eds. *Colonial Armies in Southeast Asia.* New York: Routledge, 2006.

Richards, Jonathan. *The Secret War: A True History of Queensland's Native Police.* St Lucia: University of Queensland Press, 2008.

Sessions, Jennifer E. *By Sword and Plow: France and the Conquest of Algeria.* Ithica: Cornell University Press, 2014.

Smith, Ralph A. *Borderlander: The Life of James Kirker, 1793–1852.* Norman: University of Oklahoma Press, 1999.

Streets, Heather. *Martial Races: The Military, Race and Masculinity in British Imperial Culture, 1857–1914.* Manchester: Manchester University Press, 2010.

Sweeney, Edwin R. *From Cochise to Geronimo: The Chiricahua Apaches, 1874–1886.* Norman: University of Oklahoma Press, 2010.

Truett, Samuel. "Transnational Warrior: Emilio Kosterlitzky and the Transformation of the U.S.-Mexico Borderlands, 1873–1928." In Samuel Truett and Elliott Young, eds. *Continental Crossroads: Remapping U.S.-Mexico Borderlands History.* Durham: Duke University Press, 2004: 241–272.

Vandervort, Bruce. *Indian Wars of Mexico, Canada and the United States, 1812–1900.* New York: Routledge, 2006.

———. *Wars of Imperial Conquest in Africa, 1830–1914.* Bloomington: Indiana University Press, 2009.

Weber, David J. *Barbaros: Spaniards and their Savages in the Age of Enlightenment.* New Haven: Yale University Press, 2006.

Zappia, Natale A. *Traders and Raiders: The Indigenous World of the Colorado Basin, 1540–1859.* Chapel Hill: University of North Carolina Press, 2014.

Genocide

Alvarez, Alex. *Native America and the Question of Genocide*. Lanham: Rowman and Littlefield, 2014.

Anderson, Gary Clayton. *The Conquest of Texas: Ethnic Cleansing in the Promised Land, 1820–1875*. Norman: University of Oklahoma Press, 2005.

_____. *Ethnic Cleansing and the Indian: The Crime That Should Haunt America*. Norman: University of Oklahoma Press, 2014.

Churchill, Ward. *A Little Matter of Genocide: Holocaust and Denial in the Americas, 1492 to the Present*. San Francisco: City Light Books, 1997.

Jacoby, Karl. "'The Broad Platform of Extermination': Nature and Violence in the Nineteenth Century North American Borderlands." *Journal of Genocide Research* 10 (June 2008): 249–267.

Kiernan, Ben. *Blood and Soil: A World History of Genocide and Extermination from Sparta to Darfur*. New Haven: Yale University Press, 2007.

Levene, Mark. *Genocide in the Age of the Nation State: Volume I: The Meaning of Genocide*. New York: I. B. Tauris, 2005.

_____. *Genocide in the Age of the Nation State: Volume II: The Rise of the West and the Coming of Genocide*. New York: I. B. Tauris, 2013.

Lindsay, Brendan C. *Murder State: California's Native American Genocide, 1846–1873*. Lincoln: University of Nebraska Press, 2012.

Madley, Benjamin. "Patterns of Frontier Genocide, 1803–1910: The Aboriginal Tasmanians, the Yuki of California, and the Herero of Namibia," *Journal of Genocide Research* 6 (June 2004): 167–192.

_____. "From Africa to Auschwitz: How German South West Africa Incubated Ideas and Methods Adopted and Developed by the Nazis in Eastern Europe." *European History Quarterly* 35 (July 2005): 167–192.

_____. "Tactics of Nineteenth-Century Colonial Massacre: Tasmania, California, and Beyond." In Philip G. Dwyer and Lyndall Ryan, eds. *Theatres of Violence: Massacre, Mass Killing, and Atrocity Throughout History*. New York: Berghahn, 2012: 111–125.

_____. "Reexamining the American Genocide Debate: Meaning, Historiography, and New Methods." *American Historical Review* 120 (February 2015): 98–139.

_____. *An American Genocide: The United States and the California Indian Catastrophe, 1846–1873*. New Haven: Yale University Press, 2016.

McDonnell, Michael A., and A. Dirk Moses. "Raphael Lemkin as Historian of Genocide in the Americas." *Journal of Genocide Research* 7 (December 2005): 501–529.

Moses, A. Dirk, ed. *Genocide and Settler Society: Frontier Violence and Stolen Indigenous Children in Australian History*. New York: Berghahn Books, 2004.

_____, ed. *Empire, Colony, Genocide: Conquest, Occupation and Subaltern Resistance in World History*. New York: Berghahn Books, 2008.

Smith, Andrea. *Conquest: Sexual Violence and American Indian Genocide*. Durham: Duke University Press, 2015.

Stannard, David E. *American Holocaust: The Conquest of the New World*. Oxford: Oxford University Press, 1992.

Stone, Dan, ed. *The Historiography of Genocide*. New York: Palgrave Macmillan, 2008.

Thornton, Russell. *American Indian Holocaust and Survival: A Population History since 1492*. Norman: University of Oklahoma Press, 1987.

Totten, Samuel, and Robert K. Hitchcock, eds. *Genocide of Indigenous Peoples: A Critical Bibliographic Review*. London: Transatlantic Publishers, 2011.

Weitz, Eric D. *A Century of Genocide: Utopias of Race and Nation*. Princeton: Princeton University Press, 2003.

Wolfe, Patrick. "Settler Colonialism and the Elimination of the Native." *Journal of Genocide Research* 8 (December 2006): 387–409.

Woolford, Andrew, Jeff Benvenuto, and Alexander Laban Hinton, eds. *Colonial Genocide in Indigenous North America*. Durham: Duke University Press, 2014.

Zimmerer, Jürgen, and Joachim Zeller, eds. *Genocide in German South-West Africa: The Colonial War of 1904–1908 and its Aftermath*. Monmouth: Merlin Press, 2008.

4

INTIMACIES OF EMPIRES

Born to a respected New England family in 1863, Elaine Goodale East-man functioned within a middle-class Victorian culture that tended to link white women like her with fragility, virtue, tenderness, and gentility and that expected them to safeguard the morality and respectability of their household, community, race, nation, and empire through domesticity. Very much a paragon of Victorian womanhood, Elaine embodied middle-class respectability through her writings and her role as a wife, a mother, and a teacher. She was also one of those numerous settler women who actively partook in the world-wide attempts to transplant the era's middle-class domesticity to colonized spaces and who used the domestic sphere to civilize the nonwhite world. Yet, in her own way, she also challenged the prevailing notions of propriety, stretched the parameters of white respectability, and contested narrow definitions of civilization and race.

College-educated and an avid writer from childhood, Elaine taught Native American children from the early 1880s onward. She worked at the Hampton Institute in Virginia and then in a day school she set up at the Lower Brulé Sioux agency in today's South Dakota. Later she worked at the Carlisle Indian School in Pennsylvania. Wanting the respect of the Sioux, she associated closely with them at the Lower Brulé. She preferred Sioux companions to whites and spent her vacations traveling the reservation. She also became fluent in the Sioux language and adopted some of their housing and dress. For most middle-class whites, this kind of behavior would have indicated alarming signs of racial and cultural slippage, of contamination and condition the white colonizers around the world knew as "going native." Defying prevailing conceptions of propriety even further, in 1891 Elaine married Charles Eastman, a boarding school-educated Sioux medical doctor. Their wedding was held in New York, and it proved a social curiosity that was commented on widely, including two sensationalist articles in the *New York Times*. Placed in the spotlight, the couple would go on to have six children, who were considered and who themselves identified Native. Explicitly linking her career and conjugal arrangement – the public and the private realm – Elaine represented the marriage as a logical extension of her devotion to the Native people. While interracial marriages in colonial situations were typically associated with the degeneration of the white race and the pollution of white women by nonwhite men, Elaine apparently was quite successful in extending the parameters of middle-class respectability. As historian Katherine Ellinghaus remarks, many of her white contemporaries also saw Elaine's marriage as connected to her vocation of civilizing Native Americans. Of course, it helped that she was both a middle-class lady and an educator and that her husband was a college-educated professional, a reformed and "civilized" Indian.

Attending the influential gatherings of reformers at the Lake Mohonk conferences of the Friends of the Indian, Elaine remained an activist after becoming a wife and a mother. Thus while she channeled Victorian norms of domesticity to Natives as a teacher, she nevertheless challenged those same conventions that sought to contain married women inside their households. She, moreover, went against the prevalent policy that favored the removal of Native children to off-reservation boarding schools, where the children were not only physically separated from their families, often by considerable distance, but also subjected to a curriculum and discipline that targeted the eradication of their cultures. Elaine preferred reservation day schools where white teachers could personally reach and impact the homes of Indian children. Rather than wipe out all Indianness, she, historian Margaret Jacobs mentions, strove for a more moderate assimilationist policy where Indians could take some aspects of white culture and yet retain their language and clothing, for instance. Perhaps this had something to do with her own family situation, as her biracial children were potential candidates for removal and assimilation themselves.

Back in Amherst, Massachusetts, in the early 1900s, the Eastmans struggled to uphold their middle-class veneer as Charles's medical career was repeatedly hindered by racial barriers. Yet, they ran an "Indian-style" summer camp for white girls in the New England wilderness, published numerous writings, and engaged in lecture tours where Charles related his Native cultural heritage and experiences to white middle-class audiences eager for "authentic" Indianness. Charles's extramarital relations caused the couple to split in 1921, but they never officially divorced. Through her writings, Elaine kept on building a public image of herself as an angel of civilization working on the front lines of Native American assimilation. She claimed identity as a maternalist, a savior of Native lives, and a promoter of Native cause and humanity. She was hardly a "rebel" or social outcast, but rather every bit the middle-class lady who embraced, tested, and operated the intimacies of empire on multiple planes. Preoccupation with the civilizing mission, interracial sex, middle-class respectability, domesticity, and whiteness were themes that resonated far beyond the Eastmans and the settler colonial West. In fact, they spanned across the global colonial map and demonstrated how power rested and operated in the intimacies of empires.

The central tension at the heart of colonial projects in the modern era revolves around the rule of difference. This typically manifests itself in the seemingly paradoxical preoccupation with creating distance, of differentiating and excluding "Others," especially Natives, on the one hand and the urge to close that gap, to civilize those "Others" and make them more like us (meaning whites of European extraction) through erasing their cultures and identities on the other. To put it differently, efforts to establish frameworks of difference that distinguished whites from nonwhites/Natives operated together and in tension with a civilizing mission, a determination to erase difference (at least to a degree) through the universalization of white norms, customs, and practices. This, in turn, would potentially validate colonialism as a benevolent enterprise. Thus, as colonial empires in the 1800s and 1900s were driven by the idea of Euro-American (white) identity as superior in comparison with all the nonwhite peoples and cultures, they tried to make the world to better correspond to their notions by importing their norms, values, and practices and making these the universal standards. In these processes built on asymmetries of race, class, and gender, as discussed by anthropologist Ann Laura Stoler, colonial rule infiltrated the most intimate domains in people's lives, turning households, leisure, education, conjugality, and sexuality – the social fabric of the everyday – into dense transfer points of power and anxiety. Matters of the intimate and affective dimensions – respectability, sentiments, desires, and bodies – in fact served as the very grounds for the creation and maintenance of colonial power, historians Tony Ballantyne and Antoinette Burton remark. Played out across the transnational imperial terrain, crossing borders, connecting empires, given new meanings in specific colonial social orders, and riddled with, Stoler points out, tense and tender ties, these intimacies of empires were products of accumulating interconnections within a specific global field. Fueled by transnational anxieties, they both marked and blurred community/racial membership, management of self and subject peoples, and the boundaries between "us" and "them." They also linked the West and the world.

Performing Whiteness

When reaching across the globe, white settlers, administrators, soldiers, traders, missionaries, and other representatives of the colonial powers formed heterogeneous and disharmonious communities riddled with class divisions, competing political and economic agendas, and contending ideologies and discourses. In this context, whiteness itself was contested, stratified, and hierarchical, and it was closely associated with power. Gentleman's status had traditionally rested on possession of landed estates and on personal disdain for labor coupled with devotion to leisure, while success in commerce made the bourgeois elite. While Britain's gentry possibly set something like the global norm for middle-class gentility in the nineteenth century, in colonial situations whiteness equaled something that was performed on a daily basis as men and women of varied vocations and backgrounds positioned themselves as heirs of Enlightenment, bearers of civilization, brave liberators, honorable gentlemen, true ladies, cultured, and moral. They did this hoping to matter as emblems of a transnational middle-class, Victorian, culture and to establish difference against the host populations in the colonies.

Some whites carved common ground, for instance, through the ideology of Anglo-Saxonism. They found authority in notions of self-proclaimed ethnic, political, and moral superiority of individuals and traditions of British origin. The Anglo-Saxons ostensibly excelled in the Darwinistic contest between men, representing the highest form of culture and civilization and conquering lands in all corners of the planet. While notions of Anglo-Saxonism indicated hierarchies of privilege and power, these kinds of rankings characteristically revolved around "respectability" in colonial situations. Respectability in turn was a tenuous shorthand for a whole range of desirable character traits and habits. It denoted standards of living and a set of cultural competencies; it correlated with profession, family, home, personal outlook, leisure, socializing, and character. People could gain respectability through their lifestyles, living arrangements, and appearance; by embracing certain values and practices. They could also lose it; "go native," become poor "white trash," and risk their whiteness altogether. Fluid, liminal, and subject to negotiation, respectability and with it racial identity habitually denoted more than skin tone alone. To acquire European legal equivalence in the Dutch East Indies in the 1880s, for instance, one had to be a Christian, speak and write Dutch, have a European upbringing and education, and demonstrate suitability for European society. It was also possible to acquire white status through marriage to or adoption by a European.

White middle-class women held a key role in the communication and validation of respectability, race, and civilization. According to the Victorian-era norms, it was the job of the woman to "create home," to "revitalize the community," and to "build the nation" wherever she went. However, white women occupied an ambiguous position across the colonial terrain. Perceived as paragons of racial purity with an instant civilizing impact, women were also depicted as highly vulnerable and in need of constant and vigorous protection against the dangerous colonial environment and the primitive sexual aggressions of Native men. Thus the entry of white women often caused great anxiety, or it was closely monitored or restricted. When traveling overland to Arizona in the 1870s, Martha Summerhays, a New England wife, was given a gun by his husband. He made Martha swear that she would use it on herself in case the Apaches attacked because if captured a fate worse than death, denoting sexual slavery, surely awaited her. In the hill stations of British India, the cultured single women, known as the "fishing fleet," who arrived from England each year to locate husbands among the bachelor officers and civil servants, were tightly chaperoned during their stay, so as to prevent intimate transgressions and to guard them against Indian men. Several European and American commercial enterprises – including tobacco companies and banks – operating in Africa, India, and Southeast Asia limited marriage among their white employees during the first years of service, while some prohibited it altogether. Furthermore, white enlisted men in colonial armies, including the U.S. frontier army, were often recruited among the bachelors and were strongly encouraged not to marry during their service.

These policies not merely served to protect white women from Native aggression but were also meant to prevent the proliferation of a lower-class white population, a proletariat who would not afford a "respectable life." In many colonies, there existed a growing anxiety that poorly paid white workers would not have the money needed for maintaining a respectable marriage, a household, and a lifestyle suitable to a white wife. This could in turn lead to poverty and prostitution to white women being sullied by the touch of non-white men. What these anxieties actually did lead to was a shortage of white women. This gender imbalance in the colonies, in turn, actively contributed to the prevalence of interracial sex and concubinage as white men turned to Native women for intimate companionship.

While these commonplace apprehensions over white women applied to settler colonial projects alike, it was also the case that settler colonialism especially depended as much or more on founding mothers as on founding fathers. To put it simply, no white women meant no settler colonial futures. Thus, rather than restrict their presence, settler colonies tried to lure respectable female settlers through promotional literature, assisted emigration, and cheap land. It comes of little surprise that in this cultural fabric women were again closely associated with the roles of the wife and the mother. Their status was often defined by their sexual restraint and dedication to their home, husband, and children. In the American West, women's literature at large praised the merits of domesticity, maternalism, virtue, purity, and passivity, or what historians refer to as "true womanhood." In French, British, and Dutch colonial manuals, the message was very much the same: white women were offered detailed instructions to ensure a happy home, proper social order, and good hygiene. They were also to prevent any laxity in morals. As historian Margaret Strobel observes, in colonialism white middle-class women became associated with daily rituals of racialized rule, elevated standards of living, and more insulated social spaces built and moderated according to metropolitan norms. They would lead the civilization of the colonial spaces through personal example and their presence put new demands on white communities to clarify their racial and class boundaries and mark out their social space.

In colonial armies, where marriage was by and large the privilege of officers, wives often had no official status. Yet, they enacted social norms, modeled appropriate racial, gender, and class relations, and confidently executed their duty as domestic imperial agents. For the wives, the home operated as a microsite of empire, historian Verity McInnis contends. In the American West and in British India, the wives commanded the household and subordinated domestic workers through racial discrimination and the feminization of male servants, while simultaneously enacting the social norms of the metropole. In German Southwest Africa, historian Lora Wildenthal explains, the German middle-class wife was purportedly able to preserve and strengthen the German race. Her presence was necessary to reinforce the moral backbone of German male settlers tempted by local women and to counteract interracial relations (as German men supposedly always preferred German women over Natives). She was needed to steer and motivate German men toward productive enterprises and other pioneering activities. Moreover, it was essential to produce racially pure offspring and nurse and educate a moral and hardworking next generation of settlers. The list of stock features and tasks of this "ideal" German colonial woman would suit any number of other settler colonial locales, including the West.

Expected to produce prudent, ordered, and spotless family spaces, women often faced an uphill struggle. In the summer of 1871, Lieutenant Frederick Phelps and his new bride Mary arrived at Fort Bayard, New Mexico. Coming from established Ohio families of college-educated teachers, lawyers, and judges, the Phelps' felt unease in the isolated post hundreds of miles from the closest mark of civilization, the railroad. Their social circle was restricted to the few officers and their wives stationed at the post. Besides, there was nothing "proper" to eat as government rations entailed beef, coffee, bacon, sugar, and little else. Also, if not for a bachelor officer who let them have his house, the Phelps' home would have been a tent. Even this house seemed hardly worth the title. It was originally meant as a stable. Renovated, it now came with a parlor that had one wall of stones, one of adobe, one of pine logs set on end, and one of slabs from the sawmill. Rough boards covered the floor, canvas acted as the ceiling and mud as the roof. The only window had an immovable sash. The smaller room in the house had no window at all, and its floor was of hard smooth mud. This was hardly the ideal middle-class residence. Phelps' home also included two tents, one used as a dining room and the other as a kitchen. Furthermore, the house looked very much occupied: by a number of tarantulas, centipedes, and the occasional snake.

Ideally for middle-class Victorians such as the Phelps, home mattered as an important symbol that expressed the respectability of its inhabitants by showing how they could emulate idealized middle-class domesticity. This is why Fort Bayard proved such a shock. And one needs to acknowledge that in colonial settings, middle-class domesticity was not merely the concern of married officers and their wives. In British India, for example, bachelor officers often joined together to rent a bungalow and furnish their home "European-style" with rented furniture. Furthermore, the concept of "home" stretched to include not only bachelor and family housing, but also boarding houses, immigrant hostels and lodges, all ideally offering residents a familiar and familial environment through their food, conversations, values, décor, and atmosphere.

Household commodities played a key role in creating a proper "home" as they marked close connections and similarities between the "civilized world" and the colonial domains. In her examination of cosmopolitan domesticity, historian Kristin Hoganson recognizes that bourgeois households proved enthusiastic for imported goods and styles, especially European artistic production and cultural attainments, but that some of them also valorized ethnographic and geographical knowledge when it came to household décor. Staging the whole civilized world in their households, many middle-class whites in the colonies arrived abundantly supplied or used mail-order houses such as Sears and Montgomery Ward that sprung up in the late 1800s. Furniture, wallpaper, matting, and portraits were used to create homes that looked welcoming, cozy, and familiar. It was the growth of transoceanic shipping and the railroads that caused consumer products, foodstuffs, and other manufactured items to flood colonial spaces, reducing their transports costs and times, and thus enabling a "home-like" diversity and elegance in selection. This meant that more and more colonial homes came armed with such bourgeois trappings as sewing machines, pianos, linen, shawls, china, chairs, mattresses, and matting for the floors. Important also were the scores of pictures, mountains of newspapers, and piles of books (from cooking manuals and dime novels to children's fairytales and literary classics).

It was not just the items, but their use that gave them meaning. In more distant outposts, books and newspapers were kept and stored and read over and over again, sometimes out loud, sometimes in private. Some resorted to rationing the meager news supply by, for example, reading one paper per day. They could place the paper on the breakfast table so that whoever read it could imagine he/she was a civilized person who lived in a civilized home "in the real world" reading the news of the day, no matter how old the paper actually was. Maintaining their "high standards" and civilized ways, Kenya's white settlers insisted on having afternoon tea and dressing for dinner, as did other colonizers across the British Wests. Whites also put a lot of stress on eating: on what they ate, how the meals were organized, and what kind of tableware was used. While colonialism fostered plenty of culinary mixing, certain food stuffs, some of them initially of non-European origin, like potatoes, butter, milk, bacon, and white flour, as well as canned delicacies like oysters, acted as markers of civilized life and were transported across the West and the world. Imported whiskey and cigars played a similar purpose, albeit one more masculine in tone. Other household and hygienic products associated with civilized whiteness abounded: body soap, face creams, powder, laundry detergent, bleach, and toothbrushes and toothpaste were part of the white people's commodities "cleansing" and "whitening" the colonized terrain. Soap especially was widely used as a metaphor for colonization, for civilizing peripheral areas and its "dark and filthy" Natives.

Thus, respectable homes and proper whiteness also concerned appearance and the body. Regardless of their actual amount of attiring, Natives were typically identified as naked, or half-clad, while whites were represented as decently and properly dressed in white people's texts. Because white skin was a vestige of civilization, the colonizers, especially women, took pains to keep their skins pale in the West and in other colonial settings. Whether the women covered their bodies with full skirts, long-sleeves, and high-necked clothing, or possibly adapted and used khaki skirts and plain white shirts, they seldom exposed their extremities to the sun. They also used brimmed hats – or, like their men and children, pitch helmets – as well as gloves to safeguard their hands from exposure to the elements.

Housing, dress, and food marked social space where whites were stratified by class distinctions but from which Natives were barred, except as servants. Servants occupied the inner recesses of bourgeois life, enabling middle-class lifestyles, keeping settler homes running, and mediating between the home and the outside space. Thousands of Europeans and white Americans migrated to colonial spaces to take jobs as house servants, nursemaids, and cooks. And there existed a constant need for white female servants, who would protect the domestic sphere from racial and cultural contamination that the use of Native servants might subject the white household members to. Furthermore, the nineteenth-century practice of indicating social distance between middle-class and working-class white females by reserving the title of "ladies" to the former also applied to the colonies. Yet, the paucity of white women willing to work as domestics and the fact that new hires were often quickly lost to marriages complicated the divide and enabled upward mobility among working-class white women. Moreover, more often than not the servants proved a racially mixed lot, and they included plenty of men as well as women. Army officers had their batman (British India) and striker (American West) to provide invaluable service, yet both groups of soldier-servants were feminized by the officers' wives. Often the middle-class people hired whomever they managed to get. They brought with them former black slaves or employed Mexican or Chinese men and women. Unlike in the Eastern states, the Chinese made up a large part of the household servant pool in the West, especially in urban environments.

The drive to transplant and perform respectable whiteness – to both reinforce the barriers between respectable people and others, whether lower-class whites or colonized others, as well as to reduce the imagined difference between colony and metropole – also reached outside of homes to leisure and public spaces. Leisure functioned as a vital ritual consisting of carefully orchestrated performances, often to restricted membership. There was nothing better than proper dances, dinner parties, masquerades, picnics, and amateur theatricals to showcase class and racial sensibilities and level of respectability.

Social calls were equally imperative in performing whiteness and practiced routinely by army officers and civilians alike. So was clubbing. Most famous in the British Indian context, it also spread worldwide and entailed networking, social cohesion among the elite, and specific customs built around coffee- and tea-drinking, eating, card playing, cigar-smoking, and whiskey-sipping.

While sweating and toiling was unbecoming of a gentleman, many middle-class whites, especially in British India, were enthusiastic toward sports, notes historian Byron Farwell. They engaged in polo, cricket, poon (badminton), and, of course, hunting. In the nineteenth century, hunting was widely considered a sport suitable for gentlemen. There being no foxes in India, the wily jackal proved an adequate substitute. In the American West, well-to-do businessmen and European aristocracy organized numerous hunting extravaganzas on the Plains (see Chapter 5). The U.S. Army officers' corps also included many enthusiasts who would go hunting anytime and anywhere. They prepared hunting trips that lasted several days or weeks. Sometimes a supply of horses and dogs were used, copycatting European aristocratic practices.

And then there were the retreats. Hot and humid climates were perceived as especially dangerous to white women and children. Developed in the early nineteenth century as sites for military stations and sanatoriums, hill stations in cooler altitudes in British India proved hugely popular. Importantly, they provided home-like environments. The Nilgiri railway in South India en route to the hill stations of Konoor and Ootacamund had stations such as Allderly, Hillgrove, Runnymeade, Wellington, and Lovelade whose mere names resonated with familiarity. With their modest yet English-looking buildings, these stations echoed the comfort and quiet of far-off, rural, England and signified the attempted recreation of home away from home. In the North, on the foothills of the Himalayas, Simla was for six months a year the practical capital of British India for both the military and civilian upper echelons. In 1903, Simla had a Gothic-style church, a promenade (forbidden to Indians), and numerous shops offering British and other Euro-American goods. It also boasted a Royal Hotel for the visitors, as well as over 1,400 European houses.

In the West, the scale was perhaps more modest, but the idea very much the same. Take, for instance, the army officers from Fort Grant, Arizona, who had a retreat built for themselves up in the 1880s in the nearby Mount Graham for use during the hot summer period. This quickly became a favorite resort for officers, their families, and visitors, who, with the necessary servants, went to enjoy the grassy flat bordering a small stream of cold water and surrounded by pines, aspen, and other trees. Unsurprisingly, enlisted men were ordered to cut trees and construct log cabins for elite use. When the soldiers labored, officers and their guests often ascended the summit of Mount Graham to catch the grand views of mountain ranges and long broad valleys that reached Mexico. The evenings they spent around campfires talking and singing, as soldier cooks prepared lofty meals for them. A special pack train operated between this retreat and the fort, keeping the former amply supplied.

Colonial urban enclaves in the American West and in places such as Victoria, Australia, Nairobi, Kenya, Windhoek, German Southwest Africa, Calcutta, India, Hong Kong, or Singapore, identified with civilization through architecture, through imposing administrative buildings, churches, and elegant private homes modeled after the metropole. The choice of building materials played a similar function as whites preferred brick, mortar, or wood and contrasted them with Native "mud" or bush structures. The layout built around the grid and public parks, and street design with their straight lines and wide streets and avenues further cemented the community's association with civilization and respectability. Living apart from the civilian population, the cantonments and forts of colonial armies represented experiments in modernity where middle-class ideas and ideals of public space and domesticity, as envisioned and transplanted by the officers and their wives, were played out. The typical U.S. Army posts in the West displayed a village-like layout. It promoted mastery over nature – exemplified by the urge for landscaping and other improvements – and proper social divisions thorough hierarchical housing. The masses (enlisted men) lived in inferior, stuffy, and overcrowded barracks and the elite (officers and their families) in individual homes of refinement and taste. All this was meant to offer an example of what a respectable civilized settlement looked like. Many other colonial communities also displayed a hierarchical and segregated layout in housing. Respectable peoples were secluded from lower classes and from the nonwhite neighborhoods of "China towns," "Mexican towns," or "Native quarters."

With their elegant homes, imposing structures, organized layout, straight lines, and orderly public spaces, communities were meant to signal modernity, power, and white prestige when imposing Euro-American forms on formerly indigenous spaces. Those uncolonized spaces were connected with images of vacant emptiness or wilderness, while certain kinds of landscapes, quite frequently deserts, were represented as wastelands. Native villages, in turn, frequently stood for dirty, unordered domains of mud houses, bush dwellings, or holes in the ground. For Sarah Harris, an English settler in New Zealand, the Maori domestic spaces were more fitting for animals than for humans, while Frederick Phelps thought little better of the Apache homes he saw in New Mexico. Still, many white colonizers were forced to live in tents or huts with sand floors, mud walls, and shrub roofs. The Plains had their sod huts and the Southwest borderlands teemed with adobe structures, while settlers in Kenya built *bandas*, made of wattle and daub in the fashion of black Kenyans. The urban atmosphere was also often far from gentile with saloons, gambling halls, brothels, and rowdy residents occupying public spaces. The daughter of a colonial administrator, M. H. Hamilton, remembered how towns in interwar Kenya could "only be likened to the towns of the old American West" with "their reckless Wild West atmosphere (Figure 4.1)."[1]

---

1 Quoted in Riley, *Taking Land*, 92–93.

FIGURE 4.1   Custer County, Nebraska Historical Society_NHS10766. "My little German home across the sea."

In their efforts to domesticate and claim control over the colonized terrain, whites also tried to shape the land to meet their expectations. They turned out enthusiastic amateur scientists: gazing, sampling, and collecting flora and fauna. They brought seeds and planted gardens of vegetables, rolling green laws, and flowers. Rows of familiar trees surrounded settler homes and communities whether on the Australian Outback or on the Great Plains. Often little regard was given to the suitability of the natural surroundings to any particular kind of plant. For a colonial place to be claimed "civilized," it needed European greenery. One woman in Kenya explained that "it was proverbial of the English that they love to make two blades of grass grow where there was one before."[2] It was also equally proverbial of the settlers entering the West, those invading French Algeria, and numerous others places.

> You can scarcely conceive what pleasure it gives us to walk out and see so many houses, gardens with corn growing, fine roads and boat building, in less than two years, when we landed no houses, no cattle, no poultry, no vegetables but native potatoes and pumpkins, no roads, in fact nothing but pigs and potatoes.

2 Quoted in Riley, *Taking Land*, 128.

claimed Sarah Harris when describing the conditions in the 1840s at New Plymouth on the west coast of New Zealand's North Island.[3]

Marred by constant fears over losing their sense of self as well as home and of losing touch with civilization in a strange land, respectable whiteness was also about connections. Affective ties of home and family, colony and metropole, were performed in private letters. They allowed a person to bridge the separation created by distance and to occupy and meditate between the familiarity of the metropole and the strangeness of colonies. As historian Angela Woollacott shows, personal correspondence was a lifeline that created and funneled knowledge and embodied connections between the settlers place of residence – in her example, the Australian colonies – and the globalizing world – including India, the West Indies, Canada, and beyond. Correspondence thus conjoined personal stories and lives with the story of the nation and the world. Given the need to maintain contacts, home leaves also were important. Such stints offered opportunities to "tank up" on civilization, to rejuvenate family ties, embark on civilized activities, and recharge self-belief so that one could then return to the colonial ground full of energy and confidence.

Whites strived to show that colonial spaces participated in the Victorian prescriptions for middle-class respectability and that good people could perform proper whiteness practically anywhere in the world. It resulted not merely in unpredictable outcomes but in what seemed like a perennial struggle against the colonial milieu as one sought to bridge what was often a considerable gap between desirable level of refinement and reality. Colonizer lifestyles were often far from practical. Heavy clothing, food that was hard to digest, expensive, difficult to obtain, and that went rancid characterized everyday lives. As did furniture that retained the heat, rotted, and fell apart. Proper leisure failed to materialize as the lack of social peers meant a corresponding lack of entertainment. Whites typically were forced to improvise in home décor. Homemade furniture was "dressed up" with flower and other decorations, newspapers acted as wallpaper, and curtains were made from old sheets or petticoats. They also had to rely on packing crates as furniture, making boxes and chests into chairs, lounges, sofas, cupboards, wardrobes, desks, and bookcases. Following weeks of improvements, their house at Fort Bayard became quite cozy and comfortable, Frederick Phelps assured. It was now suited for a middle class to live in, socialize with their peers, and to showcase as proof of their status. Still, others were never satisfied. What troubled them was that the houses did not live up to the standards or provide much security against the elements. Not only snakes and other wildlife, but fires as well damaged homes. Locusts stormed settler spaces with devastating intensity from the Great Plains to Kenya. Martha Summerhayes remembered her life at Ehrenberg on the Colorado River in the 1870s: "the desert literally blew into

---

3 Quoted in Cozzens, "With a Pretty Little Garden at the Back," 515.

the house," leaving "a deep layer of sand on everything on the room, and on our perspiring bodies." One storm was "so bad," Summerhayes noted, that her servant "had to use a shovel to remove the sand from the floors."[4]

As middle-class domesticity sought to create islands of civilization amidst a sea of darkness, it not merely enabled the creation of a series of others but was meant to control whites. One sphere of anxiousness was to prevent social lapses and racial degeneration that would result from "going native." Closely entangled with an overriding concern over white prestige, "going native" meant different things in different colonial situations. It usually signified fears that whites would adapt local customs and habits, thus blurring who was who. This would result in an absence of boundaries, of falling beneath one's class status or losing one's whiteness. This was seen as a potential pitfall for particularly lower-class whites. The concern over the presence of poor, "unfit" whites was a widespread phenomenon on different colonial frontiers. In British India and the Dutch East Indies, European pauperism was a real social problem, reportedly affecting as much as half of the white population. South Africa was calculated to have some 300,000 poor whites in the 1920s. Many of these were sent back home, others were forced into workhouses, while various relief organizations were set up to feed them.

Yet, middle-class peoples also needed to convince others and themselves that residency in the colonies had not reduced them to savagery. In these cases, degeneration was often seen as a result of distance from civilization and respectable white community. Colonial medicine affirmed a version of this slippage as a mental disorder, often diagnosed as Neurasthenia, a major problem in French and Dutch colonies. It could reveal itself through social choices: for instance, if a person mingled with the wrong crowd or cohabited with a Native woman. This "disease" claimed a victim also when a white person embraced nonwhite lifestyles, appearance, and dress. White children who played with Native peers and mimicked their dress and behavior were thought especially vulnerable, in danger of absorbing local languages and customs at the expense of their own white cultures. Much anxiety also surrounded the use of Native nursemaids and house servants who possibly introduced white children Native customs, foods, and languages. Making sure their offspring would grow up "white," scores of middle-class parents sent their children to Europe, or back "east" in the American West, for schooling.

Going native could also be a sign of individual resistance and defiance against middle-class social protocol. Expressing a willingness to question middle-class norms and conventions, it could signal an escape toward the formation of alternate, hybrid, identities. There were educated men like Johann Baptist von Anzer, a German missionary in late-1800s China, who represented himself

---

4 Quoted in Lahti, *Cultural Construction*, 166.

as a hybrid of a Chinese mandarin and a Catholic bishop through his attire, customs, and living arrangements. Von Anzer further shocked the middle-class audiences and earned their criticism by advocating indigenous priesthood. While doing fieldwork at the Zuni Pueblo, the anthropologist Frank Hamilton Cushing engaged in mimetic modern escapism by dressing as a Zuni and participating in their rituals. He became something of a celebrity through his open performance of a Zuni identity and when decorating his New York apartment in what he perceived was the authentic Zuni fashion for a kiva. While this kind of cross-cultural boundary hopping, of becoming the "Other," was viewed with suspicion, playacting and dressing in Indian costume, building teepees, and living "like a Native" in the outdoors also hit the mainstream. It was especially poignant with the Boy Scouts, a movement initiated by the English Lord Robert Baden-Powell, a veteran of several colonial wars in Africa, and other such transnational organizations that encouraged youngsters to act out the Native and settler experience. In these situations, performing whiteness actually entailed performing "nativeness" by copycatting and appropriating indigenous customs, dress, and cultures for the benefit of the settler societies.

Parameters of Race

In colonial settings, whiteness was seldom self-evident, and this is why it needed such stringent performing and safeguarding. And this urgency and uncertainty was made evident in the preoccupation with middle-class respectability and its manifestation through domestication, the fears over poor whites and "going native," as well as in the ambiguous position of white women. Shaping the performances and parameters of whiteness were also multiple entangled discourses over miscegenation, interracial relations, land use, and the civilizing mission. They concerned assigning and claiming identity when realities potentially straddled, muddled, and entangled the boundaries of race and crossed the lines supposedly separating "us" and "them."

In the early 1860s, Fanny and Ellen, two Strait Salish Native women in the Pacific Northwest, married European immigrant men who originated from the Danish-German borderlands. These two women came from a world where interracial relationships between Native women and Euro-American traders had been common for generations and where lives typically spanned both sides of the international line between the United States and Canada. In fact, the San Juan Islands, their home, were jointly occupied by Britain and the United States until 1872, when Kaiser Wilhelm I of Germany settled the boundary issue. When both sisters gave birth to their first children in the mid-1860s, interracial households remained the norm. Soon thereafter, historian Katrina Jagodinsky explains, the influx of white settlers saw the emergence of new social attitudes and legal structures that sought to limit the choices of Fanny, Ellen, and their offspring.

Native-white unions had actually been first banned by Washington State already in 1855, but this miscegenation stature was ignored and actually reversed in 1868. Still, in 1876, as Fanny's husband died, federal law in the United States ensured that Natives could not inherit the property of their white husbands or fathers, though courts did make some exceptions granting biracial children as legitimate heirs. But it was possible to return to live in the Native communities. The 1876 Indian Act in Canada, in turn, declared that those Native women who married white men had their Native status revoked. Thus, if Fanny, Ellen, or their children chose to join kin in British Columbia, they became non-Natives by definition. But if they joined relatives in the Lummi Reservation, in Washington State, attended federal boarding schools, or married Native neighbors south of the borderline, they became full Natives and wards of the government disposed of their homelands in the Straits Salish. As it happened, Fanny's and Ellen's biracial children were subjected to forced removal. White educators took them from their nonwhite parents and exposed the children to schooling as well as indentured labor and sexual assaults. This later led to a dangerous cycle where these biracial children negotiated poverty, premarital pregnancy, and hard work and exploitation as domestic servants. It also led the children to marry white men and mixed-race women.

In negotiating the new realities of the settler colonial West, the lives of Fanny, Ellen, and their offspring were characterized by deep racial ambiguity and shifts in racial identity. In census records, Fanny and her children would consistently claim British Columbian origin and Canadian status. Ellen and her kids would alternate between U.S. and British/Canadian identities for several decades. By 1900, compelled to choose a singular racial identity, some of Fanny and Ellen's family members reclaimed Native status and enrolled in tribes. Others ignored their Native heritage and wanted to be recognized as whites.

As this case demonstrates, the imposition of national borders and the creation of settler colonial spaces not only partitioned many homelands but recalibrated intimacy and shaped affective economies. Like Fanny and Ellen, many communities with interracial marriages and biracial children faced difficult choices between whiteness and nativeness. They balanced between an effort to maintain their kinship networks and tribal social status on the one hand and carving a more secure legal standing in the eyes of the settler colonial government on the other. These borderlands peoples with complex, shifting identities included the Metis communities on the Red River of the North. Comprising of heterogeneous groups of peoples, their roots lay in the old North West Company, numerous indigenous communities, and the northern Plains fur trade. The Metis were assigned status as Canadian halfbreeds – habitually neglected by the Canadian government – or as American Indians – who went typically unrecognized by the settler nation. For good measure, both settler states regarded the Metis as border-crossing interlopers. In the Southwest, the

O'odham living in Arizona became recognized as Indians with their own reservation, while their kinsmen in Sonora did not enjoy similar status but occupied the lower rungs of the Mexican mainstream. Both the Metis and the O'odham faced increasingly hard times from the 1860s onward as incoming settlers, boosters, businessmen, government representatives, and armies took up their space. Their right of belonging was questioned as settler colonial states drove these groups to the margins of society. Metis families sought various trajectories between white and Indian worlds on both sides on the border. They, for instance, worked as laborers, scouts, and teamsters for the North American Boundary Commission in the 1870s. The O'odham also occupied a liminal cultural and political space between settler nations. They as well used the border that divided their homeland to their advantage and sought wage labor and economic opportunity on either side of it. In their varied ways, the Metis and the O'odham resisted and refused to choose a single national identity or place to live (or to vacate the borderlands) as state officials sought to control the border and regulate the lives of its peoples.

The emotional entanglements of borders, race, and whiteness also occupied the center stage when Anglos in the mid-1800s married into, usually prominent, Spanish-speaking families from California to Texas. Scholars have viewed this mixing as serving the economic motives of white men more than to indicate any incorporation to the Hispanic culture. While this was not always the case, it is an easy conclusion to reach, especially as, while not shying away from forming sexual relations with Mexican women, numerous whites showed open contempt toward all things Mexican. In the process, white borderlanders produced a discourse of miscegenation where the Mexicans were no longer Spanish but represented European empire-building gone terribly wrong. This discourse held that the Spanish had permanently lost their whiteness, "gone native" for good, when becoming Mexican. What used to be Spanish and white had by the 1800s become a swarthy, copper-colored, half-Indian, and an inherently flawed, treacherous, lazy, and intellectually handicapped race. The long list of intimate markers designating Mexican inferiority in Anglo eyes included chili-flavored food, crooked streets, dirty adobe "mud" houses, and weird sports. It also entailed poverty-stricken people, naked and repulsive children, and sexually licentious women who in their dress and behavior grossed the boundaries of decency just by, for instance, smoking tobacco and exposing their arms, necks, and ankles. Thus in the eyes of many borderlands whites, the borderlands Hispanics were failing in performing respectable whiteness on multiple levels. It is revealing of the weight placed on proper whiteness in settler colonial situations that while there had been those Americans who wanted more or the whole of Mexico at the zenith of the U.S.-Mexican War, those arguments prevailed that cautioned against this approach largely because whites felt Mexico had too many Mexicans who could potentially contaminate the whiteness of the U.S. settler empire.

Different colonial situations adopted quite diverse takes on interracial intimacies. In general, the fur trade society that spanned inland North America across the Pacific to New Zealand in the 1700s and early 1800s represented spaces where European empires and independent Natives relied on interracial sexual encounters and racial mixing to further trade, diplomacy, and cross-cultural networking. In this context, Native women played a pivotal role in ensuring their white husbands' success, access to hunting grounds, skins, and Native kin networks. Native communities, in turn, were motivated to monopolize the benefits transnational trade brought by ensuring that visiting French, British, Russian, Spanish, American, and other white traders fancied their women over neighboring groups for casual encounters or long-term unions. In this social fabric, sex was a major diplomatic and commercial asset, even if white men tended to view Native women as natural resources sexually available for the taking, and even if violence and captive-taking cast its long shadow on cross-cultural intimate relations. Interracial intimacies also frequently proved short and transient, discarded after their economic and social function waned. It is this heritage that Fanny and Ellen carried as their lives were altered by the settler colonial projects.

In fur trade societies, as well in other trading colonies around the globe, interracial sex and marriage did not necessarily lead to the assimilation and/or incorporation of white men to the Native world or vice versa. Moreover, it did not ease nervousness over racial boundaries and membership as colonial projects became increasingly nationalized projects in the late 1800s. Referred to as *nyai* in Java and Sumatra, *congai* in Indochina, and *petit épouse* throughout much of the French Empire, Native women living with European men as concubines proved the most common domestic arrangement in many nonsettler colonial situations. This lasted until the early twentieth century and, in many places, beyond. Decrees limiting concubinage were enacted, but they were largely left unforced, for instance, in the Dutch East Indies and throughout the British Empire (where concubinage was officially banned in 1910). The reason: concubinage was seen predominantly as a stabilizing force. It kept the white men – a mixed lot of shopkeepers, traders farmers, eccentrics, soldiers, sailors, and civilian administrators – out of brothels and sick wards and thus disease-free. It offered a good-enough substitute for home life and emotional comfort, which in turn made the men better businessmen and workers. Culturally, local women provided a prerequisite to speedy acclimatization, useful entryways to local languages and societies. Importantly, concubinage curtailed homosexual relations, often seen as "unnatural" and immoral, between European men.

A noticeable shift concerning metissage and concubinage happened unevenly and at different times in different places. Oftentimes the question who was European and who was not concerned name, upbringing, education, lifestyle, domesticity, home milieu, and respectability. All persons born in French Indochina, for instance, who had at least one parent presumed to be French, could claim recognition as "la qualité de francais." Yet there was a growing attack among colonial states against the intimate arrangements with Native women. These relations were seen to lower white men as they contracted immoral proclivities and susceptibility to uncivilized lifestyles. Soon these liaisons and the mixed offspring became perceived as a danger to the European community and the white race as such. The biracial offspring especially occupied a precarious ground between cultures, "dangerously" straddling the division between white and Native, between ruler and ruled, blurring that line and making it irrelevant. The cure to all this: legislation and white women.

In the Dutch East Indies, the law of 1898, stipulating that biracial children would receive European status only if their white fathers recognized them, tried to curtail the fact that concubinage remained the domestic arrangement of choice. It was also meant to curb another development that saw some European women choose to cohabit with non-European men. In German Southwest Africa, mixed marriages were officially forbidden in 1905. And this law took force retroactively, thus nullifying existing marriages and stripping biracial offspring of their rights as Germans. Similar laws were soon enacted in other German colonies. Besides laws, the "seduction" of white men by Native women needed to be curtailed by happy family life with white wives. Efforts targeted the prevention of racial degeneration as well as stemming the radicalization of the working class. Preference moved to hiring white recruits already married to white wives. Many of the imperial companies and colonial governments that previously banned white women began to welcome them with open arms by the early 1900s. One unintended consequence throughout Africa and much of the British Empire proved a growing hysteria over the "black peril," a metonym indicating the threat to colonial order caused by the "primitive sexual urges" Native men had toward white women. Take New Guinea, for instance. There the White Women's Protection Ordinance of 1926 provided the death penalty for rape or attempted rape of a European woman. Under these circumstances, "attempted rape" could mean pretty much any kind perceived transgression of social space.

In the American West, the term "miscegenation" was not coined until 1863, when the racial contact between whites and emancipated black slaves became an issue due to fears that racial mixing would reduce and contaminate the white race. Legislatures in almost all states introduced laws to prevent racial "amalgamation" and "miscegenation," and scientists and physicians warned of the risks that mixing brought. These measures reflected widely held social beliefs, but they mostly concerned the relations between whites and blacks. While blacks were coded as a sexual threat to the purity of the whole white settler project, Native Americans never were depicted in quite the similar manner. Yes, fears of Native male sexuality and rape of white women abounded in captivity narratives. And white men who married Native women were increasingly ostracized as "squaw men" in the eyes of the settler society, and their offspring despised as no good "half-bloods." Still, Natives were also at least sometimes close to acceptable spouses for whites, subject to acculturation and incorporation.

Only 12 states legislated against white-Native marriages in the United States, writes Katherine Ellinghaus. More typically, white-Native relationships and the offspring they produced could be understood in terms of assimilation to the settler society, or as a way for white men to gain access to tribal property rights. For a white woman marrying a Native man who lived an "Indian life" in a tribal society, things looked instantly more precarious. However, if Native men appeared more reformed, then the marriages could again make more sense in terms of assimilation. This was very much the case with Elaine Goodale Eastman's marriage to Sioux Charles Eastman. In Australia all sorts of inter-racial relationships – especially if long-term and "serious" rather than casual sexual encounters – were in turn seen as outside the bounds of normal society. Or they were interpreted as means for biological absorption, outlets toward whiteness as white men engaged in sex with nonwhite women were "breeding out the color." In the 1920s and 1930s, however, there rose public concerns that the growing mixed-race population could instead possibly threaten the nation's whiteness.

In settler colonial projects, notions concerning interracial sex and misce-genation were habitually linked with the drive to assimilate the Natives and with the fluid parameters of racial designation and membership. These tensions concerning the parameters of race and the assimilationist drive also regularly entangled with notions of land ownership and use. Here again perceived racial difference evoked policies of exclusion and ordered the realities of interracial intimacies into simpler dichotomies. While sovereignty in Euro-American eyes was theirs by virtue of discovery, the question of Native property rights, meaning whether land could be seized from the Natives or whether it needed to be purchased, was the subject of differing policies. In the steppe, Russians followed long-standing practices and simply declared property state land. The British treated Australia as terra nullius, unowned land, a definition that gave no legal recognition to Aboriginal land rights and indicated that land was free for the taking for whites. Even the critics of terra nullius, historian Stuart Banner shows, suggested only compensating the Aborigines and set-ting aside reserves for them. Encouraged by the precedent set in their North American colonies, Britain acknowledged the New Zealand Maoris as own-ers of all land, and the government acquired it through purchase from tribes until 1865. It helped that the Maoris practiced farming, which was always in white eyes a sign of civilization, had organized rights to particular lands, and proved militarily powerful. All these factors reduced the arguments for terra nullius and supported purchases. In Canada, land acquisition saw British Columbia treated as terra nullius, while other western provinces often obtained land through government purchases. The largest land exchanges were worked through the 11 numbered treaties made from 1871 to 1921 between the crown and indigenous communities in the Canadian West. Compared to the United States, historian Roger Nichols asserts, such treaties gave the tribal people less land, tiny annuities, and fewer benefits, but they were the product of intense negotiation where Native communities made successful demands for provisions such as hunting rights.

In the United States, powerful tribes, like Red Cloud's Sioux in 1868 or Cochise's Chiricahua Apaches in 1872, could make demands as equals. More often treaties and reservations were dictated by whites on Native groups who were militarily defeated, hit by diseases, impoverished, and/or internally divided. Sometimes the necessary signatures to make the treaties valid could be lured from the acculturated and/or biracial tribal members. Under American law, the federal government was the only lawful purchaser of Native land. Private purchasing was illegal. The government made treaties with Native tribes and then funneled the land to white buyers. This practice lasted until 1871 (the year Canada started making treaties) and after that the policy continued through other agreements that also ostensibly at least required the consent of Native tribes for any land transfer to take place. It has been calculated that the Louisiana Purchase landmass was taken over piecemeal in over 200 (222) cessions from 1804 onward. Still, there were exceptions. Jointly occupied by Britain and the United States, Oregon was in legal limbo before 1846 as white settlers poured in and took lands without any government purchase. California, Banner comments, was treated as terra nullius. The government got to California too late as a violent settler intrusion due to the gold rush in 1849 saw the Natives stripped of their lands. Furthermore, the early treaties negotiated in 1851 and 1852 went unratified by the U.S. Congress, and new ones were never signed. This was in part because California Natives were perceived as being more primitive than other Native Americans; they did not pose a military challenge and did not farm.

Numerous treaties made by federal representatives in the West went unratified by the budget-stingy and indifferent U.S. Congress. On the ground, land acquisitions were often riddled with structural inequalities, trespassing, and fraud that revolved around racial difference. Exploitation was so systematic that historian Jill St. Germain in her comparative analysis of U.S. and Canadian practices refers to a tradition of broken treaties. In her research, she juxtaposes the Treaty of 1868 between the Lakota Sioux and the United States and Treaty Six (1876) between Plains Cree and Dominion of Canada. St. Germain notes that the United States sought not only to arrest conflicts and bring land to white settler use but also to settle the Lakotas and start "civilization" measures aiming for their assimilation. Lakotas, in turn, wanted to protect as much of their lands as possible and secure hunting rights and compensation for any lands lost. For Crees, short on game due to white competition, protection and help in subsistence from Canada were the key issues. Canada's focus was on getting Cree lands as cheaply as possible. In both cases, whites approached the negotiations with a sense of superiority and an appearance of benevolence. They proclaimed to act for the good of the Indians while simultaneously projecting images of future ruin if the indigenous peoples would not comply.

From the Cree perspective, Canada did not hold up its end of the bargain. Crees first blamed ignorance and tried to make their grievances known and actively approached any Canadian official willing to listen. Their access, however, was more limited than the Lakotas, who sent several delegations to Washington. Frustrated Crees began to think that Canada knowingly deceived them. These frustrations were vented during the Northwest Rebellion in 1885. In the United States, the presence of independent Lakotas and the controversy over the ownership of the mineral-rich Black Hills, sacred to the Lakotas, led to the Great Sioux War in 1876. Afterward, the reduction of the Lakota reservation marked a new era of unilaterally developed and implemented Indian policy where the Lakotas had little say. In Canada, Cree and Canadian interpretations of Treaty Six remained as far apart as they ever had.

In the 1860s, Britain had already forged new rules in New Zealand. It wanted to quell Maori resistance to land sales by individualizing Native title, which meant that individuals could from now on sell their lots regardless of tribal opinion. In Canada, the Indian Act of 1876 organized an attack on tribal government. It called for Native enfranchisement and saw the crown issue location tickets giving individuals rights to particular plots within the reserves. In the United States, general allotment became the norm after 1887 and the Dawes Act. Allotment was also carried out at the Kat River Settlement in South Africa, at New Norcia in Western Australia, and elsewhere in places such as the steppe, where the Russian government deemed allotment the most efficient means to civilize the Kazakhs. According to the Dawes Act, each Indian head of house was eligible to receive a 160-acre tract of land; single individuals over the age of 18 would get 80 acres, and children under 18 would be given 40 acres. Authorities promoted allotment as a way to reduce government expenditures and to promote indigenous assimilation and the eradication of tribal structures, which supposedly held the indigenous individuals back in a permanent state of barbarism. The results were much the same: white land rush with numerous fraudulent sales well below market value coupled with Native alienation, alcoholism, poverty, and desperation. While in 1861 the Maori owned 22 million acres in the North Island, by 1911 their land mass had been cut down to seven million acres. In the United States, Native tribes owned an estimated 138 million acres in 1887, of which 52 million acres remained theirs in 1934 when the United States changed its policies in favor of tribal self-government. What was left was often the most barren lands. Not unlike the Native Americans, Kazakhs were forced to settle in the desert, on hilltops, and on mountainsides.

If the thinking on Native property rights varied, the general sentiment among whites across different settler spaces around the world was that they deserved the land: Natives did not use the land properly, but kept it as un-used wilderness. Many also believed that the Natives would somehow "nat-urally" disappear when coming to contact with a superior white civilization. Christian notions of "God's plan" were mixed with evolutionary theories as this line of thinking took on the guise of a more "scientific" discourse in the late nineteenth century. The accepted wisdom that "autogenocide" was taking place among Natives traveled remarkably well, circulating throughout North America as well as Australia, New Zealand, Tahiti, and French Algeria.

Comparing American and Russian civilizing mission of the northern Plains and the Kazakh steppe, historian Steven Sabol describes how each imperial gov-ernment considered their respective region to be underutilized, sparsely populated by a "vanishing race," and suitable for extensive agricultural development and settlement by the industrious and civilized white settlers. Seeing the Kazakhs in Russia as the "Red Indians of the West Siberian steppes," the Scott John Foster Fraser, known for his round-the-world bicycle outing, stated that the Russians "have conquered them, and pushed them upon the least fertile tracts of land to make room for immigrants. The race is decreasing in number, and will one of these days disappear from the face of the earth altogether." The Kazakhs must either die or be civilized so that Russia may exploit "land capable of immense agricultural possibilities, great stretches of prairie waiting for the plough... I saw a country that reminded me from the first day to the last... of the best parts of western America."[5]

While some authors across the global colonial map saw Native disappear-ance as inevitable, others worked on a theory that in order to prevent the "vanishing" from happening the Natives needed saving by whites. This civ-ilizing mission, and its goal assimilation, also appealed to those who realized that Native populations would not naturally "vanish" and that their continued presence represented a problem if nation-building rested on white homogene-ity as it often did in settler colonial projects. Utilizing concepts like primitive-ness, backwardness, and underdevelopment, assimilationists saw Native present as white past and thus turned the concept of time into a vehicle of power. Good-intentioned whites could pull the Natives up the evolutionary ladder through Christianity, education, and work. The colonial ideology in France, for instance, tended to celebrate its civilizing mission in Africa, especially in Algeria, with its large European population. It was able to draw from a globally applied stock of parental images: great white fathers, white mothers, and Native children. Together, these made for one happy family. In the Dutch East Indies, terms such as moral tutelage and parental guidance were inseparably linked to any commentary on Dutch presence in the area. Certainly these notions were familiar throughout the American West as well. Whether operating in

5 Quoted in Sabol, "Comparing American and Russian Internal Colonization," 40–41.

the West, or within the Russian, French, German, or British empires, those who believed that "civilizing" the Natives was not just possible, but the "right" thing to do, often employed an ambivalent desire to justify conquest and the taking of Native lands by seeing it as a civilizing mission offering backward peoples the benefits of the dynamic imperial culture. To be humanitarian in the 1800s was not to believe that Native cultures were equal to white culture, but rather to believe that with white tutelage and good training Natives could be elevated and become one day (nearly) as civilized as whites were.

Still, assimilation was not a universal goal, even in the settler colonies. By the early 1900s, France moved from a position of assimilation to association in its Muslim colonies. This policy stressed respect for local customs and segregation of the colonized from the Natives. It was criticized by socialists and feminists for denying French civilization to colonized peoples. Most nonsettler British colonies also relied on association rather than assimilation, as did the German colonies in the Pacific.

Yet, on the Great Plains and on the steppe, assimilation, Sabol explains, became the goal as the Americans and Russians denigrated and destabilized the sociopolitical structures of the Sioux and the Kazakhs. Civilian agents, army officers, and missionaries were part of a process of interference and efforts to change indigenous cultures. There were few more important tools in this process than the Bible. Translated into a whopping 500 languages by the end of the nineteenth century, it proved the most obvious path from barbarity to civilization in the colonial world. Missions involved religious ceremonies, teaching in schools, medical outreach and hospitals, agricultural projects, and printing ventures. They proved extremely active in promoting their version of colonialism and advancing it on the ground.

In the West and elsewhere, segregated Native spaces, known as reserves, reservations, or camps, became spaces for Native assimilation. Moreover, they became spaces for white control and refashioning of Native lives where whites told the Natives how they should live and work, what they should look like, and how to worship; in general, what to do, and where, when, and how they could do it. Management of subject peoples happened through the reorganizing of Native living space and the regulation of labor and cultural practices. Many reservations, for instance, insisted that Natives live in "civilized" houses, not in their own dwellings. They also imposed strict temperance campaigns designed to stop indigenous alcohol production and consumption. Native cultural practices such as the Sun Dance were outlawed not only in the United States but also on the Canadian Plains. These forms of power operated in concert with extensive farming programs that gave little consideration to indigenous practices (even if the Natives had been farming for generations) or the suitability of the land for agriculture. The design also included flipping Native gender roles. Native men should be placed in farm work through individual freeholds (thus replicating the settler dream of yeoman lifestyles), and women's place was the domestic sphere in accordance with Victorian values.

Reservation regeneration was grounded on notions that Natives were by their nature lazy, dishonest, frivolous, brutal, and impulsive and that these behavioral patterns of "unruly children" needed to be eradicated through strong "parental guidance" by the whites. Parental images abounded as Natives were referred to and treated like children, ignorant, if not innocent, wards who needed stern parental guidance. Native women were often represented as helpless drudges and the men as tyrannical loafers prone to polygamy. Used to assert the validity of colonial rule, parental images were not unique to colonial situations. Instead, notions of unruly children who needed civic education before being capable of self-government as adult citizens were widely used in the public discussion dealing with peasants and working-class people in Europe and the eastern United States.

Erasing hundreds of years of savagery took firm measures. Intimidation, violence, and surveillance became the standard in many places. So did tags. At the White Mountain Reservation in Arizona in the 1870s, each Apache man was numbered and had to carry with him, day and night, his metal check, with the number and designation of his tribe stamped thereon. The officer in charge then had a corresponding record with the number of members in each family and a personal description of every man. Obviously, day-to-day policies varied quite a bit. At some reserves, for instance in New Zealand, the Natives were not subject to surveillance and control measures like they were in the West, Australia, and Canada. Also, while the United States demanded that all Natives become small farmers, seeing farming as a step upward from hunter-gatherer lifestyles in human evolution, officials in Canada at least recognized that ranching often represented a more plausible option on the Plains.

Furthermore, as historian Tim Rowse has suggested for Australia, rationing in colonial situations was a vehicle for surveying and controlling colonized peoples. The different goods and the ways they were distributed formed the relationship through which the forging of social routines, dependencies, and surveillance took place. Typically, the indigenous people had to gather at the agency or make the symbolic crossing to some other white-controlled space. They needed to come at regular intervals dictated by whites, not their own needs, in order to receive the white man's food and supplies. They also needed to wait where told, form lines, proceed in an order dictated by whites, and receive without complain what was given – no matter how meager, unsuited, or offensive to their cultural beliefs. In Arizona, Apaches had to gather near the agency from all sections, each band seating themselves separately, men generally distinct from the women. Army officers counted them and then distributed ration tickets, after which the 1,500 people present were admitted, in a line, to a small stockade where they received their ration of corn as it was scooped out to them as well as a piece of beef. Numerous Apaches protested with remarks of most obscene character that they wanted more and snatched any morsel they could put their hands on. In three hours, the ritual was over, and the people dispersed, the next rationing taking place in five days time.

Indigenous child removal and schooling constituted noteworthy civilizing weapons in the arsenal of the state in different imperial settings. According to historian Margaret Jacobs, in the American West "assimilation" and in Australia "protection" implied similar policies of indigenous child removal designed to "save" and "civilize" the children. While making the children "useful" members of the society, these policies aimed at reducing indigenous dependency on government aid. The method worked to break the affective bonds that tied the children to their mothers, families, communities, and homelands and regenerate the children in socially isolated institutions where they would associate with white female teachers. There the children would be regenerated and made into clones of whites: to look, dress, behave, and think like the whites. If the children did not want to go, they could be forced to participate.

Education had a broader function in enabling the success of Victorian social values across the racial and social spectrum. The authority of the middle class was secured by private schools and institutions of higher education, which, like elementary-level whites-only schools, were set up across the settler colonial terrain, from Arizona to Kenya and Australia. Education also pushed working-class offspring toward higher standards and subjected Native children to civilization. Historian Michael Coleman writes about how between the early nineteenth and the early twentieth centuries both the Native Americans and the Irish confronted systematic, state-controlled, and assimilationist educational campaigns as the United States strove to Americanize the Indians and the British government to Anglicize the Irish. To effect long-term permanent change through assimilation, the missionary schools gave way to Bureau of Indian Affairs (BIA) built day schools and boarding schools for Indian children. The British government in turn launched a nationwide elementary school system in Ireland, administered by the commissioners of national education.

By 1902 the BIA had established some 150 boarding schools and a similar number of day schools, while in Canada, 177 day schools for Native children were in operation in 1895. The schools included instruction in behavior and dress, while practical skills such as handicrafts and industrial skills were taught to boys. For girls the emphasis was on the diffusion of domesticity, reproduction and marital practices, household skills, and maternalism. White female teachers played active roles in carrying out and advocating schooling, painting it as a benevolent act. They concurrently stigmatized Native mothers as unloving and incompetent and Native families and living environments as filthy, degenerate, and backward. In all instances, the schools targeted the erasure of minority cultures and identities. The rigidly ethnocentric curriculum aimed to strip the students of tribal cultures, languages, and spiritual concepts and turn the children into cultural brokers who would carry the new order back to their own peoples. Yet in terms of social mobility, this schooling actually promised the Natives little more than a role at the bottom rungs of the settler society.

Some scholars, like historian Andrew Woolford, who has investigated indigenous boarding schools in Canada (Manitoba) and the United States (New Mexico), argue that this kind of forced assimilation constitutes a form of genocide. The results certainly were often traumatic. There was plenty of misery, homesickness, and deadly disease at the schools. Cultural alienation was common as students lost touch with their families. After school ended, problems often multiplied. Children who got out did not fit into their Native societies nor the white world. Apparently, some realized then for the first time that they were not white. On the other hand, many Natives returned home from schools determined to remain Natives. Education had brought indigenous peoples into trans-imperial circuits of knowledge, enabling them to use their knowledge of English literature and Christianity to protest and petition colonial authorities.

As the civilizing mission shook their world, indigenous communities, like so many peoples throughout world history, sought solace from religion for their everyday misery and emotional confusion. Combining Christian beliefs with Native practices, Western Apaches, Paiutes, Comanches, the Sioux, and others turned to religious revivalism in search of hope of a better tomorrow. The best known of these movements are the various manifestations of the Ghost Dance religion in the 1880s and 1890s. They typically advocated the return of old Indian practices, including abstinence, living plainly, and the return of game such as the bison. They also prophesized the return of old leaders and kin coupled with the disappearance of the whites. Like the Ghost Dance, the Boxer movement in China was part of this spiritual anticolonial struggle driven by religious beliefs that advocated a return of old ways. These movements that frequently led to violent outbursts shared stories of colonial dispossession, frustration, drought, and hunger, as well as foreign invasion and cultural infiltration. Furthermore, some Native dancers and the Boxers apparently assumed they could become impervious to Western weapons. In Africa, practitioners of Mumboism, an anticolonial movement in the Nyanza region of British Kenya, also believed that spells could repel bullets of the white settlers. Historians Dominic Capeci and Jack C. Knight write how the Sioux embraced a theology that practiced peace and used ritualized resistance of the Ghost Dance, while the Maji-Maji of German East Africa applied the Bokero Cult for similar purposes. But both movements culminated in violence. During the winter of 1890, U.S. soldiers smashed a group of Sioux dancers at Wounded Knee, while German attacks eventually killed hundreds of thousands of East Africans between 1905 and 1907.

While the civilizing mission spread across the colonial world, the United States exported its version of conquest and colonization from the Native communities of the West to its overseas empire. Sweeping aside the remains of Spain's imperial power in a one-sided war in 1898, the United States took control of the Philippines, Guam, Puerto Rico, and Cuba. Although Cuba gained nominal independence, the United States brutally suppressed Filipino resistance from 1899 to 1902 and then kept the Philippines for a half a century. It still has Puerto Rico and Guam as colonies. Pressure from the U.S. sugar industry led to the annexation of the independent Hawaii at the same time, and in 1903, American officials engineered a revolt in the Panamanian section of Columbia. The president organizing the Panama coup, Theodore Roosevelt, who had missed the Indian wars, represented himself as the embodiment of Western manhood. The coup not only fashioned Panamanian independence under American tutelage but also enabled the U.S. administrative control of the zone in which to build the canal connecting the Atlantic and the Pacific. The Panama Canal opened in 1914, boosting American influence regionally and globally. It mimicked the British actions and interests in the Suez Canal route, though Americans retained more direct control of the valuable shortcut.

Many administrators and almost all of the American generals in the Philippines had previous experience in the U.S.–Indian wars. They wanted to distinguish their own overseas empire from European rivals by modernizing and civilizing their newly acquired colony in a manner they had done already in the West. They wanted to see themselves and be seen as benevolent rulers, while the Filipinos constituted unruly children with generations of savagery that needed erasing. To this end, they built roads and dams and fostered scientific forestry. They introduced widespread schooling in the Philippines and advocated moral reform. They also strove to ban opium smoking and supported giving up this lucrative business. This made the Americans to see themselves as morally superior to other empires, and they employed the kind of self-celebratory rhetoric to that end. Their empire should not be morally stained like the British Raj, which sanctioned licensed prostitution. While realities in prostitution and in sale and use of alcohol proved different in the Philippines and elsewhere than this rhetoric, the goals supporting the moral exceptionalism of the United States were served. In 1900, U.S. senator Albert J. Beveridge defined the United States' presence in the Philippines as a chivalric mission to rescue the Natives who could not govern themselves.

As we have seen, the intimate realm was crucial as colonial powers engaged in the coercive incorporation of people into an expansionist state and invidious distinction, rule of difference, which involved hierarchies and ranking and othering of peoples based on race, ethnicity, class, gender, nationality, or religion. And none of the colonial powers acted in isolation, but the local and the global, the colonies and the metropole, and the different empires operated in entangled spaces. They were caught in circulations of ideas and knowledge and constituted relationships of rivalries, borrowing, and influence. Subject to constant negotiation and contestation, these intimacies of empire were typically fragile and permeable creations punctured with mobile identities and relations, dynamic constructs that needed to be produced, maintained, and guarded. We can see how colonial empires consisted of a maze of contradictions and instabilities, a mosaic of social differences and ethnic and religious antagonisms, of compilations of conflicting discourses and relations where communities were anything but internally coherent and identity and power were typically fragmented and unstable.

Bibliography

Performing Whiteness

Adams, Kevin. *Class and Race in the Frontier Army: Military Life in the West, 1870–1890.* Norman: University of Oklahoma Press, 2009.

Arenson, Adam. "Anglo-Saxonism in the Yukon: The Klondike Nugget and American-British Relations in the 'Two Wests,' 1898–1901." *Pacific Historical Review* 76 (August 2007): 373–404.

Ballantyne, Tony, and Antoinette Burton, eds. *Bodies in Contact: Rethinking Colonial Encounters in World History.* Durham: Duke University Press, 2005.

_____. *Moving Subjects: Gender, Mobility, and Intimacy in an Age of Global Empire.* Urbana: University of Illinois Press, 2009.

Carter, Sarah. *Imperial Plots: Women, Land, and the Spadework of British Colonialism on the Canadian Prairies.* Winnipeg: University of Manitoba Press, 2016.

_____. "Transnational Perspectives on the History of Great Plains Women: Gender, Race, Nations, and the Forty-Ninth Parallel." *American Review of Canadian Studies* 33 (Winter 2003): 565–596.

Chase, Karen. *The Spectacle of Intimacy.* Princeton: Princeton University Press, 2000.

Chaudhuri, Nupur, and Margaret Strobel, eds. *Western Women and Imperialism: Complicity and Resistance.* Bloomington: Indiana University Press, 1992.

Clancy-Smith, Julia, and Frances Gouda, eds. *Domesticating the Empire: Race, Gender, and Family Life in French and Dutch Colonialism.* Charlottesville: University Press of Virginia, 1998.

Collingham, E. M. *Imperial Bodies: The Physical Experience of the Raj.* Cambridge: Polity, 2001.

Cooper, Frederick, and Ann Laura Stoler, eds. *Tensions of Empire: Colonial Cultures in a Bourgeois World.* Berkeley: University of California Press, 1997.

Cozens, Erin Ford. "'With a Pretty Little Garden at the Back': Domesticity and the Construction of "Civilized" Colonial Spaces in Nineteenth-Century Aotearoa/ New Zealand." *Journal of World History* 25 (December 2014): 515–534.

Delgado, Grace Peña. "Border Control and Sexual Policing: White Slavery and Prostitution along the U.S.-Mexico Borderlands, 1903–1901." *Western Historical Quarterly* 43 (Summer 2012): 157–178.

Farwell, Byron. *Armies of the Raj: From the Great Indian Mutiny to Independence, 1858–1947.* New York: W. W. Norton, 1989.

Hoganson, Kristin. *Consumers' Imperium: The Global Production of American Domesticity, 1865–1920.* Chapel Hill: University of North Carolina Press, 2007.

Jackson, Brenda K. *Domesticating the West: The Re-creation of the Nineteenth-Century American Middle Class.* Lincoln: University of Nebraska Press, 2005.

Jameson, Elizabeth, and Sheila McManus, eds. *One Step Over the Line: Toward a History of Women in the North American Wests.* Edmonton: University of Alberta Press, 2008.

Kennedy, Dane. *Islands of White: Settler Society and Culture in Kenya and Southern Rhodesia, 1890–1939.* Durham: Duke University Press, 1987.

_____. *The Magic Mountains: Hill Stations and the British Raj*. Berkeley: University of California Press, 1996.

Lahti, Janne. *Cultural Construction of Empire: The U.S. Army in Arizona and New Mexico*. Lincoln: University of Nebraska Press, 2012.

Lorcin, Patricia M. E. *Imperial Identities: Stereotyping, Prejudice, and Race in Colonial Algeria*. Lincoln: University of Nebraska Press, 1999.

McInnis, Verity G. *Women of Empire: Nineteenth-Century Army Officers' Wives in India and the U.S. West*. Norman: University of Oklahoma Press, 2017.

McKiernan-González, John. *Fevered Measures: Public Health and Race at the Texas-Mexico Border, 1848–1942*. Durham: Duke University Press, 2012.

Peers, Douglas M. "Colonial Knowledge and the Military in India, 1780–1860." *Journal of Imperial and Commonwealth History* 33 (May 2005): 157–180.

Perry, Adele. *On the Edge of Empire: Gender, Race, and the Making of British Columbia, 1849–1871*. Toronto: Toronto University Press, 2001.

Prescott, Cynthia Culver. *Gender and Generation on the Far Western Frontier*. Tucson: University of Arizona Press, 2007.

Procida, Mary A. *Married to the Empire: Gender, Politics and Imperialism in India, 1883–1947*. Manchester: Manchester University Press, 2002.

Riley, Glenda. *Taking Land, Breaking Land: Women Colonizing the American West and Kenya, 1840–1940*. Albuquerque: University of New Mexico Press, 2003.

Rotchild, Emma. *The Inner Life of Empires*. Princeton: Princeton University Press, 2012.

Shadle, Brett L. *The Souls of White Folk: White Settlers in Kenya, 1900s–1920s*. Manchester: Manchester University Press, 2015.

Stoler, Ann Laura. *Carnal Knowledge and Imperial Power: Race and the Intimate in Colonial Rule*. Berkeley: University of California Press, 2002.

_____, ed. *Haunted by Empire: Geographies of Intimacy in North American History*. Durham: Duke University Press, 2006.

Strobel, Margaret. *European Women and the Second British Empire*. Bloomington: Indiana University Press, 1991.

Thorp, Daniel. "Going Native in New Zealand and America: Comparing Pakeha Maori and White Indians." *Journal of Imperial and Commonwealth History* 31 (September 2003): 1–23.

Wildenthal, Lora. *German Women for Empire, 1884–1945*. Durham: Duke University Press, 2001.

Woollacott, Angela. *Gender and Empire*. New York: Palgrave, 2006.

_____. *Settler Society in the Australian Colonies: Self-Government and Imperial Culture*. Oxford: Oxford University Press, 2015.

Parameters of Race

Adams, David Wallace, and Crista DeLucio, eds. *On the Borders of Love and Power: Families and Kinship in the Intercultural American Southwest*. Berkeley: University of California Press, 2012.

Adas, Michael. *Prophets of Rebellion: Millenarian Protest Movements against the European Colonial Order*. Chapel Hill: University of North Carolina Press, 1979.

Anderson, Warwick. *The Cultivation of Whiteness: Science, Health, and Racial Destiny in Australia*. New York: Basic Books, 2003.

Banner, Stuart. *Possessing the Pacific: Land, Settlers, and Indigenous People from Australia to Alaska*. Cambridge, MA: Harvard University Press, 2007.

Brantlinger, Patrick. *Dark Vanishings: Discourse on the Extinction of Primitive Races, 1800–1930*. Ithica: Cornell University Press, 2003.

Briggs, Laura. *Reproducing Empire: Race, Sex, Science, and U.S. Imperialism in Puerto Rico*. Berkeley: University of California Press, 2002.

Capeci, Dominic J. Jr., and Jack C. Knight, "Reactions to Colonialism: The North American Ghost Dance and East African Maji-Maji Rebellions." *The Historian* 52 (August 1990): 584–602.

Coleman, Michael C. *American Indians, the Irish, and Government Schooling: A Comparative Study*. Lincoln: University of Nebraska Press, 2007.

Conklin, Alice L. *A Mission to Civilize: The Republican Idea of Empire in France and West Africa, 1895–1930*. Stanford: Stanford University Press, 1997.

Connell-Szasz, Margaret. *Scottish Highlanders and Native Americans: Indigenous Education in the Eighteenth-Century Atlantic World*. Norman: University of Oklahoma Press, 2007.

Curtis, Sarah A. *Civilizing Habits: Women Missionaries and the Revival of French Empire*. Oxford: Oxford University Press, 2010.

Ellinghaus, Katherine. *Taking Assimilation to Heart: Marriages of White Women and Indigenous Men in the United States and Australia, 1887–1937*. Lincoln: University of Nebraska Press, 2006.

Ellingson, Ter. *The Myth of the Noble Savage*. Berkeley: University of California Press, 2001.

Etherington, Norman, ed. *Missions and Empire*. Oxford: Oxford University Press, 2005.

Ford, Lisa. *Settler Sovereignty: Jurisdiction and Indigenous People in America and Australia, 1788–1836*. Cambridge, MA: Harvard University Press, 2010.

Galbraith, John S. "Appeals to the Supernatural: African and New Zealand Comparisons with the Ghost Dance." *Pacific Historical Review* 51 (1982): 115–133.

Haake, Claudia. *The State, Removal and Indigenous Peoples in the United States and Mexico, 1620–2000*. New York: Routledge, 2007.

Hirsch, Jennifer. *A Courtship after Marriage: Sexuality and Love in Mexican Transnational Families*. Berkeley: University of California Press, 2003.

Hogue, Michel. *Metis and the Medicine Line: Creating a Border and Dividing a People*. Chapel Hill: University of North Carolina Press, 2015.

Hyam, Ronald. *Empire and Sexuality*. Manchester: Manchester University Press, 1991.

Jacobs, Margaret D. *White Mother to a Dark Race: Settler Colonialism, Maternalism, and the Removal of Indigenous Children in the American West and Australia, 1880–1940*. Lincoln: University of Nebraska Press, 2009.

_____. *A Generation Removed: The Fostering and Adoption of Indigenous Children in the Postwar World*. Lincoln: University of Nebraska Press, 2014.

Jagodinsky, Katrina. *Legal Codes & Talking Trees: Indigenous Women's Sovereignty in the Sonoran and Puget Sound Borderlands, 1854–1946*. New Haven: Yale University Press, 2016.

Kramer, Paul A. *The Blood of Government: Race, Empire, the United States and the Philippines*. Chapel Hill: University of North Carolina Press, 2006.

Laidlaw, Zoe, and Alan Lester, eds. *Indigenous Communities and Settler Colonialism: Land Holding, Loss and Survival in an Interconnected World*. New York: Palgrave Macmillan, 2015.

Levine, Philippa. *Prostitution, Race, and Politics: Policing Venereal Disease in the British Empire*. New York: Routledge, 2003.

McClintock, Anne. *Imperial Leather: Race, Gender, and Sexuality in the Colonial Contest*. New York: Routledge, 1995.

McGrath, Ann. *Illicit Love: Interracial Sex and Marriage in the United States and Australia.* Lincoln: University of Nebraska Press, 2015.

Meeks, Eric V. *Border Citizens: The Making of Indians, Mexicans, and Anglos in Arizona.* Austin: University of Texas Press, 2007.

Nichols, Roger L. *Indians in the United States and Canada: A Comparative History.* Lincoln: University of Nebraska Press, 1998.

Pascoe, Peggy. *What Comes Naturally: Miscegenation Law and the Making of Race in America.* Oxford: Oxford University Press, 2009.

Perry Adele. *Colonial Relations: The Douglas-Connolly Family and the Nineteenth-Century Imperial World.* Cambridge: Cambridge University Press, 2017.

Renda, Mary A. *Taking Haiti: Military Occupation and the Culture of U.S. Imperialism, 1915–1940.* Chapel Hill: University of North Carolina Press, 2001.

Rowse, Tim. *White Flour, White Power: From Rations to Citizenship in Central Australia.* Cambridge: Cambridge University Press, 1998.

Sabol, Steven. "Comparing American and Russian Internal Colonization: The 'Touch of Civilization' on the Sioux and Kazakhs." *Western Historical Quarterly* 43 (Spring 2012): 29–51.

Shah, Nayan. *Stranger Intimacy: Contesting Race, Sexuality and the Law in the North American West.* Berkeley: University of California Press, 2012.

St. Germain, Jill. *Indian Treaty-Making Policy in the United States and Canada, 1867–1877.* Lincoln: University of Nebraska Press, 2004.

_____. *Broken Treaties: United States and Canadian Relations with the Lakotas and the Plains Cree, 1868–1885.* Lincoln: University of Nebraska Press, 2009.

Van Kirk, Sylvia. *"Many Tender Ties": Women in Fur-Trade Society in Western Canada, 1670–1870.* Winnipeg: Watson and Dwyer, 1980.

Williams, Walter L. "United States Indian Policy and the Debate over Philippine Annexation: Implications for the Origins of American Imperialism." *Journal of American History* 66 (March 1980): 810–831.

Woolford, Andrew. *This Benevolent Experiment: Indigenous Boarding Schools, Genocide, and Redress in Canada and the United States.* Lincoln: University of Nebraska Press, 2015.

5

IMPERIAL EYES

In 1910, agent Johan Adrian Jacobsen was busy rushing to the Pine Ridge Reservation in South Dakota. This Norwegian was not the kind of agent usually mentioned in history books in relation to the Sioux; he was not an employee of the federal government. Instead, this well-known adventurer and ethnologist was in the service of one Carl Hagenbeck, a German merchant with a long career in selling wild animals – to American P. T. Barnum, for example. Hagenbeck was also an entrepreneur exhibiting "savage" populations. Since the mid-1870s, he had recruited Sámi, Sudanese, Mongols, Hindus, Australian Aborigines, Bella Coola (Nuxalk) Indians from British Columbia, and other indigenous peoples from around the world to perform in hugely popular human exhibits that toured Germany, Britain, and much of Europe. In 1907, he opened a permanent Tierpark, or zoo, in Stellingen outside Hamburg, Germany. Its attractions included exotic animals as well as exotic peoples put on display in extravagant ethnographic villages and in bloodcurdling performances. Each troupe could include as many as several hundred people. And this was the reason why Hagenbeck had hired his old friend Jacobsen, who came with massive experience in recruiting peoples for ethnographic shows, and dispatched him to Pine Ridge. His job was to get the Sioux to come to Stellingen. But Jacobsen needed to hurry because five other agents working for competing entrepreneurs were also converging on the reservation, while Buffalo Bill's representative was also reportedly on his way.

That the Sioux were in such high demand speaks not only of their experience as performers but also of the global popularity of human exhibitions featuring Native Americans. Eventually Jacobsen managed to hire over 40 Indians from Pine Ridge, among them several veteran showmen who had already toured with William F. Cody, known as Buffalo Bill, in the 1880s and 1890s. In Stellingen, the Sioux dressed in feathered headdresses and other regalia expected of them by audiences familiar with the West from dime novels and human shows. They also occupied a "traditional" teepee village. Their program, historian Eric Ames writes, comprised dances, horse-stealing acts, and ambushes of settlers and the Pony Express. With the revenge motif and last-minute rescues, it was a pretty much the standard package recycled from the "Wild West shows." In this case, familiar meant the same as popular. During their five-month stay at Hagenbeck's zoo, the Sioux were gazed at by 1.1 million visitors. It is safe to say they were a big hit among the Germans eyeing for imperial amusements.

The European and global fascination with the American West not only goes back several generations but is comprised of an expansive assortment of connections, diverse forms of mobility, and variations of entanglements. Prominent among those engaging the West were the upper-class European travel writers whose lives crossed multiple borders and who personally eyed the West from the early 1800s onward. They used it as a source of inspiration, a reference point for global empires, or as a stage for amusement. In search of adventure and the exotic, they came for wild natives, pristine and majestic wilderness, and great beasts. The first two they wanted to glimpse, draw inspiration from, take notes on, capture with pen and paintbrush, and collect material artifacts/samples from them. The animals they preferred to shoot. Armed with varying pedigrees of scientific and/or artistic knowledge and aspiration, as well as erratic hunting skills, European travelers often brought along their dogs, sporting guns, and servants, and always the attitudes and prejudices of their class. Not all published books or articles about their experiences, although many did, and most at least penned letters or kept private diaries. A good number also hauled sizable quantities of Western specimens (including bison) and artifacts back home to Europe. They also spread the word on the West through their family and social connections. In the process, these European travelers typically viewed the West in a deexceptionalized context and integrated it to the mental landscapes of global empires. Especially in the early twentieth century, American travelers similarly headed abroad, in search of the last frontier and hoping to find the equivalent of the rugged and untamed West in some corner of the increasingly colonized world.

The West also featured opulently in the imperial visions of Europeans contemplating expansion. During the *Kaiserreich*, the American westward expansion worked as an inspiration in German domestic debates relating to settler expansion and as a model for concrete colonial policies in the Prussian East (German–Polish borderlands) and in Southwest Africa. Later, the conquest of the West also stimulated many of the influential Nazis. Its role as inspiration and precedent was not limited to Europe, but perceptions of the West shaped Japanese conquests as well. In fact, only the dearth of scholarship on the American West as an imperial inspiration prevents us from seeing what other imperial regimes and colonial projects the West encouraged and played precursor to.

And then there were the human exhibitions. It was Columbus who first brought Native peoples from the Caribbean to Europe, while Hernán Cortés did the same with the mainland Aztecs. This trend was later extended, by Jacques Cartier, for instance, who exported Natives from Quebec to France, and by the English, who shipped indigenous visitors from Roanoke. An early Indian delegation from the West, from present-day Kansas and Missouri, visited the French court, performed dances at the Paris opera, and demonstrated riding skills in the royal woods. This was in 1724. These early exports of exotic peoples and their performances were mainly meant to be royal and noble amusement. As the culture industries of the 1800s extended across multiple borders, they turned the European and American fascination of the "other" into a global business that increasingly catered to mass audiences. Various types of human exhibitions displayed colonized peoples and performed colonialism as a thrilling adventure and as a noble and triumphant advance of civilization. These entertainments could be found in international expositions, and they also went under the rubric of "Wild West shows," "people shows" (*Völkerschau*), "freak shows," and anthropozoological shows (Hagenbeck's would fall under this category). Some modern scholars have lumped these exhibitions under the common name "human zoos." They gained new momentum in the late 1800s and became a hugely popular part of the *fin de siécle* era attractions, while gradually losing their zeal by the mid-1900s.

When taken together, the travel authors, interimperial inspirations, and human zoos, as well as other forms of cultural production such as novels, movies, and comics demonstrate some key points in how the West has caught the imperial eyes of Europe and the wider world. Whether Buffalo Bill, Carl Hagenbeck, Adolf Hitler, Rudyard Kipling, Isabella Bird, or *The Leatherstocking Tales* and the Italian-made Western comic *Tex Willer*, the West has displayed remarkable portability in its various entanglements with Europe and the world. The West has reached to the world, engaged it, entered its psyche, and fed its interests, dreams, and imaginations, while the world has appropriated, represented, and reacted to the West. Unquestionably, the flows and influences have advanced in multiple directions, producing histories that have operated on varied scales and occupied different spaces. Some of these connections and circulations are discussed here.

Travel Writers

It has been estimated that close to 2,000 travel books were published between 1830 and 1900 in the United States alone. The volume of travel writing exploded especially in the late 1800s as numerous books and periodicals told tales of various parts of the world to growing European and American audiences captivated by distant and exotic places and thirsting for adventure and knowledge. One of the more popular genres in English literature, travel writing has typically been underutilized, as well as overlooked, by today's scholars studying the American West and the global empires. Many simply dismiss it as biased and/or sentimental writings of perennial outsiders. They should think twice. In colonial situations, literary scholar Mary Louise Pratt explains, travel writings constituted one tool in justifying conquest and building hierarchies of difference – sometimes in the form of dichotomies – between the ostensibly civilized Euro-American spaces and the exotic and uncivilized terrains of what can be called the "rest of the world." Yet travel writings, historian David Wrobel explicates, were not always straightforward accounts justifying colonialism as dozens of nineteenth-century travelers produced complicated and contradictory portraits of the world and the role of empires in it. Some of these travelers also crossed into the West, observed and placed it in a broader global context, and used it as a springboard to champion as well as criticize empire building.

One eyewitness to the global reach of empires in the mid-1800s was the Hamburg-born German Friedrich Gerstäcker. His first visit to the United States lasted five years in the late 1830s and early 1840s and spanned Arkansas, Ohio, Texas, and Louisiana. During this time, Gerstäcker worked, for example, as a hunter, a cattle herder, and a fireman on a steamboat. Returning to Germany, his articles and novels – including such titles as *The Regulators in Arkansas* and *The River Pirates of the Mississippi* – portrayed frontier life and adventure and made Gerstäcker a household name in German-speaking areas.

From 1849 to 1852, Gerstäcker traversed the world. His route took him from the German settlements in Latin America to gold rush California, Hawaii, the British Wests in Australia and New Zealand, and the Dutch East Indies (Java). This time adopting more the role of a critical observer, he compared imperial regimes and their impacts on local peoples. His account, *Narrative of a Journey Round the World*, saw daylight in Germany, Britain, and the United States in 1853. Reaching San Francisco, Gerstäcker wrote how he was "simply bewildered" by the profusion of people, makeshift accommodations (tents), and the never-ending activity. "The eye found no time to take in all at once," he commented. Every place was packed to the max, even the bay itself.

> A perfect forest of them opened at once to our sight. Ship after ship, forming a perfect town upon the water, filled the inner bay, and hundreds of little boats and small sailing crafts were darting everywhere over the yet unoccupied places. [1]

Gerstäcker recorded confusion and excitement, as well as meetings with Mexicans, Frenchmen, Spaniards, Germans, Texans, Yankees, and Indians from India.

---

1 Friedrich Gerstäcker, *Narrative of a Journey Round the World* (New York: Harper, 1853), 135.

He thought it remarkable that the whole world was there in this rather unremarkable place that just a few months earlier had been a small, sleepy, and out-of-the-way Mexican hamlet on the Pacific coast. He drew several parallels between the California Indians and the Aboriginal Australians, rationalizing that they were the least warlike Natives in the world. He also expressed sadness and anger on how the Natives were being taken advantage and driven to desperation on the opposite sides of the Pacific, how they were killed in scores by prospectors rushing in from all corners of the world.

Captivated by how imperial expansions brought together peoples from diverse parts, yet critical of the impacts settler booms had on the indigenous peoples, Gerstäcker would go on to make a tremendously productive career as a travel writer. In 1867–1868, he once more returned to the United States on an extended journey across the continent. Traveling mostly by train this time, the trip also spanned into Mexico from where the French had recently been driven off and to West Indies, Ecuador, and Venezuela. In the course of his lifetime, Gerstäcker visited five continents, as well as several islands in the Pacific and Indian oceans, all along placing the West in a global context. In the end, his travel stories and novels numbered in the hundreds. Succumbing to a stroke in 1872, he was a widely popular celebrity author on the world stage. Still, Gerstäcker is relatively little known and certainly understudied today.

This is definitely not the case with the British authors Charles Dickens, James A. Froude, Robert Louis Stevenson, Oscar Wilde, and Rudyard Kipling. They are all eminent names, but comparatively little has been made of the fact that they all entered the West at one time or another as travel authors. Typically, Western destinations formed a slice of their larger journeys that spanned Australia, Southeast Asia, and India. And yes, they habitually situated the West against these larger imperial horizons, commenting on and contrasting its nature, peoples, and imperial traits. Take, for instance, Kipling, the hugely popular Anglo-Indian fiction author and the man behind the quintessential imperial poem "White Man's Burden." This poem addressed the U.S. conquest of the Philippines, but it resonated globally and was widely interpreted to justify colonialism as a noble civilizing enterprise. In 1889, ten years before penning his influential poem, Kipling had crossed the West on his way from India to London. Having just ended a stint as a newspaper editor in India, his travel itinerary compassed California, Oregon, Washington, British Columbia, Montana, Wyoming, Utah, Colorado, and Nebraska. En route Kipling sent numerous letters to his newspaper publishers in India, where they stirred the imaginations of an appreciative audience. He represented the West as a space of imperial fantasies. The British and Anglo-Indian readership could read how Kipling celebrated Western scenery as a prime settler destination and commented on its grand scale. He, for example, noted that England was about the size of Yellowstone National Park. Readers also saw Kipling admiring what he saw was the independent spirit of the Western settlers. But they could also pick up how Kipling felt bored by the abundant sagebrush. Or they could take to heart his remarks on places like Omaha, Nebraska, as despicable medleys of Germans, Poles, Slavs, and all the human waste of Eastern Europe, and thus as warnings against ethnic/racial mixing.

Obviously, Gerstäcker and Kipling represent just a small sampling on a long line of nineteenth-century international travel authors who have contextualized the West as part of a globe-spanning network of empires. Historian Harry Liebersohn maintains that already in the first half of the 1800s, an aristocratic discourse emerged among well-born French and German travel writers, who were fascinated with their own romanticized vision of North American Indians as a being of rank and honor like themselves. One of these early elite travelers was Prince Alexander Philipp Maximilian zu Wied-Neuwied, a nobleman and a former Prussian Army officer who gained international fame as a naturalist and an ethnologist. Accompanied by the Swiss painter Karl Bodmer, Maximilian conducted an expedition to the Great Plains starting in 1832. En route in St. Louis, the party met with the explorer William Clark. Drawing on his help and knowledge, they accompanied Clark to a meeting with Sauk and Fox Indians. Using the Missouri River as their entryway, they also met Omahas, Poncas, Sioux, Plains Crees, and the Blackfeet. The party visited Fort Union and wintered among the Mandans and the Hidatsas at Fort Clark. Already a famed naturalist following his Brazil expedition in 1815–1817, Maximilian was a compulsive notetaker and a diarist, with an eye for detail. When describing the natural riches of the Plains, he habitually compared the abundant specimen of flora and fauna as well as the peoples and places he saw with those in Europe and Brazil. He argued, for instance, that the North American and the Brazil Indians were of same race. Bodmer's paintings in turn captured the artefacts, customs, and appearance of Plains Indians. After returning to Germany in 1834, Maximilian released a famous account of his Plains travels in *Reise in das Innere Nord-Amerika* (Figure 5.1).[2]

Maximilian's party also literally blasted its way across the northern Plains as was typical of European travelers in the West at the time. Loads of buffalo were shot in each outing just because they could be had and the carcasses were regularly left to rot. One of these high-profile sportsmen was Sir St. George Gore, a wealthy Irish nobleman and the baronet of the Gore Manor in Donegal County. Guided by the famous mountain man Jim Bridger, his Western tour lasted from 1854 to 1857. It covered Colorado, Wyoming, Montana, and the Dakotas, and possibly ended up costing as much as $500,000. The exact number of animals killed by Gore for sport remains unknown. He claimed the casualty sheet comprised 2,000 buffalo, 1,600 deer and elk, and 105 bears.

---

2 A recent edition of Maximilian's writings is to be found in Marsha V. Gallagher, ed. *Travels in North America, 1832–1834: A Concise Edition of the Journals of Prince Maximilian of Wied* (Norman: University of Oklahoma Press, 2017).

FIGURE 5.1 *Indians Hunting the Bison,* Tableau 31 by Karl Bodmer. Courtesy of the Library of Congress Prints and Photographs Division/Wikimedia Commons.

Gore saw no need to rough it in the wilderness. His party included 27 wagons, more than 100 horses, 18 oxen, and 3 cows. One wagon was just for weaponry, being crammed with pistols, shotguns, and about 75 rifles. Gore also brought a large striped green and white linen tent, a brass bedstead, a rug, a portable table, and several other luxury items. He had over 40 men on his payroll doing tasks from cooking and hunting to tending greyhounds and staghounds. It was much the same kind of material wealth and entourage with Charles Murray, the second son of the Fifth Earl of Dunmore. He followed the Pawnees on their summer hunt in 1835 dressed as a British dandy. He came with his English rifle, brace of pistols, Scots valet, and a kilt. Sir William Drummond Stewart, the Lord of Grand Tully and Baronet of Murthly, and a veteran of the Battle of Waterloo, tried to merge into the fur trading scene in St. Louis in the 1830s as a cultured gentleman hunter. Yet, he also brought from Europe special cheeses, wine, brandy, and servants.

Historian Monica Rico observes how the West served as an imaginative and literal site on which Stewart and other aristocratic travelers from Europe constructed their masculinity. As late as the 1870s, most of these gentlemen hunters and nature tourists in the West were still foreigners. And they kept on shooting, as well as collecting and writing of the West as an imperial playground not unlike the African safari. On his return to Scotland in 1839, Stewart sought to recreate the West on his estate in Perthshire. For this purpose, he had imported Western plants, bison, deer, and even grizzly bears. Stewart quickly emerged as a trendsetter, and it became something of a fashion for the British gentry to have bison on their estates. Stewart also filled the Murthy Castle with Native American artifacts and tried his luck as a Western novelist. Here as well other British aristocrats followed his example.

Perhaps the most famous of these international visitors was the Grand Duke Alexis, the fourth son of Czar Alexander II of Russia. Alexis arrived in New York City on October 1871, set to begin a goodwill tour of the United States at the request of his father. Americans of higher class, historian Lee Farrow discloses, readily welcomed European nobility, fancying impressing royalty with their taste and style. Alexis was lavishly entertained as he stopped in Philadelphia and Boston, took a detour into Canada, and continued to Chicago and St. Louis. Then he went hunting. Guided by Buffalo Bill and accompanied by General George A. Custer and the Sioux leader Spotted Tail with approximately 100 of his fellow Sioux, Alexis's hunting party advanced from Fort McPherson, Nebraska. It did not take long for Alexis to kill several buffalo and become enamored with the West and the Indians, and allegedly with Buffalo Bill as well. Next Alexis continued to Denver. He practiced some more socializing and hunting in Colorado, before heading through the southern states and embarking to sea from Pensacola, Florida, on February 22, 1872. Alexis's tour, however, was not just about the West or the United States, but it was global in scope. From Florida, his party continued visitations, observations, and hunts in Spanish Cuba, Brazil, the Dutch East Indies, the British Cape, Singapore, Hong Kong, Canton, and Shanghai. On October 1872, Alexis landed in Nagasaki, Japan. Then his world tour drew to its final leg as the party set for Vladivostok and overland across Siberia. They arrived home in St. Petersburg with a rich palate of experiences and wondrous collection of specimen and artifacts representing the world's different empires (Figure 5.2).

While most of the European visitors in the West were well-to-do men, several women travelers also reached the West. Among them were British elite ladies such as Theodora Guest but also middle-class people such as Ida Pfeiffer, a lawyer's widow from Austria. Enthusiast for foreign places and cultures, Pfeiffer waited until her two sons had their own families and then used the money she earned from her regional travel publications – describing trips to Scandinavia and Iceland – for fulfilling her dreams of two world journeys in the late 1840s and early 1850s. These trips took Pfeiffer not only to California, Oregon, and the Great Lakes but also to Brazil, Chile, French Tahiti, China, Persia, Ottoman Turkey, the British Cape, the Dutch East Indies, among other places. In other words, her world tour was also an imperial tour.

After visiting Australia and Hawaii, the British writer and naturalist Isabella Bird in turn spent a good deal of 1873 in Colorado. Historian Robert

FIGURE 5.2   Alexei Alexandrovich and General Custer in Topeka. Courtesy of the Library of Congress Prints and Photographs Division, LC-USZ62–42305.

Athearn notes how Bird took in the buckskin-clothed, gun-carrying men and commotion of Denver with curiosity and felt most unimpressed by the rough town of Cheyenne, Wyoming. She also rode horseback in the wintry Plains, roughed it up Long's Peak, and in pretty much every way challenged the Victorian gender norms of her day. Still, Bird's books on her travels are filled with depictions of herself and other women that reinforce the prevalent Victorian domestic and behavioral codes of the era, geographer Karen Morin comments. Bird was also often described as sickly, short, and almost an invalid. That did not stop her from exploring in Japan, Malaya, Tibet, China, Persia, and elsewhere.

Much like Pfeiffer did, Bird cheered the expansion of imperial systems and the benefits of civilization they would bring to the world. Neither woman found much value in indigenous lifestyles. Describing the Ainu people of Hokkaido and the California Indians, Bird drew similar descriptions of savage life, of what she deemed was the lowest form of human existence. She was also keen to compare the Malay locals and Native Americans, writing how both peoples purportedly left no marks of their existence after being swept away by the tide of white civilization. Wrobel comments how Bird's "journeys serve as a good example of how western American experiences could shape the experience of world travel, just as global travels could shape perceptions of the West." Authors like Bird reminded the readers in North America that the

United States was "thoroughly connected to the world of empire building and that their western frontier served a primary stage for imperial endeavors, not an escape from them."[3]

The British Richard Francis Burton offers yet another window to international travelers situating the West in the world; that of a high-profile world-renowned celebrity explorer. An officer in the army of the British East India Company, a veteran of the Crimean War, a master of numerous languages, self-taught ethnologist, and a prolific and provocative writer who published extensively on all his exploits, Burton was at the height of his fame when he entered the West in 1860. He had visited Mecca in the Arabian Peninsula disguised as a Muslim pilgrim. He had also entered the fabled city of Harar (Ethiopia) as an Arab merchant. Just prior to his travels in the West, Burton had been part of an exhausting and highly controversial expedition to the Great Lakes region of East Africa. This journey saw Burton "discover" Lake Tanganyika and claim it was the source of the White Nile. His partner John Hanning Speke argued that the correct answer to that puzzle was Lake Victoria (Lake Nyanza), where Speke had visited on their return leg while Burton had been too ill and exhausted to make the detour. Who saw what and who held the authority as a true explorer and the hero of the British Empire became a heated public controversy as the two travelers returned to England and as Speke launched a second expedition into the area, this time without Burton. On September 1864, Speke died from a self-inflicted, yet apparently accidental, gunshot wound just a day before he was to publicly debate the Nile matter with Burton.

Before that, Burton had sought temporary escape from the heated controversy by traveling to North America and across the Plains to Utah and California. Upon reaching Kansas, his narrative was already peppered with numerous remarks juxtaposing the West with the Orient. The wagon trains he saw reminded Burton of the caravans of the Sahara, and the Plains and the Nevada deserts appeared to him as a sea of waste much like the deserts of Northern Africa and the Middle East. The Plains Indians, Burton felt, were like the Bedouin Arabs, while the Sioux seemed African-like and therefore, he felt, could not be trusted. Burton also expressed deep dislike for the mestizo population and noted that they as well as the Indians were heading for disappearance as white civilization advanced to the Plains and the Rockies. While Burton cast the Pawnees as Ishmaelites, he advocated Mormon Utah as a reincarnated Holy Land. All these and the many more similarities and linkages he observed, Burton made known to an international audience in his 1861 popular book *The City of the Saints and Across the Rocky Mountains to California*.

The West also reached toward the world via a man who was perhaps the biggest self-promoter of his era on a global stage: Henry Morton Stanley.

---

3 Wrobel, *Global West, American Frontier*, 66–67.

A journalist by profession, Stanley made the most of the peoples' appetite for the exotic and the dangerous in his highly popular writings that described his travels and exploits. Extensive publicity surrounded Stanley's 1871 "discovery" of the British explorer David Livingstone in East Africa and his 1874–1877 trans-African expedition, cosponsored by British and American newspaper proprietors and trying to settle the origins of the Nile yet again. Working for King Leopold II of Belgium, Stanley also journeyed to the upper Congo River to open trade and sign a large number of treaties with the locals, killing many of them in the process. Eyes of the world were again on Stanley when he outdid the Germans and the British and pulled off a successful yet grueling journey into southern Sudan to rescue Emin Pasha. This German-born ruler of Ottoman Equatorial Africa had been displaced by the Mahdist uprising that had similarly led to the fall of Khartoum and the death of the celebrated British General Charles "Chinese" Gordon.

A global celebrity, and feverishly disputed, disliked, but also admired, one could easily forget that Stanley had also once been a man of the West. Born in Wales, he journeyed to Louisiana at age 17 and supposedly fought on both sides in the Civil War. Then he went, as a journalist, to Colorado for the gold rush. His travels also led Stanley to write about the U.S.–Indian wars and the extermination of the bison on the Plains. While Stanley's Western phase preceded his rise to international fame, it undoubtedly influenced his racist views of the nonwhite peoples of the world as savages that should be pushed aside from the way of civilization. It most likely also stimulated his support for imperial expansions. For Stanley, a version of the West could be found in the remote reaches of Africa. The West represented a testing ground and a source of inspiration supporting white mastery over nonwhite peoples and their lands for this world-renowned imperial traveler.

By the twentieth century, travel to and from the West changed considerably. It became more easily available to an ever-broader assortment of peoples from inside and outside the United States. In their efforts to be exclusive, the rich turned to ever more exotic landscapes: Egypt, Japan, and Africa were among the places the European elite sought out. But the West still drew its fair share as well. Travel was much more comfortable than ever before when one could opt for sumptuous "palace cars," arrange overnight stays at elegant hotels even in the more remote locations, enjoy hot springs, and marvel at nature in the safety of national parks such as Grand Canyon, Yosemite, and Yellowstone. Where the rich trotted, mass tourism soon followed. Package tours, budget train tickets, and inventive advertising, together with middle-class lifestyles championing consumerism and travel as well as increased opportunities for leisure brought by the rise of living standards in the industrial world, provided the incentives for the masses to enjoy the pleasures once reserved for a special few.

Much of this travel was also fueled, historian Hal Rothman explains, by lingering ideals of westward expansion, the quest for the sublime in nature, and anxiety about modern life. Disgusted with the impacts of the Industrial Revolution and escaping urban ugliness and modern hectic lifestyles, many artists drew on modernist concepts of primitivism. They came looking for peace and serenity, trying to discover their souls in the lost Edens of the West. Many headed for New Mexico, setting up artist communities and seeking alternate lifestyles. One of the more famous destinations was Taos, where the community that the art patron Mabel Dodge created pulled an international crowd. Its visitor list saw, among others, D. H. Lawrence, an English novelist, poet, playwright, and painter whose wanderlust took him to South of France, Italy, Ceylon, Australia, Mexico, and the United States. It also included Aldous Huxley, an English writer and philosopher who visited Lawrence at Taos.

As Europeans entered the West to escape modern life, Americans who felt their own West was becoming too civilized desired to find the "West" of adventure and wilderness, the primitive and the exotic, somewhere else. One such American traveler who combined a global reach with a social conscience and a sharp mind was Mark Twain, probably the best-known American author of his era. Famous these days mostly for his novels, Twain was a passionate traveler and writer of his own exploits. In 1897, he set out on a world tour for the simple purpose of making money. Yet he ended up providing sharp commentary on the extermination of Australian Aborigines and of the brutal racial regime in South Africa. In the process, he also became highly critical toward American expansion.

The Scottish-born John Muir, who had found wilderness perfection in the Yosemite and helped to found the Sierra Club, also toured the world in 1903–1904. Dreading that wilderness would disappear in America and across the world as empires claimed and settled more space, Muir went up the Nile and experienced the Australian outback, the springs of New Zealand's Rotorua, and the volcanic cones of Hawaii. And then there was the onetime friend and neighbor of Marquis De Morés in North Dakota (see Chapter 2), Theodore Roosevelt. A frail easterner who wanted to be a rugged westerner, Roosevelt passionately sought to transform himself and project an image of masculinity through his hunting, military, and other exploits. He just needed a "West" to do it in. Seeking adventure, he famously got himself nearly killed on the Amazon in 1913–1914. Prior to this, in 1909 Roosevelt had gone on safari extravaganza in Africa, escaping modernity and killing hundreds of animals. He plunged into wilderness in East Africa that he felt resembled the Dakotas a generation earlier. Using Africa as a substitute for the West, Roosevelt drew comparisons to the West while advocating further colonization in Africa in the Western model. He was also quick to draw parallels between the American continental expansion and its overseas imperialism, depicting the former as a prelude to the latter.

Several traveling American social commentators also found the West in Australia and New Zealand, while missionaries headed to China and Africa did much the same. The American explorer George Kennan, in turn, drew connections between the American West and Russia's Siberian frontiers.

Furthermore, American, and also European, travelers also frequently located the West in Europe, when, for example, comparing the Rocky Mountains with the Alps and California with the Italian Riviera. It was also customary to come across the West in the Oriental lands of the Middle East. Historian Richard Francaviglia writes that there is a long tradition, by travelers and other commentators, of giving Native Americans Oriental identities and seeing similarities in the landscapes and plants of the Great Plains or the Southwest with the Middle East. According to literary scholar Susan Kollin, Arab-as-Native American configurations were also commonplace already in the nineteenth century. Fascinated by the Arabs as exotic yet warlike savages in the mold of the Native Americas, there was a tendency among many American sojourners to depict the whole Middle East as a place of adventure, heroism, and romance and to project their fantasies of conquest and otherness on it.

Imperial Inspirations

At the time when the U.S. conquest of the West and the European scramble for Africa coincided, the American West was widely used as a global reference point and a template epitomizing colonial expansion and management of subject peoples. It also acted as a model to emulate. Take, for instance, the national parks, a system designed to provide an assurance that America's authentic West had not disappeared. Established in 1872, Yellowstone was the first national park in the world, but in Africa, Australia, Canada, and Europe, the example was soon copied. The process was pursued with a distinct Western flair in addressing what kind of wild, often majestic, nature was suitable for preservation. National parks, however, proved just one thread in much larger and complex transnational webs as the West inspired and tempted consideration and comparison by Europeans who contemplated their own colonial ventures in what seemed an increasingly squeezed world.

According to historian Raymond Betts, what struck the imagination of those inclined toward British imperial federation, to whom the aggressive Native policy in the West usually went unnoticed, was the double vision of an extension of the American people westward and the steady absorption of newly acquired territory into a preexisting political system. The flair of the West penetrated the upper tiers responsible for the direction of the British Empire. It was no accident that in his 1907 Romanes Lecture at Oxford, Lord Curzon, the former viceroy of India, kept on referring to the West as he described the logic of empires and expansion. He even suggested that movement from the cultivated European center to the sparsely settled (by whites) periphery in the West, and elsewhere in the world's numerous colonial zones, brought with it a form of physical and spiritual vitality for white people, a type of personal energy unattainable in the metropolitan Europe or the eastern United States. Thus, for Lord Curzon, the West signified dynamism and power.

It seemed that every expanding colonial empire had its own "West" somewhere, a place compared and measured against the American West because of its dynamism, scale of opportunity, process of conquest, fierce Natives, characteristics of its settler communities, and imagined physical likeness, or any combination of these elements. The pastoral expanses of the South African veldt and the Kenyan highlands induced easy comparisons with the American prairies and plains, mimicking their sense of spatial freedom. Morocco was dubbed by some Frenchmen as their "far West," as was Algeria. Here as well spatial vastness prompted much of the comparisons, while in Algeria, settler farms and villages were also seen in likeness to the West. The diamond "rush" in the vicinity of Lüderitz in Southwest Africa in 1908 made the place an instant German "wild southwest" in common parlance and folklore. The United States itself saw the Philippines and Cuba as potential "Wests" beyond its actual West.

Hokkaido (Ezo) played the part of the Japanese West. The Japanese represented it as an uninhabited terra nullius and its indigenous Ainus as a vanishing race. In this manner, they justified colonialism and produced resilient images of a frontier between savagery and civilization as Japan extended its reach to this northern island. They also produced a forceful rhetoric of a civilizing mission, including claims that settlers, farming, and free land would make the island prosper. Commonalities also reached the actual colonizing process. The Ainus changed from sovereign, militarily powerful people to a dependent people plagued by diseases, forced labor, dislocation, and cultural assimilation programs. In 1899, Japanese law declared the Ainus as former aborigines. This was revoked and the Ainus recognized as indigenous peoples only in 2008. The Japanese also sought direct counsel from the United States. In 1870, Kuroda Kiyotaka, who would later become the prime minister of Japan, traversed to the West to learn about settler colonialism. He brought back the American agricultural expert Horace Capron, who taught farming techniques to Hokkaido settlers. He also imported cattle, fruits, and vegetables from California and suggested bringing in large numbers of settlers from the other Japanese islands.

There was also a German "far West" in southern Brazil. Starting in the 1890s, a large number of German publications suggested that the areas of Rio Grande do Sul, Santa Catarina, and Parana were the latest best West, like the American West, but, if possible, only more so. Comparisons with the American West were a defining factor in German understandings of the peoples, nature, and prospects of southern Brazil. Like the American West, the Brazilian "West" was also the land of plenty, unlimited possibilities, where all dreams could be made a reality. It promised easy access to land for individual settlers, guaranteed to make the depressed and out of luck drudge from Germany into a master yeoman of his own land to whom nothing looked impossible. Those caught in the *Auslandsdeutsche* discussion and others concerned about Germanness and German immigration demanded, like did the economist Robert Jannasch, that the Germans should "develop the far west of southern Brazil as the Americans have developed their Far West."[4] Even the killings of Brazil's indigenous peoples, the ethnic cleansing that made possible the extension of the settler domain in Brazil's "West" was typically referenced in relation to the fate of Native Americans in the American West. Both were often depicted as defensive measures or as unavoidable, preordained, disappearance of the Natives in the face of a superior civilization.

If the world was divided between empires, then power rested with those who could best find and utilize space in extraction of resources, consumption of industrial goods, and spread of its growing populations. Germans seemed particularly drawn to this kind of thinking, and for many of them, the West proved the most powerful allegory, inspiration, and concrete model for expansion, greatness, and racial survival. Numerous German expansionists toured the West personally. One of them was the geographer Friedrich Ratzel, who visited Mexico, Cuba, and North America in 1874–1875. He studied, for instance, ethnic groups of California and the lives of German settlers on the Great Plains. Writing his dissertation on the Chinese global diaspora, Ratzel was enthralled by racialization and space in the West. In 1901, he went on to coin the term *lebensraum* (living space), using it to denote the space needed to sustain a species or people. Drawing heavily from the West, as well as Tasmania and New Zealand, Ratzel posited that to survive nations need to extend their realm by emigration or conquest or face rapid decline. In short, he suggested there was an ongoing global struggle for space between empires and different races. What the West demonstrated to him was how the availability of land for individual settlement stabilized domestic policies and energized the nation and the race. Ratzel's ideas were subsequently adopted by the Nazis, who linked living space to biological survival of a race and approached it in apocalyptic terms.

Ratzel also praised the work of historian Frederick Jackson Turner, especially his "frontier thesis." Turner, in turn, seemed taken by the German geographer. He quoted Ratzel at length and cooperated with his devotees. Turner also recognized connections between German fantasies of colonies in the American West – notions voiced by politicians, businessmen, newspapers, and German immigrants in the mid-1800s (see Chapter 2 and the *Mainzer Adelsverein*) and which Ratzel also reflected on 30 years later – and its eventual acquisition of colonies in Africa and Asia in the 1880s. Where the two men differed was that Ratzel saw Turner's frontier as a global phenomenon. For Ratzel, frontiers signified places around the world where whites pushed aside indigenous peoples. Thinking that the American West represented the best example of this kind of frontier process in the world, Ratzel felt it could and should be replicated and emulated by Germans in their colonial projects. It is possible

---

4 Quoted in Conrad, *Globalisation*, 288.

that Turner agreed when he wrote that "American colonization has become the mother of German colonial policy."[5]

Many pro-colonial Germans saw that the American West offered antecedents for German settler colonialism in its one truly potential overseas settler colony, Southwest Africa, as well as fuel for the German *Drang nach Osten* (drive to the East) that, historian Robert Nelson remarks, took on a modern colonial form in the late 1800s. It was no accident that the head of the German Colonial Office, Bernhard Dernburg, held the American West as the biggest colonial endeavor in world history and as an important reference point for German colonialism. For his part, Oskar Hintrager, the Deputy Governor of German Southwest Africa, was dedicated to turning Southwest Africa into model agricultural colony after having spent years studying the farms and ranches of the Great Plains. From 1904 onward, the German Colonial Association actually financed study trips to the American West. Civil engineer Alexander Kuhn was dispatched to Arizona to learn about indigenous policies there and how they could be best adopted to Southwest Africa. Kuhn viewed the Indian reservations in the American Southwest as exemplary sites for segregating the races and civilizing the Natives and felt they should be emulated in Southwest Africa to solve the so-called Native problem.

When looking for stimulus, the *Kaiserreich's* most notorious advocate of colonialism, Carl Peters traveled to North America in 1893, as historian Jens-Uwe Guettel notes. Peters was a founding member of the German East Africa Company in 1885, leader of a violent filibustering expedition in 1888 that led to the annexation of German East Africa and the man who lost the globally publicized race to save Emin Pasha to Henry Stanley. Peters also proved an exceptionally brutal colonial administrator in East Africa. He was eventually ousted after an infamous scandal in 1897: residing near Mount Kilimanjaro, Peters had his Native mistress and personal servant executed for an alleged affair. When questioned about his cruel handling of East Africans in the *Reichstag*, Peters argued that the treatment – the subjugation, expulsion, and extermination – of locals was basically similar in all of world's successful colonies. Peters expressed that in East Africa, he had just followed the example set in the American West and in Australia. Wanting Germany to excel in its colonial projects, Peters thought that the country needed to pay close attention to the West. He was profoundly impressed by the subjugation of Native Americans and the pace and success in the spread of white settlement. Peters' reputation was later exonerated by the Nazis, who applauded him as a magnificent specimen of German colonial masculinity.

---

5 Frederick Jackson Turner, "American Colonization," in *The Eloquence of Frederick Jackson Turner.* Robert H. Carpenter, ed. (1893; reprint San Marino: Huntington Library, 1983), 190.

Another German traveler who reached the West with imperial lessons in mind was the agrarian economist Max Sering. Sent by the Prussian government to determine what possible lessons the colonization of the Great Plains could offer, Sering returned from North America in 1883 advocating German colonization of those German areas in the East such as West Prussia and Posen that had significant Polish population. His methods included small family farms and plenty of German settlers. Sering was sure that mimicking the settler expansion of the Great Plains would stop the flight of German farmers from the eastern provinces, dam the Slavic flood there, and reinvigorate the German nation. Over the next three decades, while Sering devoted his career to studying settler colonization, the German government carried out programs settling between 120,000 and 200,000 Germans in its eastern borderlands.

The notion that if the United States had a manifest destiny to fulfill in the West, Germany had a similar appointment with destiny in the European East (including areas extending beyond *Kaiserreich's* borders) gained more and more popularity in German thinking in the late 1800s and early 1900s. As a colonial ideology, *Drang nach Osten* was first popular in the 1860s. It indicated a wide assortment of beliefs, historical interpretations, and calls for German cultural, biological, political, and military expansion, forming one of the principal ideas of German nationalist movement by the early 1900s. It was connected to longstanding traditions of German settlement colonies in the European East, ranging from the expansion of the Teutonic Order in the Middle Ages to the widespread influences of the Hanseatic League, the long history of Baltic German presence, Frederick the Great's conquests, and the Polish partitions. But it also connected with the American West. The drive to the East, historian Vejas Liulevicius remarks, was seen as Germany's destiny expected to cure all national problems much like the American westward expansion. The East, like the West, was moreover a vivid dreamscape and a state of being. There was a dirty and savage "native" East marked by chaos and degradation, a promised land of tremendous future possibilities for Germans, and a frontier indicating generations of ethnic struggle.

Literary scholar Kristin Kopp describes how the influence of the West was clearly visible in German writings conceptualizing Poland as colonial space, a "wild East." It was common in the *Kaiserreich* to compare Poles to Indians and to view the Poles through a colonizing gaze and a language of backwardness and perilous contamination. In German writings such as Gustav Freytag's wildly successful 1854 novel *Soll und Haben* (Debit and Credit), which went through dozens of reprints by the end of the century, the Poles were uncivilized peoples both in racial and cultural terms. Kopp also discusses how German authors penning cheap dime novels, so-called *Ostmarkenroman* (novels of the Eastern Marches), from the 1890s onward depicted the East as an ancient German, Teutonic, ground that had become a wasteland as result of Polish influence. The *Ostmarkenroman* contained rural settings, traditional social values, a civilizing mission rhetoric and strict differences between the righteous and brave Germans and the dirty and treacherous Poles. They also contained sexually promiscuous dark Polish women tempting and targeting brave yet naïve blond German men, thus carrying messages about the danger of blurred identities and the lack of clearly defined racial boundaries. These writings had much in common with Western dime novels emerging at the time. They also shared ground with the literature describing Anglo-Mexican relations such as Charles Averill's pulp novel *The Mexican Ranchero*, in which muscular American manhood was preyed upon by Mexican bandits and seductive senoritas.[6] In all, the principal lesson in the *Ostmarkenroman* seemed obvious enough: as *Kulturvölker*, people with culture, the Germans, unlike the primitive Poles who were *Naturvölker*, people without history or culture, could make this "wild East" civilized much like the white settlers had done in the American West.

Looking for direct precedence and encouragement from the American West, policies of Germanification, as part of the Reich's *Kulturkampf* in the late 1800s, centered on land acquisition, assimilation of Poles, and border control. In 1886, the Royal Prussian Colonization Commission (*Königlich Preussusche Ansiedlungskommission*) was established to buy up Polish lands in the East, particularly in Posen, Upper Silesia, and West Prussia where the majority of the population was Polish. The state put pressure on these domestic Poles to voluntarily sell their lands to German settlers and then make the move to North America. It also encouraged and assisted German settlers in choosing settlement in the East instead of heading to the Americas. And then there were organizations like the Pan-German League (*Alldeutscher Verband*) and especially the German Eastern Marches Society (*Deutscher Ostmarkenverein*) that argued for German settler East and de-Polonization of German territory. They repeatedly urged Germans not to even think about moving to the United States, but instead to find a new home as settlers in the East. Furthermore, the use of Polish language was curtailed in schools, churches, and political organizations by increasingly forceful methods by the turn of the century. In schools, history and geography-valued and celebrated all things German while undermining and disparaging everything Polish. Not unlike the aims of assimilationist Indian policies and schooling in the West, these methods targeted the regeneration of Poles as Germans, their uplift in patterns similar to the colonial civilizing mission.

As the United States and other white settler societies started to worry about transnational labor migration, so did Germany, historian Sebastian Conrad writes. The state demanded and issued travel documents and began to differentiate immigrants according to nationality on its eastern borders. Here the fight was not against the Chinese, but Polish seasonal workers. Different than

---

6 Charles Averill, *The Mexican Ranchero; or, the Maid of the Chapparal: A Romance of the Mexican War* (Boston: F. Gleason, 1847).

the domestic Poles, these were foreign Poles, an agricultural labor force from Russia and Galicia that filled the gap left in the East by the numerous Germans moving to the Americas and the industrial regions in western Germany. In 1913, over 360,000 foreigners were employed in agriculture in Prussia. Of the more than two million Poles who emigrated abroad between 1870 and 1914, most first moved to Europe, and 90% of them went at some point to Germany. Many ended up in the industrial Ruhr Valley, back home, or in North America. Much like the Chinese in the West, the Poles were perceived as a danger. They were depicted as a flood and foreign infiltration of cheap, uncivilized, and cunning inferiors who would drive out the German workforce. The remedies proposed and implemented included forced deportations of foreign Poles back to Russia and Galicia, or onward to North America.

Yet, by the early twentieth century, there were also actual plans to bring Chinese "coolies" to Germany to replace the Polish seasonal workers. Here again the German press and numerous writers representing various political ends drew examples from the American West, as well as Australia and South Africa, to substantiate their claims that the Chinese stood for "yellow peril" and that they were totally incompatible with German culture and constituted a threat to the *Kaiserreich*. Much of this German discourse was influenced by the global panic over the Chinese and their "hidden agendas." The notion that the "the yellow race" was preparing to fight for world dominance gained most attention in Australia, but was also recurrently voiced in Germany and in the American West. Among those who warned of a military invasion from eastern Asia was the American naval strategist Alfred Thayer Mahan. Much was also made of the demographic side of the matter. Rumors and claims circulated that millions of Asians were heading to flood Europe and the American West, their arrival bound to trigger a bitter fight for existence between the white and yellow races. Although Prussian landowners made petitions to start hiring Chinese, nothing came of these efforts. The Junkers would have to settle with the Poles and the Ruthenians (Ukrainians). The latter were also meant to replace the Poles or at least reduce the dependency on them as the principal labor force of Prussian agriculture. Eventually thousands of Ruthenians reached not only Prussia but also the Great Plains of the American West.

By the time the Nazis came to power, the American West remained firmly part of the social imaginary in Germany. It conjured up notions of spatial expansion, hardy settlers, individual freedom, noble, yet racially inferior Native Americans, racial conflict, and reservations. Historians such as Mark Mazower, Carroll Kakel, Edward Westermann, and Jens-Uwe Guettel disagree to what extent the Nazi leaders looked to the West for encouragement or as tangible prototype for their military campaigns and settler projects in the European East. Many point out that Hitler, for instance, referred to Ukraine as Germany's California and equated Eastern European partisans with Native American fighters, while others suggest these types of linkages were actually very rare in his voluminous speeches and writings. Scholars further imply that Hitler's understanding of actual Western history was very limited. In the end, it seems easy to agree with Westermann's recent conclusion that there existed parallels as well as vast differences between the American West and the Nazi East as colonial projects.

Westermann suggests that while the American Manifest Destiny constituted a broad cultural belief posited in messianic terms and served to unify a divided nation, the *Lebensraum* ideology was a government-controlled national imperative often portrayed in apocalyptic terms. He also posits that westward expansion prioritized economic incentives in displacing the Natives from their lands and ultimately favored Native assimilation through education. The quest for living space in the East was in turn very much government/party-driven project, tightly controlled by the state elite, and with a strong emphasis on large-scale physical extermination of subject peoples. Assimilation and education of Slavs and Jews was discouraged and strictly limited. While there existed plenty of rhetoric about Native extermination in the West, there was no government policy stating such an aim or working toward it unlike in the Nazi East. On the other hand, imported diseases contributed significantly to the conquest of the West, while no such "help" was available in the Nazi East. In the East, the Wermacht, the SS, and local auxiliaries worked in concert, in close interaction, and under tight control of the central government in Berlin. In the West, the oversight of Washington was relatively weak, and the federal troops and local volunteers were often at odds with each other, as were the civilian Indian agents and the U.S. Army officers. Also, massacres like Camp Grant in 1871 and Wounded Knee in 1890 stand out in Western history, whereas comparable atrocities were not only much bigger but also very much routine practice in the Nazi East.

One possible way to contrast the American West and the Nazi East is through *Generalplan Ost*. Wanting to top the United States and other settler empires, this plan of Hitler's, sketched by the SS during World War II, outlined plans for future Nazi living space in the European East. From what we know of it, the plan seemed to offer an overblown and ultraviolent version of settler colonialism, but also one that had some similarities to the conquest of the American West. It envisioned a project that comprised of ethnic struggle on the frontier lasting for generations. Its focus was firmly set on the land itself, on the so-called Germanization of the soil. And it involved the substitution of millions of "natives," in this case Jews and Slaves, by German settlers. The plan also called for extermination, removal, and enslavement of subject peoples, as well as the civilizing of racially suitable (a small minority) "natives." It painted the future in broad sweeps: in 20 years, the racial border between settlers and "natives" would be pushed further east. Some 45 million non-Germanizable peoples would be removed, and another 14 million people enslaved as slave labor to make way for 8–10 million German settlers plus other racially suitable migrants from the Americas, the Baltic states, and elsewhere. While much of the plan was left unaccomplished, *Generalplan Ost* was no armchair fantasy. Not only do the Holocaust and the killing and ethnic cleansing of millions of Slavs attest to this, but by 1944, some 300,000–400,000 ethnic Germans had already settled in the annexed territories.

Arguably, more serious study on the similarities, differences, and connections between the American West and German colonialism as a whole is needed. This is also the case more broadly on the ways the American West shaped global circulations of colonial mindsets as a precedent, model, and an inspiration. The West certainly mattered as Europeans thought about empires of vast spaces and settler colonialism. In addition to these transnational flows shaping imperial mindsets and processes of empire building, the West held a key role in the emerging global mass culture that promoted, filtered, and represented the world of empires to domestic consumers in Europe, North America, and beyond.

Mass Attractions

In the scale of ambition, operations, and transnational fame, P. T. Barnum was perhaps the American equivalent to Carl Hagenbeck as an impresario in human exhibitions (the two actually had business contacts). A veteran showman originally from Connecticut, Barnum did not hesitate to launch his first European tour in 1874. With agents and buyers (of "exotic peoples") in Europe, Asia, and Africa, he also had plans of expansion to Asian markets, historian Jay Cook states. Already in 1870, he had sent the famous dwarf entertainer Tom Thumb to Hawaii, Australia, New Zealand, Malaysia, China, Japan, and Egypt, producing one of the first round-the-world tours in mass culture. Barnum was still just one impresario among others who operated on the international scene in a time when the outward impulse of mass culture in novels, periodicals, expositions, and human exhibitions, as well as popular waves of Egyptomania or resurging Sinophilia, become closely linked to colonialism and expansionist empires. These cultural forms operated in the junctures of exoticism and knowledge, fantasy and science, and education and entertainment. They helped promote and legitimize colonialism and build mental boundaries between the expanding "civilized" world and the vanishing "savage" realm, between whites on the one hand and the rest of the world on the other. They also marked Native Americans in the same sphere with indigenous Africans, Australian Aborigines, and Europe's indigenous Sámi peoples.

Billed as attractions principally for the reason of what they were and how they differed from whites, not what they did or what skills they had, the human exhibitions emphasized racial difference as a form of spectacle. They depicted indigenous peoples as vanishing races, as primitive, childlike, warlike, animal-like, and sexually licentious savages. Hugely popular as a transnational cultural phenomenon, the shows employed an estimated 2,000–3,000 performers a year on average by the turn of the century. These exhibitions came in many sizes and shapes. Troupes toured different countries on their own and/or were part of larger gatherings, such as international expositions. They included ethnic villages and performances and were staged in private or public spaces. Some groups stayed on the road for years, traveling from one country to the next and crossing the Atlantic several times.

The "supply" of performers often closely followed the expansion of the French, British, and United States empires. For instance, the Sioux become coveted performers soon after they were confined to reservations by the U.S. Army, the Tuareg were exhibited in Paris only months after the French overtook Timbuktu in 1894, and Madagascans were put on show a year after France had occupied the island. The Zulus also became a spectator success in the midst of the Anglo-Zulu Wars and in the aftermath of the Battle of Isandlwana. For colonial powers, to exhibit the other became a visible sign of modernity and imperial greatness. Besides their popularity in Europe and North America, there were also Japanese expositions and shows from the 1890s onward that featured human exhibitions. On display were the Ainus, Taiwanese, Chinese, Okinawans, and Koreans: the targets or potential targets of Japanese expansion.

London was the global capital of these exotic shows. A group of Cherokees were exhibited there in 1762 and following the showing of the Hottentot Venus, Saartjie Baartman, between 1810 and 1815, the city witnessed a growing stream of performing troupes. These included Native Americans, Sámi, Inuits, Khois (Baartman was also a Khoi from southern Africa), Australian Aborigines, Pacific Islanders, Indians from India, and several groups of Zulus. London also organized the first world fair at Crystal Palace in 1851. Thereafter numerous high-volume expositions with imperial themes followed, culminating in the 1924–1925 British Empire Exhibitions at Wembley that reportedly pulled approximately 25 million visitors.

One of the earlier promoters of the West in London and Europe was George Catlin. This onetime Pennsylvania lawyer had traveled extensively among Plains indigenous peoples between 1830 and 1838. Based in St. Louis, and hosted by William Clark, and later at Fort Union, Catlin saw the Mandans, the Cheyenne, the Blackfeet, and altogether more than 50 tribes. He produced over 500 paintings during his sojourns. Then he took his art and extensive ethnographic collection – his Indian Gallery – on the road. Catlin reached England in 1839, and the following year, he set up his Indian Gallery at the Egyptian Hall on Piccadilly in London. This was an appropriately global and imperial setting. The hall exhibited Oriental enchantment, artefacts from the South Seas collected on James Cook's voyages, and now materials on Native Americans of the West. Catlin also had a Native village pitched on Lord's Cricket Ground. He lectured and organized performances – dances and chants – to showcase his message and to make his efforts financially sound. He first hired 20 people, possibly run-of-the-mill Irishmen, "Paddy Murphy" Indians, to impersonate Native Americans. In 1843, he recruited the real thing, a group of Ojibwas and Iowas, to perform dances and demonstrate handicrafts. Offering an education-piece disguised as performance, Catlin took his entourage to Scotland and Ireland. In 1845, it was Paris and the Louvre where King Louis Philippe and the French royal family came to see them. Although drawing sizable crowds, Catlin's Indians died in alarming numbers from diseases; also being deep in debt, Catlin was forced to shut down. In the 1850s, still struggling to gain recognition and fighting off debts, Catlin traveled through Latin America, painting images of local Indians. Later he returned to explore the West.

While failing to make money or gain much fame, Catlin operated in an international market where the interest in the frontier and the West exploded. As historian Roger Nichols observes, this was largely because of James Fennimore Cooper and the rise of adventure novels and dime serial literature in his wake. Cooper, of established upstate New York background, drew influence from Sir Walter Scott's Waverley series. These were novels of historical fictions that encompassed adventure, heroism, and romance, an imaginative reconstruction of Scottish Highland traditions. They were among the most popular and widely read novels in all of Europe. Comprising tales of historical frontier adventures, primitive conditions, and resilient settlers taming the land, but this time in America not Scotland, Cooper's own work gained global fame. His first novel *The Pioneers*, published in 1823, was rapidly translated into French, German, Danish, Swedish, and Spanish. According to historian Ray Allen Billington, when Cooper's fifth and final volume of his Leatherstocking Tales, *The Deerslayer,* came out in 1841, his fame was already such that no less than 30 publishers competed for the permission to publish its German version.

Cooper's third book, 1826s *The Last of the Mohicans,* was not only an instant sensation in Europe but also eventually became one of the most popular novels ever published. Not only has it been translated into numerous languages and reprinted again and again, it has also been made into a movie several times in the United States and at least three times in Germany. The first, *Der Letzte der Mohikaner* was released in 1920 in Weimar Germany, the next version in 1965 in West Germany, and another adaptation of Cooper hit the silver screen in 1967 in East Germany and turned out a big hit in the communist bloc. As recently as 2004–2007 Cooper's book was made into an animated TV series by the Italian TV network RAI.

After Cooper, American authors flocked to fill the surging market demand with a virtual stampede of thrilling stories. Many writers upped the violence, made Cooper's noble (primitive) savages into more barbarian killers, and shifted the locale from the Appalachian frontier to the trans-Mississippi West. By the late 1850s, the short, easy-to-read dime novels started their breakthrough. They were helped by developments, such as cheap paper, fast rotary presses, and reduced transportation costs. Also significant were speedily improving literacy rates in North America and Europe, as well as expanding markets among an increasingly urban and rapidly growing populace of middle-class and workers who yearned for entertainments to fill their free time. An early giant of the industry, Erastus Beadle's publishing house sold some five million copies of these novels during its first five years. Western narratives quickly became part of a larger, international, trend of adventure and mystery stories. These publications habitually featured colonial themes and locations in Africa, India, and the Middle East. They always had larger-than-life heroes, pretty girls, exotic places, and strange and mysterious villains.

As American-made Western stories reached Europe, they inspired Western enthusiasts like the German Karl May. In the 1870s, May started penning hugely popular Western novels without ever visiting the West. Set in the Southwest, May's heroes included the Indians, especially Winnetou, the brave Apache leader, as well as Old Shatterhand, a German-born frontiersman. Relatively unknown in the United States, his writings sold millions in Germany and were translated to numerous European languages. Their fans also included Albert Einstein and Adolf Hitler. While preferring Western stories, May covered an extensive imperial terrain of exotic adventure by setting similarly bloodcurdling stories in the Middle East and Latin America. His total volume of sales is said to hover around 20 million copies, of which approximately half were in German. He is apparently the most translated German fiction author ever. Many of May's stories were also adapted to comics, plays, and movies, including several Winnetou films made in the 1960s (in German with an international cast, including American leading men).

The army scout and buffalo hunter William Cody, and several other real Western characters such Christopher "Kit" Carson and "Wild Bill" Hickok, also started to feature in the dime novels. According to Nichols, some 20 authors put Cody, as "Buffalo Bill," in at least 500 (some say as many as 1,700) dime novels of Western heroics. These novels came out in numerous languages, capturing audiences in North America and across Europe. Cody also tried stage acting, but made his reputation with his own Wild West show. With its inaugural performance in St. Louis in 1884, the show grew into a winner in the United States before going abroad. It landed in England in 1887 during the ongoing celebrations for Queen Victoria's Golden Jubilee. Cody's was no small troupe. It traveled on a specifically equipped steamship and included 200 people, half of them Native Americans, close to 200 horses, 18 bison, 5 Texas steers, 10 mules, 10 elk, etc., as well an authentic Deadwood stagecoach. Outside the show grounds, the setup included an Indian village where the public could gaze at the Indians and wander amidst the tepees. The performance itself celebrated U.S. dominion over the West and "reenacted" the great drama of civilization and savagery. It included Pony Express riders, roping, riding, and sharpshooting exhibitions, an Indian attack on the stagecoach, and a reenactment of Cody's scalping and killing of a Cheyenne leader. The show in London also featured the kings of Denmark, Belgium, Saxony, and Greece being driven around the Earls Court arena in the Deadwood stagecoach with Buffalo Bill on the driver's seat and Edward, Prince of Wales, riding shotgun.

In 1889, Buffalo Bill's Wild West returned to play London and to appear at the Paris Universal Exposition, attended by an estimated 32 million people and including the newly completed Eiffel Tower as its attractions. Now, as if to further authenticate it as an education piece, the show also restaged Custer's last stand at Little Bighorn. In Paris, Buffalo Bill shared the spotlight in a cross-imperial exhibition that also included, for example, a large "negro village." Buffalo Bill's place in the *Jardin zoologigue d'acclimatation* (Zoological Gardens) where humans on display were living complements to the flora and fauna on view, was guaranteed by the presence of Native Americans in his group. This was not unheard of at the time. When a group of Sioux arrived in Budapest in 1886, they set up their tepees and displayed their clothing, artifacts, and dances in a local zoo. The Paris Zoological Gardens had experimented with groups of Inuits and black Africans in the 1870s and would host at least 30 major ethnological exhibitions before World War I. These included various Plains Indians, Kalmyks of Siberia, and 150 "wild women" of Dahomey, a troupe of African "Amazon warriors" who proved an enormous success, for instance, in St. Petersburg, Berlin, Zürich, Brussels, London, Atlanta, St. Louis, and San Francisco.

Soon Cody took his show on a European tour: France, Spain, Italy (with a special performance in the Vatican), Austria–Hungary, and Germany. The Pope gave the party a special blessing, while in Germany, legend has it, Annie Oakley shot a cigarette out of the mouth of Kaiser Wilhelm. In Munich, Cody had sold out daily performances on the Theresienwiese, the official grounds of Oktoberfest. Europeans flocked to each show to watch this former scout portray the West with its cowboys and Indians, sharpshooters, trick riders, prairie fires, cyclones, and much more. The show also returned to Britain again in 1892, 1901, 1902, 1903, and 1904, when the majority of the performances took place in Scotland and Cornwall. The five days in Edinburgh drew an estimated 140,000 spectators. In 1905, the show played the entire season in France: opening April 2 in Paris and closing November 12 in Marseilles, while 34 Italian cities were on the program in 1906. Cody also teamed with Italian film producer Filoeto Alberini in two silent shorts, *Buffalo Bill's Wild West* and *L'arrivo a Buffalo Bill a Roma*. Cody's show in Milan, historian Renee Laegreid reveals, moved the renowned composer Giacomo Puccini to create the opera *La fanciulla del West* (*The Girl of the Golden West*) in 1910 (Figure 5.3).

Cody's was not the first or the last Western show or troupe touring Europe. For example, the American showman Frank Harvey first brought the Sioux to tour Germany in 1887, whereas the sharpshooter William Frank "Doc" Carver's Wild West toured Australia and preceded Buffalo Bill in Europe. On his second German tour, Carver, vying for spectators, claimed the available

FIGURE 5.3 Buffalo Bill's Wild West Show European tour postcard. McCracken Research Library, Buffalo Bill Center of the West, MS 327 James Wojtowicz Collection.

electric lights and set up camp on the opposite side of the street from Cody in Hamburg. The "duel" ended in Carver's triumph, while Cody, left in the dark, gave just one performance before he split town. Gordon Lillie's, or Pawnee Bill's, "Historical Wild West, Indian Museum and Encampment," reached big time in the 1890s touring Europe and the United States. Frederick T. Cummins' Miller Bros. 101 Ranch Wild West staged an Indian Congress – including "Indian battles," holdups, cowboys, and stagecoaches at the Omaha Exposition in 1907. The show also toured Europe until World War I and put on the show at the Panama–Pacific International Exposition in San Francisco in 1915. In the 1910s, the German Sarrasani Circus (which is still running and world famous today) hired several Sioux as regular performers alongside Chinese, Javanese, Hindus, Ethiopians, and Argentinian Gauchos. And there were many others. At the turn of the century, an estimated 125 to 150 "Wild West shows" of various pedigree were on the road in Europe and North America.

Wild West shows did not only stage shows in the biggest European cities. For instance, in August 1890, Doc Carver and his party, traveling on a steamboat from St. Petersburg to Stockholm, held a show in Helsinki, the small capital of the Grand Duchy of Finland, an autonomous province in the Russian Empire. With no more than 90,000 residents, Helsinki emphatically welcomed Carver's act, which had been widely advertised in local papers beforehand. Large crowds gathered at the harbor to welcome the authentic Westerners, and many more lined the streets as the performers paraded through town. Seven years later, Texas Jack Omohundro's troupe was an even bigger success as it performed in Helsinki for a month.

Reenacting Western expansion to European royalty, middle-class, and working-class alike, "Wild West shows" had such a broad appeal because they were rooted in the bigger story of European expansion and the meetings of civilization and savagery. The English saw Buffalo Bill as part of the growth of the Anglo-World, while Germans associated Cody with their romanticized ideas of nature as well as global expansion of empires. These shows left a permanent cultural imprint on the local populace. In Helsinki, the press reported how all the streets and courtyards turned into sites were young kids representing various social classes constantly played "cowboys and Indians" after Texas Jack had departed. And surely this was not just the case in Helsinki.

These shows also brought the broader imperial world on display more directly. Cody's show, for instance, featured the "rough riders of the world," including Gauchos, Georgian trick riders, Arabs, and Mongolians on its roster. According to show programs, the Georgian "Cossacks" defended the Russian frontier against the Turks and the tribes from the Caucasus and secured it from the Black Sea to the Asian plains. Pawnee Bill in turn hired Mexican Vaqueros, Japanese performers, and Arab jugglers. As the United States expanded overseas in 1898, the shows swiftly appropriated recent episodes: Buffalo Bill had a Cuban contingent, and Pawnee Bill staged incidents from the Spanish-American War such as "The Fall of Luzon." Of course, there were "real" Filipino soldiers and other actual participants from these conquests performing. In 1901, the shows in turn incorporated the Boxer Rebellion to their programs, featuring the U.S. military together with the British, Sikh, German, Russian, French, and Japanese forces storming the gates and climbing the city walls of Peking. A sort of imperial climax was reached in 1908 when the two Bill's joined forces, putting together "Buffalo Bill's Wild West and Pawnee Bill's Great Far East."

While Western shows toured Europe, colonial-themed shows with Asians, Pacific Islanders, Africans, and Latin American Natives flooded the West. In the 1880s, P. T. Barnum called for peoples of all the "uncivilized" races in existence to appear in his big show. In response, the American-born Canadian William Hunt, the man known as "The Great Farini," a onetime eminent circus performer turned into a swashbuckling promoter of human exhibitions in Britain, brought Zulus to the United States. Also, as anthropologist Roslyn Poignant writes, the showman R. A. Cunningham shipped two groups of Australian Aborigines from Queensland to San Francisco. The Zulus and the Aborigines, billed as "last of the living cannibals," as well as the Sioux, Muslims, and others, performed in a number of Barnum's exhibitions. The Aborigines also appeared at the Columbian World's Fair in Chicago in 1893 alongside the Sioux and other Native Americans, Javanese, Samoans, Egyptians, and the "wild women" of Dahomey. They also toured broadly in circuses, dime museums, fairgrounds, and other showplaces in America and Europe.

As the Columbian World's Fair in Chicago attests, large contingents of Native Americans and other colonized peoples became a standard feature in world fairs and expositions. In Chicago, it was Franz Boas who organized the ethnological exhibitions. He procured numerous indigenous artefacts, Inuits with their sealskin clothing, and Kwakiutl Indians from British Columbia to perform their daily tasks in an "authentic" village setting. As a young ethnologist, the German-born Boas had been influenced by Hagenbeck's Bella Coola show in Germany. He went on to build a distinguished career in anthropology, researching the indigenous languages and cultures of the Pacific Northwest.

The fairs moved West of the Mississippi River. First, in 1894, there was the Midwinter International Exposition in San Francisco. It was followed by the 1904 Louisiana Purchase Exposition in St. Louis, the 1905 Lewis and Clark Centennial Exposition in Portland, and in 1909 the Alaska–Yukon–Pacific Exposition in Seattle. And they always included a broad assortment of human exhibitions of "exotic savages" from around the world. For instance, in St. Louis, there were showings starring Ainus, Igorots (Philippines), Apaches (including Geronimo), and Tlingits (Alaska). Also there was Ota Benga, the famous Congolese pygmy who was controversially displayed in a cage with an orangutan at the Bronx Zoo in 1906 and who killed himself in Virginia in 1916.

The 1915 Panama–Pacific International Exposition featured a microcosm of the world. It had Hawaiians, Filipinos (the largest exhibit at the fair), and an assortment of Native Americans, including a reconstruction of a Pueblo village with authentic residents. It also had a '49 camp that recreated the gold rush. Celebrating the completion of the Panama Canal – seen by contemporaries as a realization of the centuries-old fantasy of explorers to find a water passage from the Atlantic to the Pacific – and the booming American West-Pacific connections, the exposition, historian Sarah Moore says, was designed to champion muscular imperialism and trumpeted American continental and overseas expansion. Still, the fair also represented a contested space where various groups jockeyed for explanatory power. White women, historian Abigail Markwym describes, eagerly promoted pioneer motherhood, whereas Hawaiian women challenged the supposed divide between the civilized and the primitive through their dress: they donned shirtwaists, the model shirt for the independent, working (white) women at the time. So did the Native Americans, who performed traditional ceremonies and attacked Custer, but also rode in cars and airplanes, admired the attractions of the fair, deposited money in the bank, and smoked cigarettes.

For the Native performers of these human exhibitions, the experience could be both terrifying and liberating. Signs of cruelty and oppressions were visible everywhere: poor living conditions, death of performers (mainly from disease, but also suicides), and the use of wire fences, and even cages, to separate performers and audiences. Indigenous people were also captured and kept in service against their will and forced into lop-sided contracts and prostitution. The performers and their bodies (living and dead) were also examined and photographed by anthropologists. Performers also made more intimate social contacts. Many spectators not only wanted to help the performers, by, for instance, tossing coins to them, but flirtations, sexual encounters, and love affairs were also frequent.

On the other hand, by joining the shows, colonized peoples found opportunities to escape colonial war zones in Africa and government control in the reservations and earn a living in times of desperate poverty. They also took it as a chance to see the world. Born at Acoma Pueblo in the 1860s, educated in an Albuquerque boarding school, and operator of a trading post, Edward Proctor Hunt exploited the interest in Native life during the 1920s, writes anthropologist Peter Nabokov. He traveled in Europe in the Miller Brothers 101 Ranch Circus, performing as "Chief Big Snake." In 1928, to celebrate the opening of Karl May *Indianermuseum*, Hunt partook in a large Native dance procession from Dresden to nearby village of Radebeul. The performers laid flowers and sang funeral dirges on May's mausoleum and in the presence of his widow. Other Native performers also found opportunities and a sympathetic ear. One of them was the Sioux Rocky Bear (part of Buffalo Bill's Wild West). He voiced the grievances of his peoples in the hand of the U.S. government when invited as a keynote speaker at the Munich Anthropological Society in April 1890.

After World War I, the scene gradually changed. Human exhibitions did not disappear entirely, but many that remained tended to represent the colonized peoples as trophies of the civilizing mission, as tangible proof that colonialism represented righteous endeavors, not so much as primitive savages, or trophies of colonization. Exhibitions also transformed into living images in cinema, representing a change in scale and a new form of otherness.

In Europe, the American Western movie, with its big adventure, big landscapes, cowboys, Indians, and settlers, proved hugely popular. Already in the 1910, the French, British, and German producers started making their own Westerns. In the 1960s, this fascination with Western films expanded to television shows such as *Bonanza*, *Gunsmoke*, and *Maverick*, which dominated television ratings in many European countries as they did in the United States (and which have seen numerous reruns ever since). In the 1960s there also came the so-called Spaghetti Westerns. These films were usually produced with joint European funding and shot in Spain with Italian directors and mixed European and American casts. The biggest international fame hit Sergio Leone's Dollars Trilogy starring Clint Eastwood and climaxing with *The Good, the Bad, and the Ugly* in 1966. Plenty of critical acclaim, some of it years later, was also bestowed on Sergio Corbucci's works. There were many other Westerns also being made in Europe at the time, especially in Germany. Even in smaller countries, such as Finland, local productions included several Westerns. In Finland, these films were typically set in the "frontier wilderness" of Lapland. Then, there were the *Osterns*, or "Red Westerns." These movies were set in the American West, but made in Communist Eastern Europe. They included titles such as *Lemonade Joe* (*Limonádový Joe aneb Konská opera*, Czechoslovakia, 1964), *The Sons of Great Bear* (*Die Söhne der großen Bärin*, East Germany, 1966), *The Oil, the Baby and the Transylvanians* (*Pruncul, petrolulsi*

Ardelenii, Romania, 1981), or *A Man from the Boulevard des Capucines* (*Chelovek s bulvara Kaputsinov*, USSR, 1987).

The West proved an international hit in advertisement as well. From the early twentieth century, manufacturers produced larger quantities of West-themed consumer goods, from the Marlboro man to Western clothing and toys aimed at the growing middle-class markets and to the working-class consumers. And the literature scene continued active. In France, George Fronval wrote hundreds of bestselling Western books in the interwar years, while J. T. Edson penned some 137 novels in the post-World War II years in Britain. Starting in the 1960s, the Norwegian Kjell Hallbing, writing under the pseudonym Louis Masterson, produced 83 books in the Morgan Kane pulp Western series. Fiercely independent white hero Kane captures a key role in Western history, appearing in gold rushes, Indian wars, and in taking down notorious outlaws. The Morgan Kane series has sold over 11 million copies in Norway alone, in addition to being published in ten other countries. It has been hugely popular, for instance, in Finland, where you can still rather easily find copies of old prints in most venues that sell used books. Novelists in Spain, Germany, Finland, and elsewhere also produced tons of Western pulp fiction flooding the newsstands and bookstores from the 1950s to the 1980s, much of it turning out to be extremely popular in their respective countries.

European enthusiasm for the West also hit the roof in the post–World War II burgeoning comic book market. Trendy throughout continental Europe, although less so in Britain, and scarcely making an impact in North America, the biggest comic hits included *Comanche* (Belgian, 1969–2002), *Buddy Longway* (Swiss, 1972–2006), *Ltn. Blueberry* (French, 1963–2010), *Ken Parker* (Italian, 1974–2015), *Tex Willer* (Italian, 1948-), and *Lucky Luke* (French–Belgian, 1946-). These comics have had a life span of several decades, and some of them release new material even today. Set in the wild and rugged nineteenth-century West, they both admire Native and Western characters and scenery, making the West an epic dreamscape in the process while offering sharp commentary on its history. Some, like *Blueberry* and *Ken Parker*, are indeed highly critical of U.S. conquest and its accompanying exploitation, violence, and racism. They have been translated into several languages and printed and reprinted in various forms as comic strips, serial albums, and special books.

If anything, the travel writers, imperial borrowings and preoccupations in the late 1800s and early 1900s, and the mass culture phenomenon from human exhibitions to movies and comics, demonstrate that the West has actively engaged, enthralled, and captured the attention of the world. The West has crossed borders and spanned oceans as an imagined realm, a commodity, and a dreamscape. It has crept into and occupied the minds of peoples from around the world, some who have visited it, others who have never set foot in it.

Bibliography

Travel Writers

Athearn, Robert G. *Westward the Briton*. New York: Charles Scribner's Sons, 1953.

Burke, Flannery. *From Greenwich Village to Taos: Primitivism and Place at Mabel Dodge Luhan's*. Lawrence: University Press of Kansas, 2008.

Farrow, Lee A. *Alexis in America: A Russian Grand Duke's Tour, 1871–1972*. Baton Rouge: Louisiana State University Press, 2014.

Francaviglia, Richard V. *Go East, Young Man: Imagining the American West as the Orient*. Logan: Utah State University Press, 2011.

Homer, Michael W. *On the Way to Somewhere Else: European Sojourners in the Mormon West, 1834–1930*. Salt Lake City: University of Utah Press, 2010.

Hulme Peter, and Tim Youngs, eds. *The Cambridge Companion to Travel Writing*. Cambridge: Cambridge University Press, 2002.

Jeal, Tim. *Stanley: The Impossible Life of Africa's Greatest Explorer*. New Haven: Yale University Press, 2007.

Kennedy, Dane. *The Highly Civilized Man: Richard Burton and the Victorian World*. Cambridge, MA: Harvard University Press, 2005.

Koivunen, Leila. *Visualizing Africa in Nineteenth-Century British Travel Accounts*. New York: Routledge, 2009.

Kollin, Susan. *Captivating Westerns: The Middle East in the American West*. Lincoln: University of Nebraska Press, 2015.

Liebersohn, Harry. *Aristocratic Encounters: European Travelers and North American Indians*. Cambridge: Cambridge University Press, 1998.

McLynn, Frank. *From the Sierras to the Pampas: Richard Burton's Travels in the Americas, 1860–69*. London: Century, 1991.

Mills, Sara. *Discourses of Difference: An Analysis of Women's Travel Writing and Colonialism*. New York: Routledge, 1991.

Morin, Karen M. *Frontiers of Femininity: A New Historical Geography of the Nineteenth-Century American West*. Syracuse: Syracuse University Press, 2008.

Nelson, Robert L. "From Manitoba to the Memel: Max Sering, Inner Colonization and the German East." *Social History* 35 (November 2010): 439–457.

Pagnamenta, Peter. *Prairie Fever: British Aristocrats in the American West 1830–1890*. New York: W. W. Norton, 2013.

Pomoroy, Earl. *In Search of the Golden West: The Tourist in Western America*, 2nd ed. Lincoln: University of Nebraska Press, 2010.

Pratt, Mary Louise. *Imperial Eyes: Travel Writing and Transculturation*. New York: Routledge, 1992.

Rico, Monica. *Nature's Noblemen: Transatlantic Masculinities and the Nineteenth-Century American West*. New Haven: Yale University Press, 2013.

Roe, JoAnn. *Ranald MacDonald: Pacific Rim Adventurer*. Pullman: Washington State University Press, 1997.

Rothman, Hal K. *Devil's Bargains: Tourism in the Twentieth-Century American West*. Lawrence: University Press of Kansas, 2000.

Withey, Lynne. *Grand Tours and Cook's Tours: A History of Leisure Travel, 1750–1915*. New York: William Morrow, 1997.

Worster, Donald. *A Passion for Nature: The Life of John Muir*. Oxford: Oxford University Press, 2008.

Wrobel, David. M. *Global West, American Frontier: Travel, Empire, and Exceptionalism from Manifest Destiny to the Great Depression*. Albuquerque: University of New Mexico Press, 2013.

_____. "Considering Frontiers and Empires: George Kennan's Siberia and the U.S. West." *Western Historical Quarterly* 46 (Autumn 2015): 285–309.

Wrobel, David M., and Patrick T. Long, eds. *Seeing and Being Seen: Tourism in the American West*. Lawrence: University Press of Kansas, 2001.

Zuelow, Eric G. E. *A History of Modern Tourism*. New York: Palgrave Macmillan, 2015.

Imperial Inspirations

Baranowski, Shelley. *Nazi Empire: German Colonialism and Imperialism from Bismarck to Hitler*. Cambridge: Cambridge University Press, 2010.

Blackbourn, David. *The Conquest of Nature: Water, Landscape, and the Making of Modern Germany*. New York: W. W. Norton, 2006.

Betts, Raymond F. "Immense Dimensions: The Impact of the American West on Late Nineteenth-Century European Thought about Expansion." *Western Historical Quarterly* 10 (April 1979): 149–166.

Conrad, Sebastian. *Globalisation and the Nation in Imperial Germany*. Cambridge: Cambridge University Press, 2010.

Gissibl, Bernhard, Sabine Höhler, and Patrick Kupper, eds. *Civilizing Nature: National Parks in Global Historical Perspective*. New York: Berghahn, 2012.

Guettel, Jens-Uwe. *German Expansionism, Imperial Liberalism and the United States, 1776–1945*. Cambridge: Cambridge University Press, 2012.

Howkins, Adrian, Jared Orsi, and Mark Fiege, eds. *National Parks beyond the Nation: Global Perspectives on "America's Best Idea"*. Norman: University of Oklahoma Press, 2016.

Kakel, Carroll P. III. *The American West and the Nazi East: A Comparative and Interpretive Perspective*. New York: Palgrave MacMillan, 2011.

Kopp, Kristin. *Germany's Wild East: Constructing Poland as Colonial Space*. Ann Arbor: University of Michigan Press, 2011.

Liulevicius, Vejas Gabriel. *The German Myth of the East: 1800 to the Present*. Oxford: Oxford University Press, 2011.

Mazower, Mark. *Hitler's Empire: How the Nazis Ruled Europe*. New York: Penguin, 2008.

McCarthy, Michael. "Africa and the American West." *Journal of American Studies* 11 (August 1977): 187–201.

Nelson, Robert L., ed. *Germans, Poland, and Colonial Expansion to the East: 1850 through the Present*. New York: Palgrave Macmillan, 2009.

Siddle, Richard. *Race, Resistance and the Ainu of Japan*. New York: Routledge, 1996.

Steinweis, Alan E. "Eastern Europe and the Notion of the 'Frontier' in Germany to 1945." *Yearbook of European Studies* 13 (1999): 56–69.

Tyrrell, Ian. *True Gardens of the Gods: Californian-Australian Environmental Reform, 1860–1930*. Berkeley: University of California Press, 1999.

Usbeck, Frank. *Fellow Tribesmen: The Image of Native Americans, National Identity, and Nazi Ideology in Germany*. New York: Begrhahn, 2015.

Walker, Brett L. *The Conquest of Ainu Lands: Ecology and Culture in Japanese Expansion, 1590–1800*. Berkeley: University of California Press, 2002.

Westermann, Edward B. *Hitler's Ostkrieg and the Indian Wars: Comparing Genocide and Conquest.* Norman: University of Oklahoma Press, 2016.

Wunder, John R. "Looking After the Country Properly: A Comparative History of Indigenous Peoples and Australian and American National Parks." *Indigenous Law Journal* 2 (Fall 2003): 1–42.

Mass Attractions

Ames, Eric. *Carl Hagenbeck's Empire of Entertainments.* Seattle: University of Washington Press, 2009.

Billington, Ray Allen. *Land of Savagery, Land of Promise: The European Image of the American Frontier in the Nineteenth Century.* New York: W. W. Norton and Co., 1981.

Blanchard, Pascal, Nicolas Bancel, Gilles Boëtsch, et al., eds. *Human Zoos: Science and Spectacle in the Age of Empire.* Liverpool: Liverpool University Press, 2008.

Boisseau, Tracey Jean, and Abigail M. Markwyn, eds. *Gendering the Fair: Histories of Women and Gender at World's Fairs.* Chicago: University of Illinois Press, 2010.

Bold, Christine. *Selling the Wild West: Popular Western Fiction, 1860–1960.* Bloomington: Indiana University Press, 1987.

Calloway, Colin G., Gerd Gemunden, and Susanne Zantop, eds. *Germans and Indians: Fantasies, Encounters, Projections.* Lincoln: University of Nebraska Press, 2002.

Campbell, Neil. *The Rhizomatic West: Representing the American West in a Transnational, Global, Media Age.* Lincoln: University of Nebraska Press, 2008.

Cook, Jay. *The Arts of Deception: Playing with Fraud in the Age of Barnum.* Cambridge, MA: Harvard University Press, 2001.

Eisler, Benita. *The Red Man's Bones: George Catlin, Artist and Showman.* New York: W. W. Norton, 2013.

Feest, Christian, F., ed. *Indians and Europe: An Interdisciplinary Collection of Essays.* Lincoln: University of Nebraska Press, 1999.

Flint, Kate. *The Transatlantic Indian, 1776–1930.* Princeton: Princeton University Press, 2008.

Frayling, Christopher. *Spaghetti Westerns: Cowboys and Europeans from Karl May to Sergio Leone.* London: I. B. Tauris, 1981.

Haberland, Wolfgang. "Adrian Jacobsen on the Pine Ridge Reservation, 1910." *European Review of Native American Studies* 2 (1988): 11–15.

Hausdoerffer, John. *Catlin's Lament: Indians, Manifest Destiny, and the Ethics of Nature.* Lawrence: University Press of Kansas, 2009.

Hoffenberg, Peter H. *An Empire on Display: English, Indian, and Australian Exhibitions from the Crystal Palace to the Great War.* Berkeley: University of California Press, 2001.

Kasson, Joy S. *Buffalo Bill's Wild West: Celebrity, Memory, and Popular History.* New York: Hill & Wang, 2000.

Lindfors, Bernth, ed. *Africans on Stage: Studies in Ethnological Show Business.* Bloomington: Indiana University Press, 1999.

Laegreid, Rene M. "Finding the American West in Twenty-First-Century Italy." *Western Historical Quarterly* 45 (Winter 2014): 411–428.

MacKenzie, John, ed. *Imperialism and Popular Culture.* Manchester: Manchester University Press, 1986.

Makharadze, Irakli. *Georgian Trick Riders in American Wild West Shows, 1890s–1920s.* Jefferson: McFarland, 2015.

Markwyn, Abigail M. *Empress San Francisco: The Pacific Rim, the Great West and California at the Panama-Pacific International Exposition*. Lincoln: University of Nebraska Press, 2014.

———. "Beyond the End of the Trail: Indians at San Francisco's 1915 World's Fair." *Ethnohistory* 63 (April 2016): 273–300.

McGrath, Ann. "Playing Colonial: Cowgirls, Cowboys, and Indians in Australia and North America." *Journal of Colonialism and Colonial History* 2 (Spring 2001) DOI:10.1353/cch.2001.0010.

McNenly, Linda Scarangella. *Native Performers in Wild West Shows: From Buffalo Bill to Euro Disney*. Norman: University of Oklahoma Press, 2012.

Moore, Sarah J. *Empire on Display: San Francisco's Panama-Pacific International Exposition of 1915*. Norman: University of Oklahoma Press, 2013.

Nabokov, Peter. *How the World Moves: The Odyssey of an American Indian Family*. New York: Viking, 2015.

Nichols, Roger L. "Western Attractions: Europeans and America." *Pacific Historical Review* 74 (February 2005): 1–18.

Oliphant, John. "The Cherokee Embassy to London, 1762." *Journal of Imperial and Commonwealth History* 27 (January 1999): 1–26.

Parezo, Nancy J., and Don D. Fowler. *Anthropology Goes to the Fair: The 1904 Louisiana Purchase Exposition*. Lincoln: University of Nebraska Press, 2007.

Penny, H. Glenn. *Kindred by Choice: Germans and American Indians Since 1800*. Chapel Hill: University of North Carolina Press, 2013.

Poignant, Roslyn. *Professional Savages: Captive Lives and Western Spectacle*. New Haven: Yale University Press, 2004.

Reddin, Paul. *Wild West Shows*. Urbana: University of Illinois Press, 1999.

Rydell, Robert W. *All the World's a Fair: Visions of Empire at American International Expositions, 1876–1916*. Chicago: University of Chicago Press, 1987.

Rydell, Robert W., and Rob Kroes. *Buffalo Bill in Bologna: The Americanization of the World, 1869–1922*. Chicago: University of Chicago Press, 2005.

Warren, Louis S. *Buffalo Bill's America: William Cody and the Wild West Show*. New York: Knopf, 2005.

EPILOGUE

The world today continues to engage with as well as entangle and embed in the West and vice versa. Up until at least the 1970s, it was very common for kids from many corners of the globe to be taken by the imagination of the West. This applied equally to Finland or Germany, as it did, say, to Australia. Historian Ann McGrath notes how, when growing up during the 1960s in Brisbane, the subtropical capital city of Queensland, Australia, "cowboys and Indians" was simply what all the neighborhood kids played.[1] Testifying to the portability of the West, and colonial culture more broadly, the game looked much the same wherever it took place: it involved plenty of chasing, hiding, and pretend killing and dying. Plastic bows and arrows and knives were the weapons of choice. So were cap guns with a loud bang and a "gunpowder" aroma. The play could include some dressing up in store-bought or homemade costumes, although this might be as nominal as wearing a feather in your hair. Also part of the act were character acting and scenarios that relied upon a dichotomy between the "good" and the "bad."

In the twenty-first century, much has changed in this respect. In fact, already when I was growing up in the 1980s Finland relatively few of my buddies gobbled up the Western comics, loved the films, read the novels, and played cowboys and Indians as I did. The release of new Western movies had dwindled since the early 1970s, and the number of novels was also in decline. Today, the Western comics have moved to the cultural margins, and practically nowhere you see kids playing cowboys and Indians. The West no longer captures the attention of kids in Europe, who, rather than let their imagination run wild

---

1 McGrath, Ann. "Playing Colonial: Cowgirls, Cowboys, and Indians in Australia and North America." *Journal of Colonialism and Colonial History* 2 (Spring 2001) doi:10.1353/cch.2001.0010.

with the West, engage in social media content and play video games. To today's kids, the West is something archaic and definitely unhip. Most young adults and fresh parents probably agree. They may regard Western movies as outdated and performing cowboys and Indians as culturally insensitive, if not outright racist and comparable to blackface, and thus as something they do not encourage their kids to pursue. In this they have a valid point. Curiously, this does not seem to prevent the many "Indian dances" or the wearing of "Indian costumes" that are still popular in today's kindergarten and school holiday festivities in Finland and elsewhere.

As a cultural commodity, however, the West is still far from dead. It just finds most of its audiences today among the adults. In other words, some of today's forty- and fifty-somethings and older, who grew up consuming a steady diet of Western films, books, and comics still yearn for more. Lucky Luke, "the man who shoots faster than his shadow," just celebrated his seventieth birthday in 2016, with two new comic book albums published in France and instantly translated to numerous European languages, including Finnish. The fast-shooting, hard-fisted, and righteous Texas Ranger/white Navajo chief Tex Willer also remains an ongoing success. Sergio Bonelli Editore in Italy publishes a steady stream of fresh stories, written and sketched by multiple artists. According to my calculations, no less than 30 different Tex Willer comic book releases hit the stores in Finland in 2016. Some were new stories, others reprints of classics from the 1960s and the 1970s. Altogether, these Tex Willer releases in 2016 contained some 5,600 pages of Western adventure. That is quite a lot even for a Western enthusiast in Finland to handle. But the trend with Tex Willer has been the same for years; its popularity is steady not just in Finland. Panini released new collectible Tex Willer trading cards in Europe in 2016, while a Tex Willer Monopoly board game came out the following year. You may ask who buys these things anymore? The answer is middle-aged men like me.

You can also experience the West firsthand throughout modern Europe in various theme parks. In Kent, England, there is a Western replica town called Laredo, complete with townsfolk and cowboys. There is also one in the small municipality of Muhos, Finland. In Italy, the Cowboys' Guest Ranch and theme park, outside the town of Voghera, has organized American-style rodeo and Wild West shows since 1995. Spain's Almeria boasts a Mini-Hollywood, a Western theme park that features daily cowboy stunt shows, a mock bank raid, and a reenactment of the final moments of Jesse James. In all, Almeria is not unlike Old Tucson in Arizona. It was also first a shooting location for Western movies, in this case the Spaghetti Westerns. In Germany, you can attend a "Grosse Apache Live Show" on the Damerower See or a "Bisonfest" in Stuttgart. You can also purchase Indian tipis or Western-style clothing in big cities such as Hamburg. Also in Germany, thousands of fans meet at Bad Segeberg in Schleswig-Holstein for the annual Karl May Festival. Established in 1952, the festival has "authentic" Native villages, exciting wild West performances, and it shows movies about the adventures of Old Shatterhand and Winnetou.

Then there is, of course, the biggest entertainment center in Europe: Disneyland Paris. It not only has a "Pocahontas Indian Village" but also offers an extravagant dinner show called "Buffalo Bill's Wild West." This show is staged on a big arena and includes Native American performers. The program is essentially copied from Cody's days. There is, however, one significant addition: Mickey Mouse.

While it would appear that the global circulations of Western Americana remain potent in our times, what this book set out achieve was to show how the West has been in the world and the world in the West for generations already. The West has been and is transnational and its reach global. It has stood as a dynamic domain of convergence and conquest at the heart of multidirectional and entangled histories of colonialism and settler colonialism. It has been a magnet for peoples from practically all corners of the world, bringing the world to the West to stay or at least to visit. The world and the West have also shared plenty of common ground in the globe-spanning circulations of violence, in particular ethnic and racial violence. The same holds for the colonial civilizing mission and the spread of transnational white middle-class cultures of domesticity and respectability. The West has also joined the world, functioning as an inspiration for empires and peoples seeking to emulate or outdo it, and fueling the minds of those captivated by its colonizing potential and by its often mythic grandeur and excitement. It is these histories of exploration, far-settlement, conquest, exploitation, racism, intimacies, imperial envisionings, and cultural transfers that resonate widely in the modern world. In fact, they have made it and continue to shape it. They bind the world and the West. They are central not only to understanding the historical and contemporary West but also crucial for grasping our present global condition.

INDEX

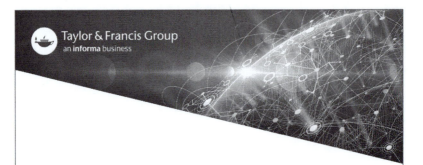